To

C000049662

Roy

CHANGE AND CONTINUITY IN CHILDREN'S SERVICES

Roy Parker

First published in Great Britain in 2015 by

Policy Press
University of Bristol
1-9 Old Park Hill
Bristol
BS2 8BB
UK
t: +44 (0)117 954 5940
pp-info@bristol.ac.uk
www.policypress.co.uk

North America office:
Policy Press
c/o The University of Chicago Press
1427 East 60th Street
Chicago, IL 60637, USA
t: +1 773 702 7700
f: +1 773-702-9756
sales@press.uchicago.edu
www.press.uchicago.edu

© Policy Press 2015

British Library Cataloguing in Publication Data
A catalogue record for this book is available from the British Library

Library of Congress Cataloging-in-Publication Data
A catalog record for this book has been requested

ISBN 978 1 44732 222 1 hardcover

Cover design by Policy Press
Front cover image kindly supplied by London Metropolitan Archives
Printed and bound in Great Britain by CPI Group (UK) Ltd, Croydon, CR0 4YY
Policy Press uses environmentally responsible print partners

'The Hope is in Children'
(*The Times*, 6 July 1908)

'We are the architects of our children's opportunities'
(Geoffrey Vickers, *The Art of Judgement*)

Cover illustration

A book's cover illustration is important. Ideally it should capture the essence of what is to follow. Yet a single picture can hardly be expected to meet that requirement and that is particularly the case when, as here, the book deals with developments over many years. Furthermore, the children's services are experienced by those involved as a series of events that not even film is capable of portraying. However, in the early years, when so many of the services relied upon institutions, it was easy to show the buildings, albeit with children in and around them, and believe that that conveyed what was going on; but, of course, it couldn't and didn't. With the dramatic decline in residential care even that illustrative option is closed off.

The visual image is a powerful means of communicating certain ideas and certain realities and can have a forceful political impact. But just how can one illustrate today's children's services when so much occurs in relationships upon which it is both difficult and, indeed, inappropriate to encroach? In what way, for example, might preventive work with families be illustrated? In the first place it is no single thing and, in the second it is a dynamic process. The documentary film might go some way to show what goes on; but that will hardly do when it comes to book illustrations.

Faced with such problems it is tempting to settle for a cover illustration that serves to catch the potential buyer's eye; but that offers no message relevant to the ensuing content. So, a word is necessary to explain my selection of this book's cover design. I chose it because I felt that it was ambiguous. What's happening? Who are the children? Are they brothers and sisters? Where are they going to or coming from? And who is the woman? Is she their mother, a foster mother, a teacher, a social worker, a neighbour or their grandmother? With their backs to the camera some of the usual clues are lost. In short, the picture is ambiguous: it poses unanswered questions. And that, it seems to me, typifies the history of our children's services. There is never enough information. Guesses have to be made. Uncertainties abound for all who are involved.

Contents

Acknowledgements

Acknowledgements are always difficult to record. My involvement in child care (now children's services) goes back over 50 years and during those years I have had the most generous colleagues, students and friends that one could want. All of them, in different ways, have contributed greatly to my education and understanding. I apologise for not naming you all, but I hope that you will know who you are and accept my gratitude.

Nonetheless, several of you have helped me in composing and improving the essays in this book and I would like to acknowledge your contributions: thanks to Dr Nick Axford, Professor Roger Bullock, Dr Bob Holman, Dr Michael Little and the late Professor John Triseliotis.

I have also had the good fortune to enjoy the generous help of the Dartington Social Research Unit, where special thanks go to Kay Turner, Fiona Mowbray and Julian Addy. I have also benefited from the stimulating meetings of the Centre for Social Policy and the friendship of its many members.

Some of the essays that follow have been published earlier although most of these have been revised, enlarged and brought more up to date. Even so, I wish to thank Barnardos, the British Association for Adoption and Fostering, Children in Scotland, the *Journal of Children's Services*, Research in Practice and Wiley for their permissions to reproduce all or part of the articles or chapters in question.

The London Metropolitan Archives gave permission to reproduce the cover photograph.

Last, but certainly not least, I wish to thank Jo, my wife of 60 years, whose unstinting help and great patience have provided indispensible support.

Preface

The subject of these essays should not need to be explained, but it does. For many years that subject was called 'the child care services' or, more often, just 'child care'. It covered those provisions that were made for the care and protection of children whose parents were unable to look after them or who were judged unfit to do so. Those who were familiar with these services understood what 'child care' meant; but for others there was some confusion. Did it include day care and nursery schools? And what about childminders? Or grandparents who looked after their grandchildren? In any case, caring for children was what parents did, wasn't it? Further complications arose from the use of the overlapping but more comprehensive term 'child welfare'.

Within the last decade, however, what were referred to as the child care services have come to be called the 'children's services', partly as a result of the Children Act 2004 which, among other things, required directors of *children's services* to be appointed to be responsible for the education as well as the child care functions of local authorities. Put simply then, these essays are about what are now called the children's services but also about what was called child care. Hence the reader will find both terms being used, but in their appropriate historical settings.

More specifically, the essays are about the political economy within which these services have been and are located. By 'political economy' I mean the political and economic influences to which they have been exposed and which have formed the contexts within which they have evolved. It follows that the thrust of the essays is towards an historical appreciation of how and why policies and services for some of society's most vulnerable children assumed the character that they have and, indeed, how both the problems and remedies came to be seen at different times. However, as the book's title implies it is not solely devoted to accounting for the changes and developments that have occurred. It also identifies and explains some of the persistent continuities.

Some of the chapters that follow have been published earlier, although in most cases what appears has been substantially revised and enlarged. Other chapters are published for the first time. One chapter found its way into the collection despite its original exclusion; that is Chapter 6, *Child Care in the Melting Pot*. The lecture upon which this was based was delivered in 1983 and reflected my assessment of the key issues that confronted the child care system at the time. Although a good deal has changed since then I have made no substantial alterations, believing that such a chapter offers a point of reference for those who wish to gain a sense of the state of these services 30 years ago and what at least one person considered to be necessary for their improvement. Indeed, the reader might wish to judge, with hindsight, what I got right and what I got wrong.

Although all the essays are concerned with issues and processes within the children's services they also make a contribution to the analysis of the politics of social and economic policy more generally. Much that can be said about one branch of these policies can be said about another and, of course, they interact in all kinds of ways. What follows, therefore, is relevant to the task of unravelling some of the complications that lie at the heart of public policy and not just the children's services.

Considerable reliance has been placed on official and other statistics. They have their limitations but, often, they are the best information that we have about the *aggregate* picture and especially about long-term trends, despite the qualifications that their use demands. Readers will doubtless bear this in mind. Where appropriate I have brought figures up to date, but because of the different times at which they are published, not all refer to the same year. Although I make no apology for the rather extensive use of the available statistics some will dispute their value. Let me call in their defence a passage from a recent article by Nigel Hawkes in the *British Medical Journal* about the cuts that are being imposed on the Office for National Statistics. This is how he explained the value of statistics: they are, he wrote, 'the stuff of history, the lifeblood of policy, the raw material of discovery, and the tribute paid by the present to the future. Without statistics we have no compass, no anchor, and no oars.'[1] The case for the preservation, compilation and use of statistics could not be put better.

I have not set out to address any one readership. Different chapters are likely to interest some more than others since each deals with a specific topic. Nevertheless, most are relevant to the fields of social work, social policy, politics, history and law and to all those who strive to improve and safeguard the lives of disadvantaged and endangered children.

CHAPTER 1

Introduction: patterns of change and continuity

This opening chapter sets the scene for what is to follow. It does not offer a detailed introduction but it does identify some of the issues that subsequent chapters address. In that respect it is intended to whet the readers' appetites, encouraging them to read on. Several themes reappear. There is the importance of appreciating the historical background of current issues. Another is the significance of the political and economic contexts within which children's services have evolved. A third is the need to *understand* how and why the problems in these services arise, rather than simply describing them and attributing blame or approbation. One further theme is the complicated inter-play of evidence, constraints, values and judgement that makes safeguarding vulnerable children and responding to troubled and troublesome adolescents such a demanding responsibility. However, we begin with an emphasis upon change and continuity.

I Legislation

Major legislation is commonly taken to reflect important shifts in the climate of opinion, in public concern or in realignments within the political system. In the children's field it is also often regarded as evidence of greater enlightenment and of an abandonment of what has been found to be unsatisfactory. This view tends to be strengthened because it is unusual for substantial controversy to arise during the passage of children's bills through Parliament, although particular clauses may be hotly contested. Of course, much will have led to a government's decision to introduce a new measure. Indeed, almost all legislation is the culmination of political processes that have been shaped by many forces, often in combination. They will have included the emergence of new information, new theories, new technology, scandal, shifts in economic conditions and in prevailing beliefs and ideologies, including those within the governing party. Yet in order for them to result in significant legislation they need to be orchestrated and politicised. Sometimes governments will take the initiative; at other times campaigning groups will be driving matters forward.

Against such a background a number of assumptions are liable to be made. One is that major reforming legislation represents a break with the past. However, there are several qualifications to be made. In the first place no children act has been comprehensive. If we take those of 1908, 1948 and 1989 for example, we see that each left certain aspects of child welfare untouched. In 1908 nothing was done about children in the care of the poor law. In 1948 issues surrounding juvenile delinquency or the approved schools were not addressed. Even though the 1989 Act was the most inclusive of these measures it did not deal with juvenile justice or the establishment of family courts. Furthermore, of course, questions concerning children's health and education are usually excluded from so-called 'children's legislation', partly to avoid unwieldiness but also to steer clear of the preserves of other central government departments.

Some parts of major legislation are incorporated unaltered from previous enactments. For instance, the Poor Law (Amendment) Act 1889 enabled local boards of guardians to assume parental rights over children in their care if the birth parents were considered unfit to resume their care. This could be done without recourse to a court, in effect by administrative fiat. It came to be known as poor law adoption. Surprisingly, the Children Act 1948 left this power intact, as did the Child Care Act 1980.[1] It was not until the legislation of 1989 that it was eventually repealed.

Like most other fresh legislation, that concerned with children's services has fulfilled, and continues to fulfil, a secondary purpose; namely, to consolidate and tidy up an array of previous enactments, many of which will have developed piecemeal in response to particular issues. That was certainly the case with both the Children Act 1908 and the Children and Young Persons Act 1933, exposing them to the criticism that they were not as innovative as was claimed. Likewise, the Children Act 1980 consolidated sections of 21 previous enactments. Consolidation can lead to already existing provisions being included in otherwise more radical measures.

One further reason for looking carefully at what new legislation does *not* change, or not change straightaway, revolves around the question of its implementation. In almost all enactments Secretaries of State are given the power to decide when particular clauses are brought into operation. This enables them to defer the introduction of those parts of an act that have not found favour because of their expected cost, their impracticality, their political sensitivity or because of an ideological change of heart, the latter tending to occur when there has been a change of government or even of a minister within the same government. For instance, custodianship orders that were introduced in the Children Act 1975 had to wait ten years before a commencement order was issued. This is an interesting example. The Act had begun life as a private members' bill introduced by David Owen when Labour were in opposition. However, Labour won the election of October 1974 and Harold Wilson invited Owen to become Under Secretary of State for Health. In that role he was in a strong position to transform his private members' bill into a government measure; but his tenure was short-lived. He was soon moved to the Foreign Office as a Minister of State, subsequently becoming Foreign Secretary. With his departure from Health enthusiasm for a full implementation of the 1975 Act waned. The guardianship provision in particular was left to one side, probably because it did not command enough support. In the event it fell to a Conservative administration that was more favourably disposed to its introduction to see it implemented in 1985.[2]

Even when legislative provisions are activated without delay they may fail to be implemented as intended by those to whom that responsibility falls. There are many reasons. One could be because such responsibilities are not mandatory. Another may be because an act has been so badly drafted that it gives rise to disputes about what *is* intended. However, as well as these explanations, there is the fact that local authorities may drag their feet, interpret what is required of them in their own way, or find that there are practical difficulties in conforming to the legislation or exercising the regulation necessary to meet its requirements. Indeed, the question of regulation may be becoming a more significant issue as services are increasingly contracted out to the private sector. Furthermore, those upon whom the *use* of a measure's provisions depends may choose to ignore it. For example, the Custody of Children Act 1891 remained largely unused after an initial flurry.[3] Similarly, when custodianship under the Children Act 1975 was finally made available there were few applications from foster parents or relatives for the necessary order.[4]

There is some children's legislation that has heralded significant changes but which tends to get overlooked. The Children Act 1963 is a notable example. It was principally concerned with making changes in the work of the juvenile courts and with strengthening the regulation of children's employment; but an extra section was added as a result of pressure from the Association of Children's Officers. For the first time a duty was placed upon local authorities 'to promote the welfare of children by diminishing the need to receive or keep them in care' and this included the opportunity to spend money on doing so. Previously, any such expenditure was illegal.[5] Henceforth, it became possible for local authorities to engage in prevention. This considerably enlarged and complicated the work of the then children's departments and continues to do so for their administrative successors.

As well as considering what changes or continuities are to be found in primary legislation there is also much subordinate legislation that has to be taken into account. Statutory instruments, regulations and rules may all exercise a notable influence over the way in which the parent legislation is interpreted and implemented.[6] They may put a new gloss upon what is done or be no more than a continuation of what existed before. Furthermore, they may be revised without changes to the primary legislation. Indeed, it could be argued that it is in their detail that the true character of the principal legislation is to be found.

Take, for example, the boarding-out rules that were first drawn up by the Local Government Board in 1889, slightly revised in 1933[7] and again in 1946.[8] The only significant changes in the 1946 version were that a person was no longer debarred from being a foster parent by reason of being in receipt of the equivalent of poor relief and the removal of the prohibition on placing more than two children (unless brothers and sisters) in the same foster home. Otherwise the previous rules (such as the one that required a doctor to certify that the child was 'suitable' to be boarded-out) remained unaltered. Likewise, the undertaking that foster parents had to sign stayed the same, including the obligation to bring up the child as they would their own and to ensure that they attended church. The next revision of the regulations occurred in 1955.[9] These were much more detailed; for example, introducing separate rules for those boarded-out for more or less than eight weeks. However, the only change to the form that the foster parents had to sign was that now the child had only to be 'encouraged' to attend church.

Further minor amendments were made in 1982 but the 1988 version did make important changes and added new requirements, the most notable of which were that henceforth a child's needs arising from their cultural and racial background had to be met, that foster parents had to be provided with more information about a child's background (such as their medical history), that they had to be given an outline of the local authority's plans for the child, that the child's wishes and feelings had to be taken into account and that, once placed, they had to be seen when a visit was made unless this was considered to be unnecessary.[10] Further modifications followed in 1991. Two were noteworthy: first, foster parents could be approved solely for looking after a specific child or class of child and, second, there was no longer a universal form of agreement for foster parents to sign. Instead there was a detailed list of what had to be covered in such an undertaking. Furthermore, there was now a 160-page handbook of guidance and regulations concerning family placements that was issued as part of the series of such documents that accompanied the Children Act 1989.[11]

Clearly, if we are to appreciate the impact of legislation upon children's services we need to include secondary legislation as well as the principal measures. However, as well as this it is necessary to take account of a variety of enactments that, on first sight, may seem to lie beyond the 'children's field'. Take, for example, two acts in the inter-war years: the allowances for widowed mothers that were introduced in 1926 and the Unemployment Assistance Act that followed in 1934. Both led to a gradual uncoupling of destitution from the need for care, a process that was eventually completed by the Children Act 1948. This is not to say that children from poor families did not come into care during the 1930s but that, for the first time, their parents' destitution alone was less likely to lead to that happening.

Of course, there are other examples of legislative change in related fields having a marked impact on children's services. The Divorce Law Reform Act 1969 could certainly be cited. The relaxation of the grounds for divorce that followed led indirectly to the rapid growth in the number of children admitted to care (and often staying there for lengthy periods) as a result of more matrimonial care orders being made.[12] This was usually the consequence of unresolved disputes between divorcing parents. In England and Wales in 1965 there were just 400 children who were in care on such orders; by the end of the 1980s there were 5,000.[13] Easier divorce also led to more re-marriages that, in their turn, increased the number of step-parent adoptions, sometimes with the intention of distancing the parent without custody even further. The character of adoption also began to change as a result of the Legitimacy Act 1967, of the Abortion Act of the same year and, later, of the Family Law Reform Act 1987. Each, together with improved methods of contraception, contributed to a marked reduction in the number of babies being relinquished for adoption.[14]

There have also been enactments in the field of social security that it is plausible to believe affected the work of the children's services; for example, the Child Benefit Act 1975 that improved the financial position of single mothers. However, it is difficult to determine exactly what effect it, or other measures affecting family income, had in reducing or increasing the number of children coming into care. There is also the potential influence of changes in housing law and policy, especially where these have affected rates of eviction or the provision of accommodation for homeless families.[15]

It follows, therefore, that the interpretation of the effects of legislative reform on children's services should be approached with caution. What appears to be a radical transformation may contain much that is borrowed from the past and may, in any case, fail to fulfil its intended purpose for an assortment of reasons, some of which will be found in the politics of an enactment's evolution. Moreover, the legislative influences on the children's services have to include much that, at first sight, might not be considered to be 'children's legislation'.

II Policy

Law and policy are sometimes confused. Legislation may certainly embody identifiable policies; but it may deal with little more than procedural matters that hardly amount to policies. On the other hand policies may be developed independently of legislative requirements, either explicitly or by default.

Central government issues many documents of exhortation (memoranda and circulars) and although these do not have the force of law the expectation is that local authorities, and indeed others, will adjust their practices accordingly. Going back some 60 years, there was the joint circular from the Home Office, the Ministry of Health and the Ministry of Education on *Children Neglected or Ill-treated in their own Homes.*[16] This 'asked' local authorities to introduce arrangements in order to co-ordinate the contributions of different organisations and thereby to make the best use of the resources available. In its appendix to the circular the government explained that it considered that there was no need 'for an extension of statutory powers'.[17] Nonetheless, local authorities were required to inform the Home Office of what they had done and for the organisations involved to bear any extra costs. This, of course, was just one of many attempts by central authorities to improve local co-ordination, an issue that has been stubbornly persistent, witness the steady flow of guidance such as the *Working Together* series.[18] Indeed, there has been a plethora of central government injunctions,[19] much of it aimed at improving practice; but such aspirations have often amounted to shifts in policy (or to its re-enforcement), not least because they seek to see certain practices *generalised*, that being the essence of policy.

Jean Packman has provided one of the most illuminating accounts of this complexity in her study, *Who Needs Care?* There she grappled with the question of how decisions to admit or not to admit children to care were made and, if they were to be admitted, which route should be chosen – the voluntary or the compulsory. In particular, she sought to assess how far these decisions were affected by identifiable policies in the two local authorities in which she conducted her research. Her broad conclusion was that even where clear-cut policies existed they exerted a weaker influence than might have been expected because of the considerable discretion vested in social workers, albeit that they were wont to complain that they were 'cramped by rules and regulations'. What the study revealed 'were workers with considerable potential autonomy', an autonomy that came from 'being the prime holders of vital information…and also from working at the boundary between the organisation and the outside world'. Furthermore, she explained, 'the complexity of the situations that they [the social workers] were required to assess and respond to defied detailed regulation or prescription… room for manoeuvre was very important if the service was to be truly individual and personal.'[20]

This captures the essential policy dilemma, both at the national and at the local level. It epitomises the problem of *implementing* policy in fields where operational discretion is imperative or is allowed. Of course, such discretion is constrained by legal requirements, by the imposition of financial limits and by what other resources are available (and by who controls them); but that leaves much which is unconstrained. That, in its turn, creates the conditions for variation. Beyond that, however, the exercise of discretion at the field level can lead to 'policy' emerging by default; that is, by enough people adopting a similar pattern of practice, but one that finds no reflection in any policy statement, possibly because none exists, because it is ignored or because it has failed to filter down to those in the field.[21] Likewise, individual social workers (particularly those lacking good supervision) may construct idiosyncratic ways of working that, to those with whom they interact outside the organisation, are assumed to be their organisation's established policy. However, it is not only the decisions of individual social workers that affect how practice, and thereby policy, evolve but also the differences that are liable to emerge between areas within an authority once administrative responsibilities are largely decentralised. Area managers in particular may adopt certain policies of their own even when overall policies are in place in the parent authority.[22] On the other hand, of course, there may be some who implement a centrally laid down policy so assiduously that it remains unchallenged or fails to be reassessed.

One important reason for both individual and area divergencies arises from the necessary imprecision of policy statements. Packman describes the matter like this: 'Policy presupposes that people, or the situations they are in, can be categorised and that general statements can be made about how to deal with this or that sort of case or set of circumstances. Yet', she continues, 'a basic tenet of social work is that help must be tailored to meet individual need';[23] hence the prevalence of 'policy guidance' or exhortation rather than detailed prescription. Nonetheless, there have been obvious movements in the direction in which children's services have headed, a point that Packman made in her follow-up study in the same authorities some ten years after her first inquiry.[24] By then there were more local 'policy statements' and managements were making greater efforts to ensure that what social workers did conformed more closely to them. Essentially, there were three policy initiatives in play: to reduce the number of children in care; to reduce dependence on residential establishments (particularly those in other authorities) and to embark on more activities that would support fragile families and hence avoid the necessity of taking their children into care. The first two of these objectives were linked to numerical targets which allowed progress to be monitored, the first being worked towards by the introduction of more systematic and effective 'gate-keeping' in which the decision whether or not to admit a child to care had to be endorsed by meetings at a more senior level. These policy goals (although pursued somewhat differently) were largely realised in both of the study authorities, although not enjoying 'universal enthusiasm or acceptance' in either.[25]

Despite the introduction of greater clarity about what was expected of them social workers continue to exercise considerable discretion, not least in the *interpretation* of the situations with which they are confronted, and hence the information that they provide and upon which decisions made elsewhere rely. Likewise, they have to do the best that they can when faced with a lack of those resources that are needed if they are to do what policies require. Furthermore, it is easier to implement overall policies when administrations are centralised (and, one might add, stable) than when they are decentralised; and, of course, decentralisation has been another favoured policy, both centrally and locally.

Although numerous policies in children's services can be identified (for example, the prominence accorded to foster care, the emphasis placed upon prevention, the need to take account of children's views or the importance of achieving closer co-operation between disparate agencies) they have not been achieved to the same extent nor realised at the same speed. Indeed, most have been developed gradually and might best be described as 'policy tendencies'. Even where policies have been codified in legislation a measure of flexibility has usually been allowed about when and under what circumstances they should be implemented.

Furthermore, not all policies are accompanied by guidance about *how* they are to be realised; but where there is such guidance it is likely to be couched in terms of the procedural steps that need to be taken. In truth, there has been a veritable cascade of documents (both from central government and within local authorities) that set out the steps that have to be followed, when and by whom, either to achieve the ends of policy or in response to shortcomings or failures of various kinds. These documents would seem to have at least two purposes. One is to secure improvements in practice such that children and their families receive a better service. The other is to provide a means by which management can exercise a measure of control over what is done beyond its immediate reach and, when things go wrong, to have a line of defence against charges that the 'systems' in place have provided insufficient safeguards. Indeed, recourse to the contention that failures arose because 'procedures were not followed', though sometimes true, has a tendency to narrow the analysis and hence to overlook more far-reaching explanations. Indeed, the successful implementation of policies requires more than procedural guidance; perhaps inspirational leadership, the mobilisation of commitment, high professional standards, additional resources or a greater involvement of those whose interests and well-being the policies are intended to serve.

Policies are described in different ways that suggest their level of generality or specificity. For example, we have had 'strategies', 'plans', 'agenda', 'mission statements' and 'targets'. All, however, whether dealing with children's services or not, describe broad aspirations, the realisation of which requires a mixture of what might be regarded as sub-policies (from time to time described as 'projects') some of which fall by the wayside after an initial burst of enthusiasm. Even so, announcements about over-arching ambitions *are* important; for example, the commitment to eliminate child poverty by 2020[26] or the Children's Plan of 2007 that sought 'to make England the best place in the world for children and young people to grow up'.[27] They are important because they have a political potency, especially when linked with financial support. Furthermore, they can be used to hold governments to account, although a different government is unlikely to attach the same significance to them as its predecessor. Such political changes are one obvious reason why some policies lose their momentum or are abandoned.

What needs to be emphasised about the crop of 'policy' documents produced by New Labour, documents such as *Every Child Matters*,[28]

Aiming High for Children and Families[29] and *Every Parent Matters*,[30] is the extent to which they focused on children and families in general (albeit with an emphasis on the more disadvantaged) rather than dealing exclusively with 'looked-after children' or those at risk. That was a welcome development although other publications were focused more narrowly; for example, *A Better Education for Children in Care*[31] and the report *Reaching Out: Think Family* that was based on a review of families at risk.[32] Some policies have straddled the two emphases (the general and the particular), most notably the 'Early Years' initiative of which the Sure Start programme became the flagship.[33] Even so, it is difficult to calculate the effect of any policy in isolation; often it is the combination of several, sometimes disparate and apparently unconnected, that has made the greatest impact. That said, however, it should not be forgotten that policies can interact in ways that are counter-productive or neutralising. And, of course, there are the unforeseen and unintended consequences of both legislation and policies that are liable to confound even the most confident expectations.[34]

III Making progress

It is rather easy to assume that little progress has been made in the care and protection of vulnerable children or the troubled and troublesome when one sees the same kind of tragedies befalling them today as befell others several decades ago. The circumstances seem distressingly similar and the subsequent inquiries make much the same recommendations; for example, that there should be better communication and co-ordination between agencies. Yet if one looks more broadly at what has happened, particularly over, say, the last century, we do see that there has been considerable progress. For example, the Children Act 1908 made substantial improvements in the treatment of young offenders: juvenile courts were established, imprisonment while on remand was abolished, as were the severest punishments. Forty years later another Children Act saw the creation of separate children's departments that were no longer associated with the poor law. At the same time the first training courses were established for what were then called boarding-out officers but who soon became known as child care officers. After 1963, as we have seen, local authorities were permitted to spend money on preventing children entering the care system rather than having their spending restricted to those already in care.

The chapters that follow explore the evolution of changes such as these as well as charting some of the reasons for the delay in introducing measures that most would now regard as having been long overdue.

One trap, of course, is to assume that all changes have amounted to progress, even though they may have been heralded as such at the time. The enthusiasm with which the reduction of residential care was embraced in favour of foster care largely ignored the contribution that the former could make for some children if it were imaginatively designed, well-funded and staffed by appropriately chosen and trained people. Certain fashionable ideas take hold but then disappear; witness the notion of the 'short, sharp shock' for young offenders that detention centres were created to administer.[35] Other schemes that were once enthusiastically embraced have eventually been recognised as having been deeply misconceived, schemes such as the organised emigration of certain poor children to Canada and Australia, a practice that continued from the 1870s until the 1960s.[36] Indeed, it was so misconceived that official apologies have been offered by the governments of the United Kingdom and Australia as well as by a number of voluntary organisations.[37] There has also been a sad catalogue of ways in which it has been thought appropriate to control children's behaviour that we now find quite unacceptable, practices that range from whipping (still available as a disposal for young offenders in the 1908 Act) to 'pindown' as a method of restraint in children's homes.[38] Unlike these examples some intended changes, although clearly in children's interests, have simply proved to be impossible to realise, measures such as that in the Children Act 1908 which sought to curb juvenile smoking. Countervailing forces are found to be too strong or the means available are found to be inadequate or unavailable, at least at the time.

Despite provisos such as these there have been undeniable improvements in services for vulnerable children, improvements that are liable to be overlooked because of an undue preoccupation with the pressing and apparently unforgiving problems of the moment. This partly arises from the fact that some changes (perhaps most) occur so gradually that they pass almost unnoticed; for example, the improvement in the nutrition and general health of children in care or the steady decline in the ravages of diseases such as tuberculosis, rickets, diphtheria, poliomyelitis or congenital syphilis. Improvements like these may also be underestimated because different damaging conditions take their place; for instance, youth unemployment, obesity or drug and alcohol abuse.[39]

One of the problems, of course, is to determine the extent to which the more general improvements in children's lives are, or could be, reflected in the lives of those who are most vulnerable. Indeed, the relationship between across-the-board policies for the betterment of all children and those aimed specifically (and therefore narrowly) at those at greatest risk remains an important underlying issue. Have general improvements in education, in the reduction of poverty or in public health also helped to improve the lives of those with whom children's services engage? Looked at historically the answer must be 'yes'. For instance, once compulsory education was in place it became easier to identify those children who were most in jeopardy, especially when the rudiments of a school health service were added.[40] Furthermore, as the standard of living began to improve it became that much more possible to distinguish conditions attributable to wanton neglect from apparently similar conditions but which stemmed from the effects of profound poverty. It is hardly feasible to embark upon policies for tackling the former (wanton neglect) until the worst features of the latter (endemic poverty) have been eliminated; and that, sadly, still remains the case.

Can improvements in the *general* standard of services for children do more than expose the particular needs of a vulnerable minority? There are three reasons to believe that they can. First, they establish a benchmark against which specialised children services can be and should be assessed, a possibility reflected in the title of the government's 2003 publication *Every Child Matters*. The second contribution that universal services can make to the amelioration of some of the problems with which the children's services grapple is by being generously inclusive. Significant steps forward were taken, for example, as more and more children in residential care attended local schools rather than having an 'enclosed' education (or training) on the premises. Likewise, we have the example of an increasing number of children suffering from a variety of disabilities being included in ordinary schools rather than being kept apart. Finally, of course, the children's services (and thereby the children whom they serve) depend heavily upon the co-operation of adjacent services like the schools, the health services, the police or housing agencies. How readily they offer their co-operation depends partly on their policies and practices but also on the extent to which they feel able to divert resources to this end; and that, in its turn, will be influenced by *their* level of development, by the weight of pressure they experience upon their primary activities and by the calls being made upon them to co-operate in yet other directions.[41]

Such patterns of inter-dependence warn us that in order to understand the changes or the continuities in children's services we have to look further afield than these services alone. As has already been made plain, what happens (or fails to happen) elsewhere is of great importance; and that includes the rise and fall of the kinds of problems with which these services are expected to deal.

IV Problems and issues

It is tempting to begin a discussion of the problems and issues that have dogged children's services from the standpoint of those who wrestle to find 'solutions'. In truth, however, we should begin with what faces the *children* who suffer from the many forms of family disruption, neglect or abuse. It is they who bear the main burdens, the heaviest of which are experienced at an emotional level. Indeed, how children *feel* about the drastic upheavals and other ills that befall them (or have befallen them) seems to have been much the same in whatever historical period: feelings of abandonment, of an insecure identity, of anger and of confusion about *why me*, albeit varying from child to child and from one circumstance to another. Even so, how those feelings play out for children of different ages and at different times may well have changed. How they manifest themselves will be influenced by the prevailing culture, by the availability of relevant information, by the extent and nature of support and by the likelihood of compensating experiences. It is important therefore that those organisations that are charged with securing the betterment of imperilled children and, if necessary, with providing substitute care, take account of their likely emotional states as well as their more tangible needs. Nonetheless, what has been *assumed* about these emotional states, as well as about the nature of children's development, has influenced the 'solutions' to their problems that have found favour.

In the nineteenth and early twentieth centuries, for example, a prevalent assumption was that children, even those who were older, were pliable, that they soon forgot their past and could be expected to adapt readily to new lives because they were not yet set in their ways. Such a conviction encouraged the practice of 'severance' if parents were considered to be 'unfit'. Children were to be separated, once and for all, from damaging or helpless parents. They were to be rescued and thereby saved; but that salvation tended to be seen as much as a religious responsibility as a practical one, especially by the voluntary organisations that proliferated in the 1870s.[42] Severance, of course, could be viewed as a form of prevention; but the Children Act 1948 added another interpretation; namely, that children's departments should endeavour to prevent children having to remain in care by working to restore them to their families if that were possible.[43] The idea of severance becomes less central. Furthermore, it comes to be seen as important to take account of what the children themselves have to say. However, that too makes certain assumptions about how children feel, not least about their desire to unburden themselves in the contexts of painful experiences and of divided loyalties. In any case, the exhortation 'to listen' goes only so far. What follows next is probably more important to the child.

As we understand more, and are more ambitious in our aspirations for severely disadvantaged children, so the complexity of the tasks confronting the children's services increases. They face political, administrative and managerial problems as well as those that turn on matters of 'best judgement'. Some of these problems arise from the need to adjust what is done (as well as how it is done) in the light of new information, new ideas or the emergence of new directives of one kind or another. Even so, much of this is influenced by the circumstances that conspire to put children at risk and by whether and how these are perceived and then acknowledged.

The process whereby this acknowledgement is accorded can be a lengthy business. For example, social services departments may have been aware of, or have been dealing with, certain problems well before they become the subject of public disquiet. What eventually brings matters to prominence depends upon many things: upon the steady build-up of information, upon the modification of public opinion, upon changing patterns of influence or upon persistent campaigning. On the other hand acknowledgement may come quite swiftly, often as a result of a particular event to which an unequivocal political response has to be made.

Bearing all this in mind, what can be concluded about the persistence or novelty of the problems or issues that have preoccupied those engaged in, or who have been responsible for, ensuring the safety and well-being of endangered or troubled children from the late nineteenth century onwards? One thing that can be said is that there have been few entirely new problems. Indeed, it is plausible to argue that the main problem remains essentially unchanged: namely, the actual or perceived incapacity of a child's parents or parent to care for them in an adequate fashion. Of course, what is regarded as adequate has changed, as have the reasons offered to explain what lies behind that inadequacy. For example, destitution, orphanhood, unmarried motherhood or abandonment loomed large throughout most of the nineteenth century, gradually to be replaced in the political and popular consciousness by cruelty and neglect. Throughout, however, there has been an ever-present disquiet about children's delinquency, a disquiet that intensifies when the statistics show an upward trend and that abates when they indicated a decline.[44]

Once a child has been taken into a care system the question inevitably arises as to how they should be looked after. Much has changed on this front, the major shift being from residential (institutional) care to foster care (boarding-out). Residential care was long seen to have many advantages, albeit as much for the providers as for the child. It was considered to offer the opportunity to exercise close control over the children's daily lives in order to instil habits of industry, to ensure a proper religious upbringing, to expose them to a disciplined regime and to prepare them for certain specific labour markets. In the case of girls this was domestic service and with respect to the boys it was the army, the navy, the merchant marine or farm work. Some boys were taught the basics of certain trades such as cobbling or tailoring which could also contribute to the reduction of an institution's running costs. The same could be said for the laundering and cleaning that the girls undertook.[45]

For those who organised the care of separated children (whether a voluntary body or local poor law guardians), however, institutions commended themselves for other reasons as well, as we shall see in the next chapter. In any case, the alternative of boarding-out was regarded by many as fraught with potential dangers while 'adoption' remained an informal arrangement until put on a legal footing in 1926.[46] Nonetheless, boarding-out did begin to be used from about the 1880s onwards. Indeed, by the turn of the century 23% of the children in the care of the poor law in England and Wales were boarded-out.[47] In Scotland, for reasons that will be explored later, the rate was much higher.[48] Among children in the care of Barnardos and the Waifs and Strays Society the rate was around 25% by 1900.[49] Other voluntary societies made a more sluggish start.

Nevertheless, several factors began to weigh in the favour of boarding-out. One rested upon a mounting criticism (most tellingly delivered by the Curtis committee in its report of 1946[50]) of the poor standards and stultifying effects on children of institutional care. Another was based on health grounds; namely, that grouping children together in large numbers encouraged cross-infection (both of illness and poor behaviour).[51] A further argument rested upon the claim that institutional life was particularly unsuitable for girls, especially if they were to be adequately prepared for life as servants, wives and mothers.[52] Indeed, there has been a consistent pattern for a larger proportion of the girls who were in care to be boarded-out than boys. In 1949, for example, 42% of girls in the care of the new children's departments were in foster homes in England and Wales compared with 29% of the boys.[53] Finally, as the costs of running homes rose there was a widespread conviction that boarding-out was a cheaper alternative.[54]

Yet there were countervailing arguments and interests at work that served to slow down the development of foster care. One was that it was virtually impossible to know, and therefore to control, what went on in a foster home. This reflected deep concerns about the selection of foster parents and their subsequent supervision.[55] More and better-trained visitors were required. A second factor that told against a shift towards foster care was the financial and personal investment that institutional buildings represented – to those who had provided them as well as to those who worked in them. Paradoxically perhaps, a third factor that slowed the development of foster care was that residential homes were 'improved'. Cottage and grouped homes contrasted sharply with the barrack-like institution, separate residential nurseries for babies promised more appropriate care and registration and inspection were gradually imposed on the voluntary sector.[56] Finally, until 1948, certain restrictions were placed on which children in the care of the poor law could be boarded-out; and some of the voluntary bodies were still recalling children placed in foster homes to their residential homes at various ages 'for training'.[57]

Of course, the question of how best to provide for children who are taken into care is more complicated than the choice between residential care and foster care and, in any case, there are subtle variations within each option, some of which turn on the age of the child, their needs and the expected duration of their stay in care. Indeed, the profile of the 'in care' population has changed significantly over the last 50 years, although the rate of children in care per 1,000 of those in the relevant age group has remained remarkably stable. For example, in 1952 it stood at 5.6 per 1,000, in 1961 at 5.0 and between 2004 and 2009 at 5.5 although rising to 6.0 in 2013.[58]

Fifty years ago, in 1962, the published reasons for children's admission to care in England and Wales did not offer a separate category for 'abuse or neglect', but they did record that in that year only 7% of those arriving in care had been committed on a fit person order (the forerunner of today's care order). Almost all the rest had been admitted on a voluntary basis.[59] By contrast, 56% of all children 'starting to be looked after' in England in 2013 had been admitted because of abuse or neglect, or both (almost all on care orders).[60]

There have been other changes in what might be termed the 'profile' of the in-care population; for example, in the age structure. In 2002, for example, 16% of all admissions to care were of children under the age of one. In 2013 the figure was 21%, but it was only 4% of those who were already being looked after. In general there are more adolescents being looked after now than there were in the past although these patterns vary from authority to authority. In 2001, for example, the proportion of children admitted to care who were under one year of age ranged from 7% to 22% in authorities with similar sized populations under 18; in this example populations of between 100,000 and 115,000.[61]

Another change in the composition of the in-care population is the emergence of minority ethnic groups that, in 2013, comprised 14% of the total. Nine per cent more were of mixed parentage.[62] However, information about the ethnicity of children looked after by local councils was not published until 2000–01 when 20% were recorded as belonging to an 'ethnic minority'.[63] Generally speaking such changes in the statistics that are collected reflect significant changes in the groups of children involved, in the solutions sought or in a sharper political consciousness of a rising issue: witness young unaccompanied asylum seekers. Ten years ago no details appeared about them in the statistics of children looked after. By 2007 they accounted for 6% of the total and in 2011 4%.[64]

As well as new categories appearing in what is recorded about looked-after children, however, some other categories have disappeared. For example, in 1963 a longer list of reasons for admission to care was provided than hitherto, among which 'confinement of mother' was to be found: it accounted for 20% of the total.[65] That classification is no longer used although it might have become subsumed under the heading 'parents' illness or disability'. Even so, those reasons only accounted for 3% of all admissions in 2013.[66] It seems clear that significantly fewer children come into care (albeit for short periods) because of circumstances associated with their mother's confinement. This would indicate that steps have been taken to find solutions other than admission to care when child care problems arise because a mother is confined in hospital or at home.[67]

This, together with a number of other examples, emphasises the growing importance being attached to social work with families in order to safeguard and enhance the lives of children. The extent to which this can reduce the number of children having to be admitted to the care system is hard to assess, partly because it is difficult and complicated work with, as yet, few reliable guidelines about how best to proceed [68] but also because the pendulum is liable to swing away from this emphasis in response to tragedies that are attributed to a failure to recognise when children must be removed for their safety. Even so, looked at historically, the shift towards prevention can be regarded as a significant change in the children's services, albeit that there remain other aspects that reflect some surprising continuities.

Given this and numerous other initiatives to forestall admission or commitment to care, together with efforts to restore children to their families or to seek their adoption, the relatively stable *rate* of children in care of the relevant age group remains an intriguing statistic. It almost suggests that as one group is removed from the care population another appears to take its place. That, of course, is too crude a proposition. Nevertheless, an explanation is worth pursuing, not least for the light that it might shed upon how changing social and economic conditions affect childhood vulnerability, but also upon some of the enduring factors that so deeply scar young lives and, indeed, the families in which they live or from which they have to be removed.

CHAPTER 2

Residential child care: an historical perspective

In Britain the Victorian era witnessed a remarkable proliferation of institutions. There were new workhouses, prisons, hospitals, lunatic asylums and barracks. Boarding schools were built for the children of the middle and upper classes and reformatories, industrial schools, refuges and homes for those of the poor. Despite recurrent bouts of economic depression, it was an age of construction that was closely associated with the development of the cities, of factory-based industry, of the railways, canals and docks. Public buildings, from baths to museums, multiplied as local government gradually acquired enlarged responsibilities, more resources and a sense of civic pride, typically captured by the many magnificent town halls that were built in the latter part of the nineteenth century.

Building labour was cheap and, apart from the central areas of the main cities, so was land. The domestic brick industry was rapidly expanding and new techniques, for example in the production of cement, did away with many of the former cumbersome and time-consuming processes of construction. However, the quality of building varied. Housing for the swelling ranks of the urban working class was built down to a low standard. By contrast, homes for the wealthy and grand edifices for corporate bodies were often of the highest quality and meant to last. There were, for example, the great railway stations that, like other such monuments, proclaimed the stability, reliability and economic prosperity of their owners. They were symbols of assertive self-confidence.

I The Poor Law influence

The multiplication of institutions for children from about the 1860s onward has to be seen against a backcloth of this history of building and building costs. Yet this alone does not explain the widespread and enduring conviction among many of those of influence that the institution was an appropriate remedy for a wide assortment of social ills. Nor are they sufficient to account for the deep repugnance with which a broad sector of the population viewed the prospect of having to be admitted to an institution. Other factors have to be added, prominent among which is the nature of the English Poor Law that survived, in one shape or another, until 1948.[1]

After 1834 the poor law system was dominated by the oppressive and frugal workhouse, the primary purpose of which was to discourage the able-bodied from seeking relief. Yet many of the inmates were children; others were old, mentally and physically disabled or chronically sick. They, along with the able-bodied, frequently bore the harsh consequences of the preoccupation with deterrence.[2]

As we move away from the 1830s and 1840s, however, the picture becomes more complicated. Gradually, and with encouragement from the central department of government, local boards of guardians began to remove children from the general mixed workhouses into separate accommodation – into workhouse schools, into large district schools shared between several poor law unions and into various residential homes. This process was driven forward by a concern to break the cycle of pauperism, an objective that it was believed could be pursued successfully only through education and training. Poor law children needed to be prepared for the labour market and thereby prevented from becoming the next generation of paupers. Nonetheless, there was resistance to these pressures in some boards of guardians (the administrators of the poor law locally) on the grounds of the expense. As a result progress was slower in some areas than in others.

II The quest for control

Other factors have to be considered together with these aspects of poor law history if the growth in the number and variety of children's institutions from about the 1860s onwards is to be understood. However, one persistent theme was the need to secure better control over the children of the poor. That problem appeared to be sharply accentuated in the middle decades of the nineteenth century. Changing technology, together with the emergence of legislation to restrict children's employment, meant that it was less likely than before that children would be employed. In many industries mechanisation had made their labour redundant (with some notable exceptions like the textile mills). Industrialisation, with its factory system, had already swept away most of the domestic economies in which children worked alongside their parents; almost all parents had become wage labourers who spent long hours away from their children. The control that had been imposed on children by the rigours of their labour weakened.

More and more children inhabited the streets, begging, stealing, doing whatever odd jobs came to hand or forming themselves into gangs.

No system of elementary education existed before 1870 to offer an alternative form of control. Indeed, compulsory education was not to be securely in place in Britain until well into the 1880s.[3] Had it been available 20 years earlier, the history of residential child care might have been significantly different. As it was, the time lag between industrial change and educational development created a vacuum of child control at the base of society that was viewed with dismay from the upper reaches of the class pyramid.[4] The spectre of a fast-breeding and dangerous underclass merged with the fear of the kind of revolutionary upheavals on the continent that had been anxiously observed and of which there were already sporadic indications at home.

Alarm, however, at the absence of control over certain classes of children also took another form that was closely associated with the wave of religious revivalism that swept the country from the end of the 1850s. The zeal and evangelical fervour that it generated found expression in a deep but practical concern with moral reclamation. The task among the adult population seemed overwhelming, but with children, whose habits and thoughts might not yet be set, the prospect was considered to be decidedly more hopeful.

In reality the fear of social disorder and the desire to secure children's spiritual salvation often went hand in hand; but whichever concern predominated, it appeared that what was needed was a new environment in which religion played a part. It seemed obvious that this could be achieved only by removing deprived and 'debased' children from the contaminating influences that surrounded them to a controlled space that would ensure their rehabilitation. To those unable or unwilling to contemplate the more radical structural changes in society that the alleviation of these conditions demanded, the residential home appeared to be an attractive solution.

There were, however, two problems to be faced. One was how to gather the children most at risk into such establishments. The other was how to keep them there once they had been admitted. A legal framework was crucial. Its first elements appeared in the 1850s when courts were enabled to commit certain children either to reformatory or industrial schools set up by voluntary bodies that usually had distinctive religious affiliations. Offenders who had been imprisoned could be sent to reformatories while those (some as young as five) who were found wandering, begging or in the company of criminals went to the industrial schools.[5] From time to time the grounds upon which children could be committed to these establishments were extended, the most important extension being associated with the introduction of compulsory education. Children who repeatedly failed to attend school could be dispatched to an industrial school, and many were. Even by the 1920s about a quarter of all the children in these schools were there for that reason.[6] It is notable that any citizen, as well as the school boards, could bring a child before the courts with the intention that he or she should be sent to an industrial school; constables, beadles, Bible-women, relieving officers, as well as parents themselves all had a finger in the pie.

For many years reformatory and industrial schools grew apace. By 1873, for example, there were already 65 reformatories in Great Britain and 104 industrial schools that, between them, held nearly 17,500 children.[7] These developments owed a good deal to the fact that the enabling legislation provided for per capita government grants to be paid to support the work. Although these did not quite meet the full cost they offered considerable encouragement to set up schools of this kind and, once they were established, to keep them as full as possible. There was, therefore, little incentive to discharge children on licence before the full term of the committal order. In any case, most managers were anxious to retain their charges as long as possible in order to prevent them from returning to what they considered to be the deleterious influences from which they had been removed. As the schools filled with long-stay children so there appeared to be a need for more schools. In this and other ways the system fed upon itself. For example, between 1873 and 1883 the number of industrial schools in Great Britain increased from 104 to 139 and the number of children held in reformatories and industrial schools rose from some 17,500 to 25,350, or by 70%.[8]

One of the reasons that it was so difficult to get youngsters released from reformatory or industrial schools on licence (even after many years) was that those who were most likely to be eligible (the older and more co-operative) were vital to the internal economies of many institutions. The widespread belief in the salutary value of work (epitomised in the very idea of the *industrial* school and in the required mixture of schooling and work) encouraged the use of children to grow food, make and repair boots and clothing, do the laundry, help in the kitchens or act as servants to the staff. This obviously reduced costs. Hiring out gangs of older boys to local farmers brought in additional income, as did outside contracts for simple manufacture or tedious processing on the premises. It was well into the twentieth century before certain limitations were imposed upon the extent to which school-age children in such institutions could be employed in these ways.[9]

As the courts were provided with additional options for dealing with troublesome children, most notably by the reforms introduced in the 1908 Children Act (including the establishment of juvenile courts), the importance of the industrial schools and reformatories began to wane. However, it was a slow and erratic process. They often had influential patrons and, from time to time, a surge in juvenile delinquency led to a renewed call for their services.[10] Furthermore, legal changes in the 1930s allowed older children to be admitted to the industrial schools (then renamed approved schools; that is, schools approved by the Home Office).[11] This boosted their intake. Despite such reprieves these institutions had been in decline from about the 1890s, hastened by the decision of the Home Office in 1919 to move from a per capita form of financial aid to annual fixed grants.[12]

III The influence of the voluntary children's organisations

The period from 1870 to about 1885 witnessed the creation of the large voluntary children's organisations (such as Barnardos, the Methodist National Children's Home, the Church of England's Waifs and Strays Society and Quarriers in Scotland[13]). The issues that concerned their founders were remarkably similar to those that had persuaded others to set up the reformatory and industrial schools and, similarly, virtually all were inspired by strong religious convictions. Likewise, since it was seen to be imperative to keep children away from the pernicious influences of unfit parents and corrupting localities, the residential home became the keystone of their system of care.

There are, however, several reasons for the nineteenth century growth in the number of residential homes provided by the principal voluntary societies and for their longstanding prominence. First, there was demand. From the outset most of the societies received many more referrals than they could accept.[14] These came from various sources: from their local branches, from the employers of domestic servants who were anxious that their employees should not be encumbered with dependent children and from parents or relatives whose desperate circumstances led them to part with their children (temporarily, they usually hoped) but whose distaste for the poor law led them to approach the voluntary societies. Other referrals came from the guardians themselves and, after the first legislation in 1889 to protect children from cruel parents, from the courts that placed such children in the care of the societies on fit person orders.[15] This complicated referral network was a far cry from the popular image of child-saving in which enthusiastic missionaries went on forays into the streets, particularly at night, to gather in ragged, homeless and hungry children.

The second vitally important impetus for growth in the provision of voluntary children's homes was sectarian rivalry. This took several forms, one of which was the antagonism between the Protestant evangelists and the Catholic Church. Many of the voluntary children's societies drew their strength, as well as their financial and political support, from those who were imbued with a combination of evangelical fervour and passionate anti-Catholicism. For its part the Catholic Church regarded the growth of such societies with grave misgivings. Examples of Catholic children being taken into the care of these organisations, and the fear that others might follow, elicited a surge in the provision of Catholic institutions that, as well as receiving children directly, also took those who were transferred from the care of local boards of guardians, often at the request of parents encouraged by their priests.[16]

The sectarian rivalries were, however, spread more widely than this. Suspicion and distrust grew among the Protestant societies. They vied for public support and often adopted a distinctly competitive stance towards each other. That competition often manifested itself in comparisons of the number of children saved. Yet more children could not be rescued unless there were more residential places.

To understand the importance of these rivalries to the growth in the number of children's homes in the nineteenth century it is necessary to take account of two other factors. One is the constant struggle that all the societies faced to secure charitable donations; the more similar their denominational character, the more intense the competition was likely to be. There were also trend-setters like Barnardo whose approach to the problem of gaining such support was inventive, aggressive and flamboyant. Other organisations felt constrained to follow suit, and so the process continued. However, in order to attract and keep public support the societies had to demonstrate that they were successful in what they claimed to be doing; namely, saving children. The institutional building was at once the symbol and the proclamation of that success; foster care or preventive work possessed no such qualities.

An additional reason for the spread of residential homes for children was the unwillingness of the societies to restore children to their families. Rescue implied severance, and thus most children were kept in these homes until they were ready to be employed. Like the reformatory and industrial schools therefore, the voluntary children's homes faced the problem of accumulation. In these circumstances vacancies were limited and the admission of further children was correspondingly restricted. Yet a sustained or rising number of admissions were almost as powerful an image of success in child-saving as the institution itself. If children were turned away support might be lost. That problem created a constant pressure for more institutions; but it also led to the adoption of other solutions, the most notable of which was emigration. In the last half of the nineteenth century tens of thousands of unaccompanied British children were sent, mainly by the voluntary children's societies, to Australia and New Zealand, but principally to Canada.[17] Emigration was, as Barnardo described it, the back door that enabled the front door to be kept open.[18] Associated in the public mind with a new start and with the patriotic duty of Empire settlement, child emigration became a popular cause and yet another activity in which the societies competed for favour and recognition.

As the number of residential homes grew they increasingly became the symbols of active child care. Their very existence made it extremely difficult to develop other forms of help for children, particularly any type of preventive work that did not automatically entail the child's removal from their family. Investments became embedded in the 'residential solution'. It attracted income, it created support but, perhaps more important still, it drew upon the loyalty of a staff that was not easily put to other work. Most of those who undertook the day-to-day care of the children in the homes were women who were often unmarried. Many looked upon their work not only as a religious vocation but also as a means of earning a living as well as acquiring accommodation.

The supply of such women was increased by the gigantic casualty lists of the First World War that left many without the prospect of marriage. They were also weakly placed in both the labour and housing markets. Residential employment of various kinds offered a solution. In many ways therefore that cohort of single women sustained residential homes for the best part of 30 or 40 years, finally disappearing around 1960.[19] As well as this, some of the voluntary societies were able to call upon religious orders to provide and staff residential services. Typically, the orders were often already organised as residential communities, the members of which were unmarried, cost little to employ and were unlikely to leave.

The financial feasibility of voluntary children's homes thus owed a good deal to the low cost of staffing them. Later, as the pool of single women shrank, as new opportunities became available to women in the labour market, as religious zeal subsided and as training came to be seen as necessary, the costs of running institutions mounted, to become a major reason for the retreat from residential child care that began, albeit erratically at first, after the Second World War.[20]

Even so, residential homes remained a feature of voluntary children's services for some years, notwithstanding that foster care became more common. However, as fewer children were admitted to their care, mainly because local authorities referred fewer to them, the emphasis changed to various kinds of community activities that were mainly aimed at support and prevention. Had the voluntary children's societies not placed such a heavy reliance upon institutions from the start and, instead, had followed this course, the history of British children's services might have developed somewhat differently.

IV The inter-war years

Several factors served to restrict the growth and development of residential provision for children, especially from the 1920s onwards. Within the poor law, for example, there had always been strong pressures to prevent children having to be supported 'on the rates' and equally strong pressures for parents (and relatives) to resume the responsibility for looking after their children. A common measure of success in the public sector was how *few* children had to be kept in care. As far as possible, demand was to be held in check, particularly in the face of the severe restrictions on public spending, epitomised by the National Economy Act of 1931.[21]

There was a remarkable decline in the number of children in the care of the poor law authorities between 1920 and the late 1930s.[22] This may have been partly attributable to a falling birth rate but, more plausibly, to the gradual separation of public cash relief from the provision of public care, most notably because the resources of local boards of guardians were quite insufficient to cope with the scale of relief payments that mass unemployment brought in its wake. Central government was obliged to accept responsibility for the financial support of those without work, a process that was virtually complete by 1934. As a result, family destitution less often brought children into the care of the poor law system.

The reduction in the number of children they had to care for in the inter-war period might have been expected to have led to the closure of public assistance children's homes and, given the severe restrictions that were imposed upon public expenditure, to the vigorous development of foster care. In fact, the use of foster care declined and, although some children's homes were closed, others took their place. This happened for two reasons. The first is to be found in the radical reform of local government that occurred in 1930 that, among other things, abolished hundreds of small boards of guardians and concentrated their responsibilities in far fewer local authorities. Larger pools of residential accommodation were thereby created under the control of single authorities whose inherited responsibilities from the boards of guardians were now discharged through their public assistance committees. Some homes were sold and some put to other use, but the remainder could now be used more efficiently.

The second factor that forestalled a reduction in the provision of residential care in the public sector in the 1930s was the quest to improve its quality. Many of the large institutions were closed but were replaced by smaller establishments, sometimes private houses bought cheaply in a depressed housing market. In this way much of the criticism of public institutional care for children was met (and deflected) by the greater use of accommodation that was, it was maintained, run on family lines.

Similar arguments were deployed in defence of their residential establishments by the voluntary societies, many of which claimed that the village-like complexes that they had created and divided into family groups avoided the detrimental effects upon children that were associated with large monolithic homes. Of course, smaller homes did not guarantee loving care and accounts of the experience of living in them in the 1930s suggest that their isolation, and the autonomy allowed some of those who ran them, could lead to oppressive regimes.[23]

Although, like the public sector, some of the voluntary societies had developed the use of foster care it had little effect on the scale of their residential provision. There were several reasons. One was the practice of removing children from their foster homes to be returned to an institution during adolescence or even earlier.[24] There was also, as with some boards of guardians (that, as we have seen, later became the public assistance committees of counties and county boroughs), a certain pride taken in the buildings. Indeed, typically, the photographs included in the voluntary societies' annual reports showed buildings, albeit with children in or around them. A further reason, as in the public system, for the modest use of foster care by the voluntary organisations, and therefore for it not reducing the amount of residential care, lay in the question of *relative* costs. Although the unit cost of boarding-out a child was lower than a place in an institution, the marginal cost usually worked in the opposite direction; that is, if a vacancy existed in an establishment then admitting one more child cost very little.[25]

In that respect the under-occupation of homes could be one reason for the sluggish development of foster care.

Apart from some of the changes that have been mentioned, the inter-war years were largely a period of inertia in child care, especially among the voluntary societies. Their charismatic founders had died, usually to be replaced by cautious administrators. Their incomes had become problematic, the introduction and increases in personal income tax discouraged charitable giving, as did the decline in popular religion. Furthermore, central government began to tighten its control over the activities of voluntary societies, to inspect and register their homes and to impose detailed requirements upon those which accepted children from the public sector. In short, by the 1920s the dynamic, confident and rather self-righteous societies of the Victorian era had become formal organisations that relied heavily upon the legacies of the past. They continued to do much of what they had always done. Furthermore, their children's homes seemed to provide secure anchorage in times of uncertainty.

V The post-war years

The history of residential child care in Britain since 1945 has been dominated by five inter-related factors: first, by the considerable emphasis placed upon fostering as the preferred form of care; second, by the decline of the voluntary societies as care-providing agencies; third, by new attitudes towards the treatment of juvenile offenders; fourth by concern about the quality of care provided and, finally, by rising costs.[26]

The reforming legislation of 1948 accorded pride of place to boarding-out. Indeed, it placed the new local authority children's services that it created under an obligation to arrange foster homes wherever possible. Yet, despite constant encouragement from central government rates of boarding-out remained stubbornly fixed at around 40% for many years, although there were wide variations between authorities.[27] The reasons for this are complicated and are discussed in the following chapter; but, in short, foster homes were less easy to find than had been expected. More married women were now in paid employment. The housing shortage, accentuated by wartime losses and damage, was severe. Overcrowding was common and when the slums began to be cleared they were replaced by the cramped high-rise developments of the 1960s. Added to which it also became apparent that many foster home placements failed, requiring new arrangements to be made for the child.[28] This often meant a return to a children's home. Paradoxically, therefore, residential care was to some extent sustained by the desire to place as many children as possible in foster homes. The combined effect of these and other factors weakened the undermining effect of the post-war foster care policy upon the residential sector; foster care was unable to supplant residential care even though it reduced its prominence.

The second factor that influenced the fortunes of residential child care in post-war Britain was the decline of voluntary sector care. Whereas in 1945 the voluntary societies looked after about a third of all separated children that proportion fell rapidly thereafter. In 1970 it was just 15%. This largely reflected the fact that voluntary organisations received fewer referrals from local authority children's departments. By 1978, for example, of the 7,800 children in the care of voluntary societies, 89% had been referred and paid for by the public sector.[29] As their care activities declined, the children's homes that had formed the backbone of the voluntary movement began to empty. Some were sold or used for other purposes. The societies began to reassess their policies, most deciding to shift their resources to various community-based schemes.

A third important influence upon residential care that emerged in the 1960s is to be found in the changing political assumptions concerning the treatment of juvenile offenders. In policy terms these were associated with an incoming Labour government in 1964, the main shift arising from the party's earlier re-assessment of the nature of delinquency.[30] Juvenile offending was regarded as but one of several manifestations of deprivation and family disruption. Since it sprang from similar causes as, for example, child abuse or neglect, so the argument went, it should be dealt with in a similar fashion; that was, by the application of welfare principles. Prosecution was to be avoided in preference to, say, police cautioning, and those who were brought to court should be given non-custodial sentences. Such practices affected the role and function of institutions for young offenders. At first these consequences were slow to be felt; but, as policies for deflection (such as intermediate treatment) began to take effect, fewer young offenders were committed to approved schools, leading to some being closed and, in 1973 those that remained being re-classified as 'community homes with education'.[31]

The fourth factor shaping the fortunes of residential care was disquiet about the ill effects that residential provision was liable to have on the well-being of children looked after in this way. That concern was of longstanding and overlapped with similar misgivings about other kinds of institutions, most notably those provided for people with mental illness or mental disability.[32] In that context the 1950s saw concern being expressed about the ravages of 'institutional neurosis'.[33] That began to be associated with a growing disquiet about the abuses that could be perpetrated in residential situations, abuses that were increasingly exposed and then investigated in the public inquiries that usually followed.[34] The general effect of all this was for residential care to be viewed as an unfortunate last resort. That has been sustained by continuing problems of providing appropriate training for those employed in these settings and in attracting them to the work in the first place.

Residential care has laboured under a legacy of disapprobation that has been hard to dispel and which has impeded efforts to engage in the dispassionate consideration of what *exactly* it could offer, to *which* children and in *which* circumstances. If residential care is to play a part in our children's services it has to be good enough to become a positive choice for certain children at certain times rather than a residual facility. Encouragingly, there are signs that both policy and practice are moving in this direction.[35]

Finally, rising costs have exercised a considerable influence over what has happened to residential care in the last 50 years or so. The increase was attributable to several causes. First, since in a local authority, debt is pooled and an average interest charged to all projects, both old and new, residential homes were not exempt from the substantial increases in the cost of capital borrowing. Second, the cost of labour also rose as improvements were made in staffing ratios and as units became smaller and as homes were increasingly provided for boys and girls together. Unionisation won improved pay and conditions of work, and these were usually incorporated in national agreements. Third, other running costs increased because of the increasing cost of such things as heat and maintenance. Raised standards also raised unit costs, not least because of the imposition of more stringent fire regulations. Furthermore, the higher cost of residential care when compared with foster care (and, of course, adoption) has been a constant argument in favour of the latter, although much depends on just how the relative costs are calculated.

At different times rising costs have been combined with intense pressure to reduce public expenditure. In the 1980s, for example, its effect was to encourage local authorities to find alternative forms of care and thereby to be able to sell their residential establishments. An added incentive for doing this was the escalation of land prices. Many homes occupied sites that commanded handsome prices on the open market. With auditors, accountants and the government continually stressing the need to obtain 'value for money' both the disposal of such valuable assets and the virtues of fostering and adoption were accorded renewed priority. These forces coincided with a fall in the number of children in care in the 1980s, offering further encouragement for a reduction in the amount of residential provision.[36]

The history of residential provision for children has witnessed its rise and fall. What is clear is that these movements have been attributable to the influence of many factors operating in both directions, and more or less forcefully at different times. However, there have been two influences about which little has been said so far. One is the improvement in the general standard of living of the bulk of the population and particularly of the poor. Harsh and frugal though conditions in children's institutions in the past may seem to have been they have to be judged by the standards and beliefs of their time. A second general influence on the unfolding history of residential homes for children has been the parallel history of the public boarding schools. Not only did their number grow rapidly in the middle years of the nineteenth century (between 1840 and 1869, for example, 31 were founded[37]) but the assumptions that underpinned them were often shared by those who shaped how the vulnerable or threatening children of the poor were to be dealt with. The emphasis was upon the creation of a *system* set in a controlled space in which behaviour was to be moulded by a mixture of discipline and religious exhortation.[38]

VI What of the future?

Looking towards the future there are several reasons to foresee a modest revival of residential care, if not in its numerical contribution to the care of looked-after children at least in its character and status. First, there is the enduring problem of the behaviour of some deeply disturbed children to be confronted, behaviour that is unlikely to be able to be contained or treated in the wider community. Second, some children do express a preference for residential care when they have to be apart from their families and such preferences need to be understood and taken seriously. Third, there is the question of providing secure accommodation for youngsters who have committed the most serious offences and who remain a danger to others as well as to themselves. Lastly, and reflecting most of these issues, there remains the matter of treatment of whatever kind it might be. Where will it best be provided, by whom and for how long? It may be that this too will necessitate a period of residential care if it is to be successful.

A new 'shape' to residential children's services is already evident, however, most notably the growth in provision by the private for-profit sector. In England between 1995 and 2000 the number of these establishments increased from 182 to 256; that is, by 40%. At the same time the number of local authority-run community homes declined, falling from 741 to 672, or by 9%.[39] Since 2000 that trend has become more pronounced. As at March, 2013, there were 1,718 children's homes in England of which 1,347 were provided by private agencies; that is, 78%. Thus, since 1995 the number of these homes has risen by 1,165,[40] although it must be borne in mind that many of them provide for only a few children. Even so, these are significant changes that are explained in various ways: by local authorities seeking a cheaper alternative to in-house provision,[41] to the willingness of the private sector to offer more specialised services (particularly for children with demanding behavioural and physical problems), by the opportunities being seized by venture capital and for family investment. It is still difficult to disentangle the relative importance of these rather diverse factors.[42] However, there are marked similarities to what has happened in the provision of residential care homes for the elderly and others from which certain lessons might be drawn.

Of course, what exactly happens over the next several decades will, as in the past, be determined by a combination of political, economic and professional forces. Looking back, however, we should remind ourselves of the extent to which the residential sector has declined. In England at the end of March, 2013, there were 7,910 looked-after children in children's homes, hostels, secure accommodation and residential schools, or 12% of the total at that date.[43] Forty years ago there were 37,627, or 59%.[44] This is a remarkable social change.[45]

Furthermore, certain *types* of homes that were once considered to be cornerstones of the child care system, indeed improvements on the past, have quite disappeared. Residential nurseries have gone and we have already noted the dismantling of the approved school system. But a particularly good example is to be found in the rise and fall of residential assessment. In 1946 the Curtis committee recorded that they had 'received almost unanimous recommendations' from their witnesses 'in favour of what [were] variously described as reception homes, sorting homes, or clearing stations'.[46] That led them to propose that there should be one such home in each authority. It is interesting to consider why this was thought to be so important. In the first place there was the legacy of the common poor law practice of admitting a child first to a 'receiving centre', the purpose of which was for them 'to be cleansed and treated for skin diseases and other minor ailments before being placed in a children's home'.[47] The contamination of other children had to be forestalled. However, by the time the Curtis committee reported that concern had been overtaken by an emphasis upon the need to obtain more information about a child before a decision about the most appropriate placement was taken and that, it was concluded, could only be done after a close study of the child and their needs. This, in its turn, was assumed to be most effectively undertaken in a residential setting and by the application of tests of various kinds. Indeed, in 1951 the Home Office maintained that such assessment should be 'the keystone of a local authority's child care arrangements'.[48] This emphasis was reflected in 'reception' homes soon being re-named 'observation and assessment' centres.

Ideas about the nature and process of assessment have changed however, in particular about where and how it should be done. It began to be recognised that the most appropriate decisions about children's well-being needed to draw on a much broader band of information than could be obtained simply by testing and observing children in a contained setting. This, together with other factors such as concern that they should not be exposed to more moves than was absolutely necessary, led to a gradual shift away from residential observation and assessment centres to more comprehensive assessments being undertaken by social workers together with colleagues. That development is reflected in the annual statistics that recorded how looked-after children have been accommodated. For example, at the end of March, 1975, in England and Wales there were 5,300 children in observation and assessment homes.[49] Twenty years later that figure had fallen to 700[50] and by 1998 homes described as offering facilities for such assessment had disappeared altogether from the returns.[51]

Residential provision for children has been in a constant state of flux. However, the extent to which that history provides us with a guide to its future is uncertain. Nevertheless, what it does suggest is that it is likely to be the *kinds* of factors that have been described in this chapter that will determine that future. With that in mind it is interesting to speculate what role residential care for children might play in, say, 50 years time and to consider what purposes that role will be expected to fulfil.

CHAPTER 3

From boarding-out to foster care[*]

The policies, practices and disputes that have surrounded the development of foster care go back a long way. An appreciation of that history helps to place current issues in a broader context than is commonly the case. Here, we begin at 1870 and continue the account up to about 1980, albeit only for England and Wales. These years witnessed changes in both the pattern of foster care and in the assumptions that have been made about it. At the same time much remains familiar; for example, the quest for appropriate foster parents, what best to do by way of supervision and support, questions about which children should be placed in which homes and what purpose the placement is intended to serve.

It will also be apparent that there has been a longstanding inter-relationship between foster care and residential care, with each affecting the evolution of the other. Furthermore, of course, foster care in the public sector has not stood alone. Several of the voluntary societies had boarded-out about a quarter of the children in their care by the end of the Victorian period.[1] By contrast the private sphere of foster care has been informal and unorganised but is now moving to a more commercial footing. This has had, and will continue to have, a significant bearing upon foster care in the public arena, an issue that will be explored further in the final chapter. Likewise, the different history of foster care in Scotland warrants a separate examination although it will be touched upon in what follows.

I Boarding-out and the Poor Law in the nineteenth century

Little attention was paid to boarding-out as a method of providing for poor law children in England and Wales until the 1860s when the number of them under the age of 16 in poor law institutions rose steadily from some 43,000 at the beginning of the decade until, by 1869, it had reached an unprecedented peak of 58,000.[2] The extra

---

[*] This is a considerably expanded version of Chapter IV of my *Away from Home: A Short History of Child Care* (1990). Ilford: Barnardos (commissioned).

numbers, together with the growing insistence that children should be kept separate from adult paupers, confronted many boards of guardians with the prospect of having to embark upon new building programmes. Boarding-out began to find favour as a less expensive option. Had the numbers continued their upward course, the financial argument might well have accelerated the development. As it was, the economy began to pick up after 1870, the number of children in the care of the poor law system fell and the pressure on residential accommodation eased.

Nevertheless, the campaign for boarding-out that had been mounted mainly by a group of influential women in the latter years of the 1860s (and which was to become the National Committee for Promoting the Boarding-out of Pauper Children) was sustained. Florence Davenport Hill's book, *Children of the State* (published in 1868)[3] provided much of the evidence upon which those who advocated boarding-out relied. A major theme was the need to protect young children, especially girls, from the damaging effects of institutional life. Indeed, the boarding-out associations that were formed by groups of middle-class women in various areas were frequently the result of their disquiet at what they saw as members of local workhouse visiting societies.

Yet, as a class, these ladies were also keenly aware of the shortage of reliable domestic servants. Boarding-out offered a promising means whereby pauper girls might be rescued from the adverse influences of workhouse surroundings and, at the same time, be fitted for employment in the lower ranks of servant-keeping households. It was believed that an infusion of additional labour at this level would have a generally beneficial effect by increasing the overall supply.

It must be borne in mind, however, that the boarding-out campaign was chiefly aimed at persuading the central Poor Law Board (and, after 1870, its successor, the Local Government Board) to permit the local poor law guardians to board-out children beyond their boundaries (they could already be placed in foster homes within their area without such permission). The idea was that children should be removed from the physical and morally dangerous surroundings of the cities to the countryside where they could live with respectable cottagers.

Hence, there were several interwoven threads in the case that was made for boarding-out. Different emphases were used in different settings and, of course, different aspects appealed to different groups. Whatever the arguments used by a deputation of lady lobbyists to the president of the Poor Law Board in 1870, they met with some success.[4] The group delivered a petition signed by over 3,000 women. It was agreed that the Board would allow a limited experiment in boarding-out 'beyond the union' and a General Order to that effect was issued in the same year.[5]

This concession was made with a good deal of reluctance, for although it was acknowledged that a properly conducted system of boarding-out could bestow great benefits on pauper children, it was also considered to be open to 'abuses of a deplorable character' and 'result in moral and social evils of the greatest magnitude'.[6] These fears were expressed by the Poor Law Board's secretariat and especially by its inspectors. Their misgivings were of two kinds. First, there were those that sprang from a pervading concern with efficiency, an efficiency that was to be secured mainly by successfully controlling the use of poor relief. This, in its turn, meant avoiding any major departures from the principle of less eligibility (that is, that the condition of those receiving poor relief should not be made better than those who were not) as well as retaining as much central control over local activities as possible. Boarding-out was regarded as a dangerous departure from these objectives. In particular, the circumstances of the boarded-out child might become more favourable than those of the child of the poor but 'independent' labourer. The alarming conclusion drawn by the Board's officers was that more parents would be encouraged to seek poor relief by the prospect of their child being boarded-out in a comfortable cottage home.

Yet it would be a mistake to believe that the central Board, at least on the part of its senior civil servants, particularly its inspectors, took this negative view of boarding-out only because they feared that it would threaten the principle of less eligibility. They also expressed anxieties that in placing children outside the unions – often at considerable distances – the local guardians would not be able to exercise adequate supervision over their treatment and general well-being. In an institution schooling could be assured, over-work could be proscribed and proper food and clothing made subject to detailed regulation. Boarding-out carried unknown risks and dangers that would not be easy to detect or to correct. Worst of all the inspectors could not oversee what went on in the same way that they could when children were collected together in residential homes.

The general distrust of boarding-out that was felt by the central Board's officers was vividly reflected in the limited coverage of the 1870 Order and in the detailed regulations that it contained. Boarding-out beyond the union was only to be allowed in a limited number of unions, mostly those in congested urban areas. These authorities were permitted to place children outside their areas provided that they had made arrangements with a voluntary boarding-out committee in the reception area that was prepared to find foster homes and offer supervision. The children were to be visited at least at six-weekly intervals. In order to prevent any possibility of 'farming-out', not more than two children were to be placed in any one home unless they were brothers and sisters. All boarding-out in larger towns (of over 15,000) outside the union was to be avoided. School attendance was to be compulsory (remember that it was not yet compulsory for other children) and placements were not to be more than a mile and a half from a school. The schoolteacher was to furnish quarterly reports on children's progress and proper provision had to be made for their medical treatment.

Not all children were to be eligible for boarding-out – only those who were 'practically orphans' because of a parent's death, desertion or permanent disability. This was 'to avoid severing or weakening in any way the ties of family, even where, owing to the character of the parents, it might be thought that children would benefit by removal from their control'.[7] The eligible children were to be boarded-out as early as possible after two years of age, but not later than ten. In order that the voluntary committees could keep an adequate oversight of children in remote areas, no child was to be placed in a home which was further than five miles away from that of some member of the local committee.[8] The foster parents were also required to sign a detailed undertaking that specified their responsibilities and which set out the terms upon which they received the child (a maximum payment of four shillings a week was to be allowed, plus clothing allowances, medical and school fees).

These remarkably detailed regulations covered all the possibilities of neglect or ill usage that administrators at the commencement of the 1870s could have been expected to foresee. They imposed a standard that, if achieved in practice, certainly placed the well-being of the boarded-out child at a level beyond what might have been supposed to have breached the principle of less eligibility. Thus the regulations illustrate the tension that existed in the central poor law administration throughout the last quarter of the nineteenth century; a tension between the legacy of 1834 (with all its trappings of less eligibility, means-testing and fear that the system could be open to abuse) and a concern to safeguard the welfare of children who were the responsibility of a multitude of individual boards of guardians that were often regarded as potentially wayward and slack in their administration.

Notwithstanding the new regulations the poor law inspectorate continued to regard boarding-out with misgiving throughout the 1870s and 1880s. For example, Andrew Doyle, the Inspector for Wales, prepared a report in 1875 on how the system was operating in Swansea.[9] The Swansea guardians had rejected his proposal to join with other unions to build a district school on the cottage home pattern. They argued that they were pursuing the alternative policy of boarding-out. Doyle, however, contended that they had only done this in order to avoid having to make new and separate residential provision for children. He visited all the children who were boarded-out (most of whom were in the town) and compiled a catalogue of unsatisfactory conditions. These included the exploitation of children's labour by foster parents, gross over-crowding, irregular school attendance and poverty-stricken surroundings.

Partly as a result of Doyle's report the Local Government Board took new steps in 1877 to control boarding-out within the unions. A similar Order was issued to the one that had been drawn up in 1870 to control boarding-out beyond the union. However, there were certain differences. No age restrictions were imposed and instead of a voluntary boarding-out committee undertaking the supervision it was to be done by a relieving officer and the medical officer of health.

These regulations were introduced in order to combat what the central Board saw as great laxity in the way in which local boards of guardians exercised their responsibility for ensuring the well-being of boarded-out children in their care. They were not intended to promote boarding-out within unions. Indeed, central government continued to be concerned about the poor standard of care being provided to foster children. One consequence was that a special woman inspector (Mary Mason) was appointed in 1885 with an exclusive responsibility for visiting these children. Her reports confirmed the central Board's disquiet. For example, it was concluded from what she presented that a 'strong warning is necessary for the protection of children against ill-treatment or neglect by persons who have taken them for use or profit'.[10]

With notable exceptions, such as Liverpool and Birmingham, there was as little enthusiasm for boarding-out beyond their unions among boards of guardians as there was at the Local Government Board. Even by 1880, in England and Wales, only 500 children were placed at long distance and although the figure doubled in the next five years it never matched the scale of boarding-out within unions. For example, in 1877, of the 93 voluntary boarding-out committees that had been approved by the Local Government Board only 49 were actually responsible for any children.[11] Ladies in the country towns and rural areas were more ready to form committees than the urban guardians were to use them.

However, in spite of the misgivings expressed by the central department and its inspectorate and the reluctance of many local guardians to do other than use the places in institutions that were available to them, boarding-out began to emerge as a distinctive system for looking after poor law children from about the middle years of the 1880s. In 1887 there were 3,300 poor law children in foster homes in England and Wales, or 11% of the total.[12] By the outbreak of war in 1914 there were 11,600, or 26% of all those for whom the guardians were responsible.[13] There were several reasons for this development.

By the first years of the 1880s, following rapidly rising unemployment in 1878 and 1879, the number of children in the care of the poor law authorities began to mount once again, rising to a new peak in 1888.[14] Thereafter, except for a few years, the upward trend continued until, in 1913, boards of guardians were responsible for 84,000 children.[15] The conflict between providing sufficient places in institutions and developing boarding-out became less marked: given certain safeguards boarding-out was seen as preferable to the new capital investment that would have been required to accommodate the rising tide of children. However, there were other influences that also began to cast boarding-out in a more favourable light.

Although full-time education up to the age of 14 did not become universal in England and Wales until 1918, an Act to make it compulsory between the ages of five and ten was passed in 1880. The chances that the boarded-out child would be sent to school were thereby increased. The claim that only by being in a poor law residential school could the education of the poor law child be ensured began to lose its force. This was important because education was regarded by the central poor law authority as the most effective means of breaking the cycle of inter-generational pauperism.

In addition, the critics of institutional care sitting on local boards of guardians also became more numerous, especially as more women were elected.[16] The cause of boarding-out, particularly of girls, was now more often championed by women from within the poor law system rather than by those at a distance who lacked any political foothold in the local administration.

The boarding-out system received additional encouragement from the publication in 1886 of the Mundella report on the maintenance and education of poor law children in the Metropolis.[17] The commissioners recommended that boarding-out should be expanded and suggested, among other things, that more women inspectors should be appointed (a proposal that was duly accepted) and that the age restrictions should be removed (something that was not done until 1911). However, other recommendations, such as that the ceiling of four shillings a week on what could be paid to foster parents should be removed in the case of children under two or for those who had special needs were not taken up.

Nevertheless, the scope of boarding-out was extended by new regulations issued in 1889.[18] Additional classes of children became eligible, most notably those who would henceforth be 'adopted' by guardians as a result of the 1889 Poor Law (Amendment) Act which, for the first time, allowed local boards to assume parental rights and duties over children in their care who were orphans or whose parents were unable to look after them or were considered unfit to do so.

Yet despite these favourable influences the women inspectors of boarding-out continued to emphasise its disadvantages and risks as much as its advantages. They were particularly concerned about the true motives of foster parents. Despite that, as we have seen, over a quarter of poor law children were boarded-out by the outbreak of war in 1914 and the central authority had cleared away many of the restrictions that had formerly been imposed. However, they still insisted that only orphans, deserted, or illegitimate children and those for whom the guardians had assumed parental rights could be placed with foster parents. Even so, there seemed no reason why, after the disruptions caused by the First World War, the use of foster care should not continue to grow. That did not happen. Indeed, the number of children boarded-out by the poor law guardians in England and Wales dropped from 12,000 in 1914 to about 9,000 in 1920, rose slightly to 10,500 in 1925 but then fell again to 5,700 by 1939 – a level similar to that which had prevailed in the middle years of the 1880s.[19] Why was this?

II The inter-war years

One obvious reason for the decline of boarding-out between the wars was that the number of children in the care of the poor law system declined. By 1920 it had fallen dramatically by over 20,000 since the pre-war years.[20] Further reductions occurred, particularly after 1927, so that by 1939 there were only 37,500 children in the care of public assistance authorities in England and Wales; that is, about 45% of the level in 1913.[21] It was inevitable, therefore, that some reduction in the number of those who were boarded-out would occur – but the reduction was disproportionately large. Whereas one in four of all poor law children were boarded-out in 1913 this ratio had fallen to one in six by 1939. Obviously, other factors were also at work.

It has been suggested that local boards of guardians only turned to boarding-out when their institutions were full.[22] Consequently, as there were fewer children to be looked after during the 1920s and 1930s so the incentive to find foster homes would have been weakened. Furthermore, residential homes, as we have seen, were relatively cheap to run. There were no pressing reasons to close them in favour of boarding-out. However, by the 1930s the picture had become more complicated.

The implementation of the Local Government Act 1929 in April 1930 was an important event in the history of the public child care services.[23] Under its provisions county councils and county borough councils took over the functions of the boards of guardians, functions that now became the responsibility of the public assistance committees that were established within these local authorities. An important result of this reform, as we saw in the previous chapter, was that public assistance was located in much larger units of administration, especially in the conurbations and the counties. In London, for example, the London County Council assumed responsibilities that had previously been carried by 25 separate boards of guardians. This provided the opportunity for a considerable pooling of institutional resources and therefore, with the firm encouragement of the Ministry of Health (to whom the responsibilities of the Local Government Board had passed in 1919[24]), for a more detailed classification of homes and residential schools. It also provided the chance to close the least suitable homes and to remove children who still remained (illegally) in the general workhouses. In the first five years after the introduction of the new arrangements 120 children's homes were closed; some were sold and some were put to other uses.[25]

Yet there is little evidence that this was achieved by the increased use of boarding-out. Typically, as we have seen, the thrust of reform was to replace the old, large-scale accommodation with smaller units; that is, by 'scattered homes' or small grouped cottage homes. The combined effect of a reduced number of children in care, a larger pool of residential accommodation, the low cost of acquiring property and of building new small units continued to make it relatively easy (despite the economic stringencies under which local authorities were obliged to work during the 1930s) to close unfit or redundant homes without resort to boarding-out. Nevertheless, there were a few areas, notably London, where special efforts were made to increase its use.

At least four other factors also need to be taken into account however, if a convincing explanation for the failure of the public sector to develop boarding-out during the inter-war years is to be found. One was the availability of an alternative overflow system. In 1931 there were some 250 voluntary children's homes in England and Wales that were certified for the use of the public assistance committees. Many had vacancies. The Ministry of Health's annual report for 1931–32 pointed out, for example, that these were homes that local authorities could and did use in suitable cases if they were unable to incur the expenditure necessary in making their own provision.[26]

A further factor that contributed to the sluggish development of boarding-out between the wars was the absence of any special staff to engage in the recruitment of foster parents or to undertake the subsequent supervision. In 1934, for example, although 27 councils and 47 county borough councils employed women officers who devoted part of their time to boarding-out visiting, they were usually health visitors, district nurses, assistant relieving officers or clerical assistants. In the remaining 26 authorities, the visiting was done by women members of the boarding-out committees (by then sub-committees of the public assistance committees).[27]

It was the problem of inadequate supervision, especially when undertaken by elected members that, probably more than anything else, deterred the Ministry of Health from promoting boarding-out. Instead, advice and guidance were concentrated on the reform and improvement of residential care. The attitude was almost certainly reinforced by the results of a general survey of boarding-out that Ministry of Health inspectors had carried out in 1934. Its main conclusion was that it was important to have 'regular and systematic inspection by a visitor sufficiently trained and experienced to protect the child from a plausible foster mother who might deceive the kindly and well-meaning visitor' and that 'whilst boarding-out with a good foster mother is almost certainly the best means of dealing with the normal child who is left without parents of its own, this system can be a real danger unless properly supervised'.[28] Echoes of the anxieties that had been expressed repeatedly by the nineteenth century poor law inspectors continued to be heard; indeed, after the 1934 report they became distinctly louder.

Another factor that impeded the development of foster care for children in the care of local authorities' public assistance committees between the wars was the prevailing notion that some children were unfit to be placed in private homes. The practical manifestation of this was to be found in the longstanding requirement that the local medical officer of health had to certify that a child was physically and mentally fit enough to be fostered. Obviously, different doctors interpreted this injunction differently but, to all intents and purposes, it debarred those who suffered from chronic illnesses as well as the physically and mentally disabled. As a result, perhaps as many as 1,500 children who were certified as 'mentally defective' and looked after by the public assistance authorities were accommodated in institutions of various kinds.[29] Indeed, there was a profusion of specialised homes in the voluntary sector to which public assistance committees could send the 'deaf and dumb', the 'blind', the 'crippled' or the 'delicate' children for whom they were responsible. There was also a general view that older children were difficult to place in foster homes and that those who were 'coloured' could hardly be placed at all.[30]

Three considerations might well have softened the view taken centrally however, and often locally, about the desirability and feasibility of developing boarding-out. First, there was the Scottish experience. In that country there had been, and continued to be, a strong reliance on the boarding-out system. In 1875, for example, 78% of the children in the care of the poor law north of the border who might have been eligible for boarding-out were so placed.[31] This had risen to 86% by 1914.[32] Although the proportion had fallen by the time of the Clyde committee's report in 1945 it still stood at 68%.[33] The scale of boarding-out in Scotland might have been expected therefore to have lent considerable encouragement for its more active development in England and Wales; but although the reports provided by the Scottish inspectors[34] and by those who visited Scotland from London[35] endorsed the potential benefits of boarding-out they also sounded many notes of caution about the actual practice.

Another reason why boarding-out might have come to be regarded in a more favourable light in the inter-war years was because a parallel system of public child care was inaugurated after the First World War under the auspices of the Ministry of Pensions (covering the whole of the UK) in order to support the care of war orphans or those whose widowed mothers were unable to look after them. Except for a small number who were placed in institutions for the physically or mentally 'defective' all were boarded-out. In 1920 that amounted to nearly 20,000 children, some having been transferred from the poor law.[36] The centrality of boarding-out in this system owed much to the fact that the Ministry of Pensions had no residential resources at its disposal and was loth to use the poor law system for the children of those who had 'died for their country'. The policy was also facilitated because many of the children were looked after by relatives. Nevertheless, in some areas the Ministry of Pensions' regional children's officers (working to a central children's branch) competed with the local poor law authorities for foster homes – principally by offering better allowances. Indeed, it was because of this that in 1920 local boards of guardians were released from the constraint of a nationally determined maximum boarding-out allowance, recognising that foster mothers were expressing 'a desire to receive "pensions children" instead of "poor law children"'.[37] Although the number of children for whom the Ministry of Pensions was responsible gradually declined throughout the 1930s, the Second World War reversed the trend. As a result, by 1946 (in England), 7,000 children were in foster homes overseen by the Ministry of Pensions.[38]

There was yet a third development in the mid-1930s that could have and did provide a boost to boarding-out. After the Children and Young Persons Act of 1933 children who were committed to the care of local authorities by the courts on fit person orders (forerunners of today's care orders) because they were considered to be in need of care or protection became the responsibility of the Home Office centrally and of education departments locally, *not* the Ministry of Health and the public assistance committees. Furthermore, the Act required that committed children be boarded-out unless there were good reasons why this was impractical or undesirable.[39] As a result, by 1945 60% of those subject to fit person orders (in England and Wales) were living in foster homes supervised by local education department staff of various kinds.[40] In contrast, the rate was a mere 15% among those in the care of the public assistance committees.[41] However, because these latter children were much more numerous than the committed group (33,000 to 10,000 in 1945) the combined rate of boarding-out remained low – at about 25%.[42]

In fact, none of these three examples of an active boarding-out policy – in Scotland, by the Ministry of Pensions and by the Home Office – seem to have dispelled the suspicions about it that existed at the Ministry of Health and locally in many public assistance committees. Nevertheless, it might be thought that certain events associated with the outbreak of war in 1939 would have cast boarding-out in a more favourable light.

III The war years and after

The war-time evacuation of British children from towns to the country on an unprecedented scale might have served to restore confidence in boarding-out. Clearly, it was feasible to find foster homes (and at short notice) for a great number of children. However, there was some reluctance to take in other people's children and even when this was done willingly some of the hosts were confronted with difficulties of one kind or another. There was the undeniable fact of some children's deep unhappiness at their enforced separation. Bed-wetting was one issue. Disturbed behaviour was another that necessitated the placement of some evacuated children in special hostels and nurseries. Nevertheless, many children found warm, sympathetic and caring foster parents with whom they prospered. Yet the evidence from this vast 'social experiment' was ambiguous with respect to the future of boarding-out. Much seemed to turn on the quality of the foster home and the needs of the children.[43]

In 1939 the Refugee Children's Movement (the Kindertransport) had brought some 10,000 young Jewish victims of Nazi tyranny to Britain and had placed about half of them in foster homes.[44] This might have been taken as evidence that an enlarged programme of boarding-out could and should be mounted for other children in the care of public authorities; but, of course, half of the Jewish children had not been found foster homes and, in any case, it could be argued that, as a group, they were not comparable with the children who were 'in care' in Britain. Indeed, the same might have been said about the evacuees.

Thus, war provided somewhat conflicting evidence about the possibilities of boarding-out. Neither the evacuation scheme nor the re-settlement of Jewish refugee children offered unequivocal guidance. The issue was further complicated by so many different policies and practices: in local authorities, in the voluntary organisations and, not least, as between various central government departments. There was little co-ordination and a good deal of competition. Furthermore, there was no reliable research that might have helped to point the way forward.

Uncertainty and, indeed, official uneasiness persisted and was further deepened by the death of 13-year-old Dennis O'Neill in January 1945 from starvation and beating at the hands of his foster father. The tragedy seemed to confirm the misgivings that had been expressed repeatedly about the quality of foster homes and the standard of their supervision. Dennis, and his older brother Terence, had been committed to care and were therefore subject to the Home Office injunction that, if possible, all such children should be boarded-out.[45] This much publicised tragedy hardly augured well for a vigorous post-war policy to promote foster care.

So, by the end of the war the evidence about the feasibility and, indeed, about the wisdom of boarding-out was still decidedly mixed. Despite such uncertainties and different standpoints, foster care, as boarding-out gradually came to be called, assumed a central position in post-war child care policy. Plans for the break-up of the poor law had begun to be made from 1943 onwards. If there were to be a national insurance system such as Beveridge envisaged, it would supplant the income maintenance work of local public assistance committees. That meant that its other functions – the care of the old and children in particular – had to be reallocated in the administrative uncoupling of care from the payment of cash. Proposals were prepared within government for the establishment of county and county borough children's committees that would have an exclusive responsibility for separated children. However, a protracted battle developed in Whitehall about which central department should have overall responsibility. The contest involved the Home Office, the Ministry of Health and (at a later stage) the Ministry of Education. In the end, and after disputation at the cabinet level, the Home Office, with its already established children's branch, emerged as the victor.[46] This was important to the future of foster care because, as we have seen, the Home Office was more enthusiastic about boarding-out than the Ministry of Health.

These developments occurred in 1947. In the meantime, a powerful group of child care lobbyists, almost all of whom were women, had launched a campaign for the better care of children, especially young children. The Women's Group on Public Welfare[47] was prominent and so too was the National Council for Maternity and Child Welfare. The child guidance movement was also important as were a number of individual psychologists, magistrates and educationalists. The best known example of the considerable pressure that they were able to exert was Lady Allen of Hurtwood's letter to *The Times* in July 1944 calling for a committee of inquiry into the poor standards and lack of integration of services for deprived children. The target of the attack was chiefly the ill effects of institutional life upon the mental health and sound development of young children. It was mainly as an outcome of this sustained pressure that two committees of inquiry were announced in December 1944, one for England and Wales and one for Scotland.

The first of these, chaired by Myra Curtis, delivered its report in September 1946.[48] The companion report on Scotland, led by Lord Clyde, came a little later.[49] Apart from proposing the creation of separate children's departments in all counties and county boroughs the Curtis report did three things that were to steer child care policy towards a preference for foster care over other forms of provision.

First, although it was acknowledged that standards were not universally bad, the report catalogued grave deficiencies in residential care, both in the public and in the voluntary sectors. Not only were many buildings considered inadequate but the regimes were often unimaginative, harsh and stultifying. Frequently there were insufficient staff and virtually none were trained. Many proposals were made for improvements.

Second, although foster care was regarded as the best way of providing for separated children, major criticisms were made of the way in which foster homes were selected and supervised. It was made plain, therefore, that only when children were 'suitable' and only where 'entirely satisfactory' homes could be found should boarding-out be arranged. Yet such criteria could only be met if the children's officers who led the new children's departments had a sufficient staff of trained visitors. So, third, detailed proposals were made as to how such training should be organised.[50] One-year courses would be located in universities and recruitment was to be under the guidance of a central council and aimed at those who already had relevant background qualifications – people such as graduates in psychology or philosophy, those with social science diplomas or certificates, trained health visitors, non-graduate trained teachers and so on. The training of 'well-educated people' was the precondition for the 'safe' development of foster care as the flagship of child care policy. These recommendations were adopted and an emergency programme launched soon afterwards. It laid the foundation for a profession of child care that, in time, was to make a major contribution to the establishment of the wider profession of social work.

With some notable exceptions, the recommendations of the Curtis and Clyde Committees were incorporated in the Children Act 1948 and, in terms of the treatment of children in the care of local authorities, foster care was accorded pride of place. In the explanatory circular that accompanied the Act, authorities were urged 'to use every effort to arrange for boarding-out in suitable cases'.[51] This set the scene for what was to become a vigorous campaign, especially on the part of the Home Office children's department that, as we have seen, now had overall national responsibility. As well as the factors that have already been discussed two others imparted a special impetus to this policy in the years that followed.

One was the acute shortage of building materials and building labour and the high priority that had to be given to housing repairs and then to the housing drive. For instance, after stressing the value of boarding-out for the child a Home Office circular in 1952 pointed out that its expansion 'should relieve pressure on accommodation in children's homes and residential nurseries, at a time when restrictions on capital investment limit severely the improvement of existing premises'.[52] These constraints lasted at least until the mid-1950s and meant that it was difficult to improve or replace existing residential accommodation;

but the number of children in care rose sharply from the end of the war until 1953, thereafter remaining at much the same level until the second half of the 1960s.[53] If the aim to avoid placing or retaining children in unsuitable or overcrowded residential accommodation was to be realised then many of the extra children had to be found foster homes. As the Home Office pointed out in 1951, 'in most areas all the children's homes are full, and in some areas the number coming into care is rising, with the result that newly acquired premises are immediately filled up', adding that 'an important contribution to the solution of the problem of unsatisfactory buildings is to pursue a vigorous boarding-out policy'.[54]

The other additional factor that served to promote foster care, and one that is still influential, was the coincidence (or so it seemed) that the most desirable provision was also the cheapest. For example, a Home Office circular in 1952 ended by emphasising that 'boarding-out is the least expensive method of child care both in money and manpower, and in the present financial condition of the country it is imperative to exercise the strictest economy consistent with a proper regard for the interest of children'.[55]

The policy of boarding-out received further support on these grounds from the Select Committee on Estimates whose report on the child care service was also published in 1952. It emphasised, for instance, that 'local authorities are under a specific obligation to use boarding-out as the normal method of providing for children in their care with an implied obligation to give it an overriding priority and to make it the main objective of all their work in this connection'.[56] In their reply to this report the Home Office claimed that they were 'at one with the Committee in wanting to secure a large expansion of boarding-out and to see this achieved in all suitable cases, bearing in mind that expansion cannot be forced unduly without risk of unsuitable placings and consequent damage to the children'.[57] The reply went on to add that renewed instructions would be issued to local authorities to the effect that boarding-out was, with due safeguards, the primary objective.

Some local authorities embraced the policy more wholeheartedly than others however. Some faced different local traditions and different attitudes towards fostering, while some had better opportunities for recruiting foster parents than others. It did not follow that because the Home Office continually emphasised the policy that individual children's committees of the county councils and county borough councils accepted it blindly, ignoring local conditions and their own beliefs and attitudes. Rates of boarding-out varied considerably between authorities. For example, in England and Wales in 1952 the highest rate was 82% and the lowest 20%.[58]

Nonetheless, despite considerable encouragement and chivvying from the Home Office through its inspectors, neither the number nor the rate of children boarded-out increased very much after an initial surge that seemed to have been exhausted by about 1954. The rate only rose from 45% in that year to a peak of 48% in 1964, after which it declined steadily and continued to do so throughout the 1970s. In 1974 the rate stood at 32% – roughly what it had been at the inauguration of the Children Act in 1948.[59] Given the enthusiasm with which the policy of foster care was promoted in the post-war years, its lack of expansion through the 1960s and 1970s needs to be explained. As is so often the case, there is no straightforward answer; but several intermingling factors can be identified.

As was noted in the previous chapter one important reason for the reduction in rates of fostering after 1971 was that, as a consequence of the Local Authorities Social Services Act of the previous year, the approved schools' population, numbering some 12,000 youngsters, was included in the total number of children in care. However, many of them were adolescents who were more difficult to place and they continued to be accommodated in former approved school buildings, by then renamed 'community homes with education'.

Another reason for the sluggish development of foster care was the dearth of trained staff who could take the policy forward with confidence. Even by 1960 only 28% of child care officers working in local government were professionally qualified.[60] Yet increasingly their tasks were becoming more diverse than the authors of the Curtis report had foreseen. More work was being done with the families of children and with children who were not in care. There were also responsibilities for adoption and for working with children in residential homes. There was other work to be done besides finding and supervising foster homes. Indeed, the graduation of 'boarding-out visitors' to 'child care officers' was more than a change of title; it reflected a much wider range of responsibilities.

Satisfactory foster parents also seemed to be in short supply, particularly in some areas. The need to understand how that supply might be increased was one of the reasons that prompted the Home Office to ask the Government Social Survey to undertake a study of the issue. The results were published in 1957[61] and represent the first systematic study of fostering in this country. Although the report drew no conclusions nor offered any suggestions for action, a profile of the foster mothers did emerge. Three-fifths of them were over 40 when the child in the sample was placed. Half had no other children at home and over a third were childless. One in eight had an adopted child living with them and, in all, a third had considered, or were considering, adoption. Virtually none was in paid employment. Most were working-class, although both extremes of income were under-represented – the upper income groups appreciably so.

The evidence suggested two conclusions. One was that the recruitment of foster mothers (little was said about foster fathers although almost all the women were married) drew upon a comparatively narrow band in terms of social class, age and family composition. The second conclusion was that foster homes were, in the terms that Holman was later to use to classify different styles of fostering, 'exclusive'.[62] That is, they were typically long-term and adoption-like. For example, the Social Survey's research found that 80% of the foster children had no contact with their mothers during the time they had been in the foster homes and that mothers had only visited 4% of them on a regular basis.

Of course, the more fostering that was long-term, the fewer foster parents there were who could be used several times over. That increased the scarcity, as did the fact that the rule about not having more than two foster children at one time (unless they were brothers and sisters) was not lifted until the boarding-out regulations were revised in 1955.[63] However, the scarcity also began to be accentuated by far-reaching economic changes.

The 'traditional' foster mothers who were portrayed in the Social Survey's study were members of a generation in which it was uncommon for working-class wives to go out to work. From the 1960s onwards a new generation of wives and mothers was emerging who were occupied in, or intending to return to, a paid labour market that was increasingly anxious to recruit them, albeit often on a part-time basis. Where the rates of female participation in paid work were high, or climbing, local authorities were liable to find the recruitment of foster parents difficult unless the boarding-out payments compared favourably with prevailing wages – and few did.

The shortage of foster parents was also aggravated by the acute post-war housing problem in many areas. Slum conditions and overcrowding were often widespread in just the localities from which children were most likely to come into care; and there was a growing disinclination to place children away from where they had been living. The post-war slum clearance drive did not really begin until about 1955, much of it leading to the high-rise developments of the 1960s that did little to increase living space.[64] Without enough space families could not readily contemplate having a foster child.

In endeavouring to understand the nature of the post-war shortage of foster homes (or shortage at any other time for that matter) account must also be taken of the rate at which they broke down. This affected supply in two ways. First, when foster homes collapsed, for whatever reason, they were unlikely to be used again – they disappeared from the pool. Second, since many children returned to residential care when breakdown occurred, there was a re-circulation of demand if they were to be fostered again.

A series of studies of foster care reported their findings in the 1960s and all indicated high rates of breakdown. In 1960 Trasler estimated that between a third and two-fifths of all long-term placements were unsuccessful[65] and in my study, at about the same time, I found a failure rate in one county of 48%.[66] At the end of the decade George reported the results of his study in three areas and these showed an overall breakdown rate of 60%.[67] Whatever reservations there were about how success and failure were defined, the size of the problem of failure (later termed 'disruption') was obviously considerable. More caution began to be taken about pressing ahead with the 'league table' of fostering in which high rates were considered to indicate that a children's department was both progressive and successful.

The idea that some children were not capable of being fostered also persisted, although in an attenuated form. Medical officers were no longer required to certify a child's fitness to be fostered but, even in 1955, instances of the successful boarding-out of 'difficult' children were sufficiently notable to be described separately in the report of the work of the Children's Department of the Home Office.[68]

At the end of the Second World War about a quarter of the children in public care in England and Wales who were boarded-out were placed with relatives. This proportion remained steady until towards the end of the 1960s. In 1968, for instance, it still stood at 23%.[69] By 1975, however, it had fallen to about 14%.[70] It is unclear why this should have happened. There may have been a deliberate policy in that direction in some areas. Furthermore, the report on the death of Maria Colwell at the hands of her step father in 1973 had pointed out the complicated circumstances that had preceded Maria's return to her mother and step father, prominent among which was the considerable animosity between the aunt with whom she had been fostered and her mother. In the light of this some authorities became more cautious about placing children with relatives.[71] However, the trend had begun its downward course before then and was only slightly accelerated afterwards. The decline may have had something to do with increasing rates of household mobility or to the higher standards being applied to the selection of foster parents in general. Nevertheless, the consequences were plain: more unrelated foster parents had to be found.

There are, therefore, several factors that help to explain why, despite periods of intense encouragement from the Home Office, foster care did not advance as fast or as extensively as might have been expected in the 25 years after the end of the war in 1945. Further developments awaited new organisational, political, financial and professional developments in the 1980s.

Important among these have been the establishment of special fostering (and adoption) teams and the growing conviction that, given enough care and energy, virtually no child was 'unplaceable'. These developments were aided by the dissemination of ideas about good practice that was encouraged by the work of organisations like the British Agencies for Adoption and Fostering and by Barnardos. Yet, as much as anything else, the rapidly rising cost of residential care imparted a renewed impetus to the quest for more foster homes. In this climate, the belief that the best form of care was also the cheapest became politically irresistible.

Nevertheless, in spite of all these favourable factors, only 50% of the children in the care of local authorities in 1985 in England and Wales were fostered.[72] However, another 17% were 'home on trial' with parents or relatives and therefore not available to be placed in foster homes although they were still in care. If this group is excluded from the total number of children in care then the rate of fostering rises to 62%.[73] Even so, a third of all children in care still remained in residential care of one kind or another[74] and many more than this would have experienced a residential placement at some time. There still appeared to be many factors that impeded the development of foster care beyond a certain level.

Let us stop here in the mid-1980s but continue an account of more recent developments in fostering and, indeed, adoption, in Chapter 7.

CHAPTER 4

The evolution of landmark legislation*

The three Children Acts of 1908, 1948 and 1989 each reflected the times in which they were enacted. Sometimes, as in 1908, politicians spoke of 'a propitious moment' or, as in 1989, of recent years having offered 'an historic opportunity' to reform child care law. What was it, therefore, in these instances, and in 1948, that created the climate in which it was judged both necessary and opportune to introduce these major legislative reforms?

I The 'Children's Charter' 1908

Although the Liberal Party had won a landslide victory in the election of January 1906 it is doubtful whether they came to power with a clearly formulated programme of social reform. However, sufficient measures followed, such as the Children Act of 1908 and the Old Age Pensions Act in the same year, for their administration often to be credited with creating the foundations of a welfare state. Yet the reasons for this departure are complex. Some lay within the Party where those such as Churchill and Lloyd George were keen to advance the cause of social reform. Some lay in what has been termed 'the pressure from below'; that is, in a fear of the possible repercussions of working-class discontent and in the election of 29 Labour MPs in 1906.[1] Even so, there was a more pervasive influence that encouraged social reform; namely, a growing concern about the decline of British power in the world.

The British Empire, seemingly so secure in the past, now looked under threat from the military and imperial aspirations of other European powers, especially Germany. Supremacy could no longer be taken for granted, a fact that had been starkly illustrated by the

---

* First published under the same title in the *Journal of Children's Services*, 2010, 5 (2). I provide a fuller account of the politics surrounding the 1908 Children Act on the website of the Childcare History Network: www.cchn.org.uk

army's deficiencies in the Boer War (1899–1902). In future much was considered to depend upon improving the efficiency of the armed forces. Yet compelling evidence emerged of the unfitness of potential recruits. A large number of young men, not long out of school, were being rejected on medical grounds. An article written by a Major General in the *Contemporary Review*[2] in 1902 put the proportion at 60%. A year later the Director of the Army Medical Service, although questioning the exact proportion, nevertheless drew a similar conclusion.[3] The implications were clear. If the problem were to be remedied then the health of the rising generation had to be improved; and this conviction merged with growing support for the eugenics movement in influential circles[4] and for the ideas of those who promoted the case for 'national regeneration'.[5]

The evidence emanating from army sources did not stand alone, however. In 1903 and 1904 two influential reports from committees of inquiry were published: one from the *Royal Commission on Physical Education (Scotland)*[6] and the other from the *Inter-Departmental Committee on Physical Deterioration.*[7] The Scottish report was important because two large-scale studies of the health of schoolchildren had been commissioned. The purpose was to establish whether a regime of physical training could be safely introduced without damaging the health of poorer children. In fact, many were found to be in such bad health that they were not fit enough to undertake the exercises involved. The report on physical deterioration was equally disturbing. It concluded that there was ample evidence to show that a major problem of ill-health existed among the working class which, if not addressed, would steadily erode Britain's economic and military prominence. The remedy was again obvious: improve the health of children.

Furthermore, these reports, and the information from the army, were not the only sources of disturbing evidence. Between 1892 and 1897 Charles Booth had published his ten-volume study of the *Life and Labour of the People of London* charting, among other things, the nature and extent of poverty and ill health.[8] This was followed in 1901 by Seebohm Rowntree's *Poverty: A Study of Town Life* which showed that serious physical defects among the poor resulted from their inability to purchase adequate food. In the course of the study nearly 2,000 schoolchildren were examined. More than half of those in the poorest families were found to be in 'bad' physical health.[9]

Hence, by the time of the Liberal Party's election in 1906 there was well-founded evidence of the extent of child poverty and of its disquieting consequences for the future of the nation. The outgoing Conservative government had failed to make the political responses that might have been expected and, at first, the same could have been said of the Liberal administration. The Education (Provision of Meals) Act of 1906[10] was not, in fact, the result of a government initiative but of a private members' Bill supported by the Labour Party but not obstructed by the government. However, it only went as far as giving local authorities the power to provide school meals if they chose to do so. The following year the medical inspection of schoolchildren was introduced, but partly as a result of backbench pressure and partly through the determination of Robert Morant, the Permanent Secretary of the Board of Education.[11]

One of the reasons for the new government's initially slow response to the pressing issue of children's poor health lay in the fact that, until 1919, there was no Ministry of Health to take the lead. Responsibility for the health of children was divided centrally between the Local Government Board and the Board of Education. Why, therefore, should the growing concern about 'national degeneration' have influenced the Home Office in its decision to embark on framing a Bill that was to become the Children Act of 1908?

For the reasons that have been outlined, the condition of children had gained political prominence in the early years of the twentieth century. Against such a background it is not difficult to appreciate that concern about aspects of children's welfare other than their health should find a favourable political reception. That background also offered pressure groups a better opportunity to press for reforms. Nonetheless, in a busy legislative programme such reforms had to find a champion within government. That champion was Herbert Samuel, the newly appointed Under-Secretary of State in the Home Office.[12] In his memoirs[13] and in the parliamentary debates on the Bill,[14] he maintained that his interest in the question had been caught by the intercession of a Mrs Inglis. All we know about her is that she was involved in welfare work in Edinburgh and had visited Samuel in order to argue that the better protection of children required both new legislation and the creation of a Ministry for Children.[15] Samuel accepted the first of these proposals but not the second. In the House of Commons debates however he also explained that he had been much influenced by the findings of the reports that we have described, by conversations with Rowntree and by what he had heard from a number of campaigning groups.[16]

Even so, the Act of 1908 was far from comprehensive, dealing mainly with the treatment of young offenders, especially the abandonment of their imprisonment and the removal of the severest punishments. Furthermore, it required juvenile courts to be established throughout the country. However, it also dealt with the better protection of infants placed in the care of private individuals, with the prevention of child deaths as a result of being laid upon in their parents' bed or because they were burnt by open domestic fires. In addition, children were henceforth prohibited from being in public houses during opening hours. It did not cover what today would be called 'looked-after children' although it did consolidate legislation on cruelty and neglect as well as that regulating the work of industrial schools and reformatories. There were two principal reasons for these limitations.

One was that because the Bill was a Home Office initiative there was a concern that there should be no encroachment on the jurisdictions of other departments, particularly those of the Local Government Board and the Board of Education. Thus, only matters for which the Home Office was responsible were considered for inclusion. The second reason for the limited scope of the subsequent Act lay in Samuel's concern that the Bill should obtain a smooth passage through Parliament. Consequently, potentially contentious issues that could have been seized upon as grounds for opposition were omitted.

Partly for reasons such as these the Act of 1908 has often been characterised as little more than a consolidation of measures going back to the 1850s and, certainly, that was one of its purposes. Even so, it was also a response, albeit belated, to the need for reform.[17] However, it was significant because it marked a clear acknowledgement that the State had an ultimate duty to protect children from harm while, at the same time, imposing penalties (typically fines) on parents who failed to do so: the assumption being that these would induce them to mend their ways.

II Dismantling the Poor Law

It is evident that the Boer War, and then the prospect of war in 1914, had contributed to the creation of a more propitious climate for the introduction of reforming child welfare legislation in the early twentieth century. War was even more significant in creating the prelude to the Children Act 1948. First, many services (particularly medical services) had had to be made available without charge because of the exigencies of war. Domestically there were the air raid casualties and the homeless to be aided. Likewise, the armed forces had to be provided with medical and other services that most had not enjoyed in civilian life. It became obvious that after the war the previous reliance on the poor law of those in adversity could no longer continue.[18] In short, the poor law system had to be replaced, and that included its responsibility for the care of separated children.[19]

A second and related reason why the war was so important in creating the necessity for a new child care organisation arose from the fact of evacuation. At the outbreak of war in 1939 tens of thousands of children were dispersed from the danger areas to safer places. As early as 1943 the Ministry of Health had established an internal committee to consider the problems that would arise when that scheme came to an end. In particular, there was concern that some children would be left where they were. The estimate (grossly exaggerated as it transpired) was that there would be 10,000. However, it was considered politically impossible to leave this problem in the hands of the reception areas and their poor law authorities; but if the remaining evacuees were to be kept out of the poor law fresh administrative arrangements would have to be made. Why, therefore, shouldn't such a new system assume responsibility for all children in public care?

The whole issue was set out in a Ministry of Health paper entitled *The Break-up of the Poor Law and the Care of Children and Old People* that was circulated within government early in 1944.[20] Among other things it proposed that all homeless children should be the responsibility of a separate children's committee in each county and county borough, jointly appointed by health and education committees. This was interpreted in the Home Office as a bid by the Ministry of Health to assume overall control of these services and this led to a protracted contest stretching over the next few years. Nevertheless, what had been established was that there would be a single local body dealing with the care and protection of separated children that no longer had any association with the poor law or with the payment of financial relief.

At the time there was no intention of having a public inquiry to collect evidence of what exactly needed to be done and to make recommendations. The view of the Home Secretary, Herbert Morrison, was that no further investigation was necessary.[21] Eventually, however, his hand was forced by a campaign that was largely orchestrated by leading women in the fields of education and child welfare. Lady Allen of Hurtwood became the public face of the campaign and, conscious of Morrison's reluctance, she wrote to *The Times* in July 1944[22] calling for a committee to look into the poor standards and lack of integration in services for deprived children. What is less well known is that, by the end of the month, 21 further letters from prominent figures had appeared in *The Times*, as well as a leading article. Such a campaign could not be easily brushed aside.

Prompted by the obvious political need to avoid further delay in responding to the campaign, and to the growing number of questions in Parliament, a joint memorandum on provision for homeless children was drawn up by the Home Office, the Ministries of Education and Health and the Scottish Office entitled *Enquiry into Methods of Providing for Homeless Children*.[23] This was then submitted for the consideration of the Cabinet's Reconstruction Committee, mainly because it was independent of these departments. The upshot was (as we have seen in previous chapters) that two committees of inquiry were announced in December 1944 although not appointed for another three months: the Curtis committee for England and Wales[24] and the Clyde committee for Scotland.[25] However, it was firmly indicated that they should not make recommendations about the allocation of central responsibility. Furthermore, it is noteworthy that the announcement that they would be appointed was made before the tragic death of Dennis O'Neill at the hands of his foster parents. Nonetheless, the report on the circumstances of his death recounted a catalogue of accidents, delays and slipshod supervision.[26] This, together with the already widespread press coverage of what had befallen Dennis, increased pressure for the government to make radical improvements in the way in which children in care were looked after; and it became evident that this would have to go beyond a rearrangement of the administrative framework of the services.

What the Curtis and Clyde committees did was to provide evidence of the steps that needed to be taken once the separate children's departments that they recommended had been established and hence how much of this needed to be specified in forthcoming legislation; for example, that boarding-out was to be preferred to institutional care; that reception homes were required and that children in care should normally attend schools in the neighbourhood and not those attached to the institutions in which they lived.

Yet the wrangling between central government departments about which of them should assume overall responsibility for the work of these new local departments continued and was not finally resolved until the matter was referred to the Machinery of Government Committee whose decision that it should be the Home Office was eventually ratified in April 1945 despite a rearguard action on the part of the Ministry of Health and, at a late stage, by the Ministry of Education.

Although the Children Act of 1948 was undoubtedly an important step forward it fell short in the extent of its coverage. For example, it did not deal with the question of prevention, so that it was not until 1963 that local authorities were permitted to devote resources to reducing the number of children coming into care. Nor was there any modification of the longstanding provision (Poor Law (Amendment) Act 1889) whereby, under certain circumstances, local authorities could assume parental rights without recourse to a court of law.

Furthermore, the Children and Young Persons Act 1933 remained a separate measure that dealt mainly with the work of the juvenile courts and the approved schools.

In essence the local children's committees that the 1948 Act created took over the responsibilities for separated children that had previously been discharged by poor law authorities and local education and public health departments. Nonetheless, it heralded changes beyond what might have been foreseen at the time. It laid the foundation for a child care profession as specially trained officers were recruited, many of whom were women who brought a more enlightened approach to the care of vulnerable children. As we shall see in the next chapter this was no more apparent than in the appointment of many talented women to head the new departments. In short, the Act not only severed the final links with the poor law but also brought with it an infusion of new blood and new ideas that gradually saw the unfolding of new policies and practices.

III Taking reform further

Apart from a mounting dissatisfaction with the existing law and with the services being provided, the context surrounding the appearance of the Children Act 1989 was rather different from those in which the Acts of 1908 and 1948 evolved. One additional factor was 'the rediscovery of abuse'.[25] Although the tragedy of Maria Colwell, who was killed by her step-father in 1973, is considered to have been a key event in the reappearance of child abuse on the social welfare agenda,[28] it was not the first sign that the abuse of children had been re-acknowledged. In the United States, the extent and nature of 'baby battering' had been exposed in the early 1960s and, a few years later, the disquiet that it had produced began to find its way across the Atlantic. Even so, concern about abuse continued to be concentrated upon babies, as seen in the Department of Health's first guidance on the matter in 1970.[29]

So, why did Maria's death play an important part in bringing child abuse into prominence? Nigel Parton has provided us with some convincing answers. First, he points out the enormous media interest that was aroused once a committee of inquiry into her death had been appointed and goes on to argue that this reflected a growing concern about the level of violence in society. The subsequent *political* interest that Maria's death generated can be explained in several ways. One is that the public outcry was such that some kind of response became unavoidable. A second explanation, as Parton has documented, revolves around the role played by the then Secretary of State for Social Services in the Conservative government, Keith Joseph. His conviction that there was a 'cycle of deprivation' fed into the parallel conviction that its root cause was inadequate or bad parenting. It was not surprising therefore that Maria's death captured his keen interest. This in turn encouraged more robust measures to be taken to curtail the rights of failing parents, for firmer decisions to be taken about whether or not children in care should be restored to their families and therefore for permanent substitute care to be arranged for those for whom this was judged to be unlikely or undesirable. This theme was echoed in Rowe and Lambert's widely read book *Children Who Wait*, published in 1973.[30]

What we see at this time therefore is what Ray Jones has called 'a battle of ideas and ideology'.[31] On the one hand there was the established emphasis on working to support families, either to prevent children entering care or to engineer their restoration, while on the other there was now mounting opposition to this approach and a call for endangered children to be better protected: if that entailed permanent separation then that, it was concluded, was what should happen, and without undue delay. This view gained in force and found legislative expression in the Children Act 1975 which made it easier for children in care to be adopted or remain in long-term foster care, if necessary against the wishes of their parents. As Parton has put it, 'The Act emphasised the needs of the child over and against those of parents, and reflected a less optimistic view about the solution of family problems than prevailed in 1948 or 1963.'[32]

Concern about the spread of violence had not abated and, in 1974, the select committee on violence in the family was appointed, at the time principally to report on the plight of battered wives,[33] but its enquiries exposed the seriousness of violence to children as well. Seized by such evidence the committee asked to be re-constituted in order to review that issue as well. This was done at the beginning of 1975 and led to their report on *Violence to Children*, published in 1977, in which, among other things, it was pointed out that there was considerable dissatisfaction with the law and with the legal procedures for dealing with non-accidental injuries.[34] However, that dissatisfaction extended to the piecemeal manner in which child care legislation and judicial decisions in general had developed. This had created what Cretney and Masson described as a 'system which was complex, confusing and unsatisfactory with far-reaching (and often adverse) consequences for the welfare of children' and which gave parents only 'very limited rights in care proceedings'.[35] Indeed, there began to be a movement to reassess the position of parents in these proceedings.

This was the climate in which, in 1982, the Social Services Select Committee of the House of Commons decided to undertake a general inquiry into 'children in care' to be chaired by the Labour MP Renée Short. It is, of course, important to understand why the committee chose this issue. Cretney and Masson have argued that the work of pressure groups, such as the Family Rights Group, the Children's Legal Centre and the National Association for Young People in Care were influential in this respect, and that was probably the case.[36]

At the outset, however, the Short committee did not intend to examine the legal mechanisms by which children came into care, or the structure of the courts; but the evidence that it received convinced them that there was a need 'for a review of the constitution, procedures and powers of the juvenile courts, as they affected children in care and their parents, and of the whole legal structure of care'.[37] A comprehensive reconsideration of child care was required, from practice to policy and from policy to law.

This recommendation was quickly accepted and a working party, drawn from the Department of Health, the Home Office and the Lord Chancellor's Department and chaired by Rupert Hughes (Assistant Secretary in the Department of Health) was set up to explore in more detail what needed to be done in order to improve the law as it affected the care and protection of vulnerable children. The group included Brenda Hoggett (now Baroness Hale and a Supreme Court judge) from the Law Commission and a specialist in family law. The working party produced a number of discussion papers, commissioned several pieces of research and, in 1985, issued its *Review of Child Care Law* containing over 200 proposals for reform, many reflecting the recommendations of the Short committee.[38]

At much the same time as the working party was formulating its recommendations the Law Commission[39] was conducting a review of private child care law. A question that arises, of course, is why this should have been happening at the same time. One explanation, as Eekelaar and Dingwall have put it, lay in 'the uncoordinated development of legislation and its interpretation by the courts [that] had created a hodge-podge of rights, powers and duties and a confusing array of court orders'.[40] Another explanation is to be found in the fact that the Law Commission viewed the reform of child care law as an opportunity to reaffirm its usefulness after many of its reports 'had been piling up on dusty shelves'.[41] Nor should Brenda Hoggett's role in this, and as a member of the Law Commission and the working party, be overlooked.

For the moment, however, we should return to that working party's *Review of Child Care Law.* This was largely accepted by the Conservative government and formed the basis for its 1987 white paper, *The Law on Child Care and Family Services,* which spoke of achieving a better balance between 'the State and individual parents', emphasising that the prime responsibility for children's upbringing rested with the latter, but that if there were a need to transfer these responsibilities to a local authority it should be through 'a full court hearing following due legal process'.[42] Furthermore, the report recommended that parents should be properly represented when this happened. What we see here is a shift from the interventionist approach that tended to be favoured in the 1970s to one in which that was to be kept to a minimum unless there was clear evidence that a child had suffered harm or was at risk of being harmed.

It is evident that the inter-departmental working party's recommendations thus formed the basis for the Children Act 1989, together with the Law Commission's work in respect of private child care law, the aim being to bring the two elements together in a single enactment. Even so, what was recommended and eventually adopted fell short of a comprehensive consolidation of the relevant legislation. For example, the working party's report omitted the treatment of young offenders, adoption and the question of establishing family courts. The first may have been excluded because the scope of the reform was already considerable and juvenile justice was regarded as a separate area that could wait upon a later re-examination. On the other hand it may have been omitted for fear that some of the contentious matters that would be involved would lengthen both the process of consultation and the Bill's passage through Parliament.

The reason for the omission of adoption (except for one or two amendments to existing legislation) seems to have been rather simpler; namely, that a separate review was pending and had the Act waited upon these findings its completion would have been delayed. The establishment of family courts was excluded partly for the same reason but also because some of their advantages were to be obtained by the easier transfer of cases between magistrates' courts and the high court ('concurrence' as it was called). Finally, the scope of the Bill in these and other respects may have been somewhat restricted because of the constraint imposed on those who framed it; namely, that it had to be kept to no more than 80 clauses (eventually 108 in the Act).[43]

IV The process of reform

Of course, we have only looked at three among many of the Acts that have affected children's services. Other people, such as Harry Hendrick,[44] have provided more comprehensive accounts that also cover a longer period. Nonetheless, our three-way comparison does permit some conclusions to be drawn. One common feature is that each Act was shaped by what (in translation) Antoine de Saint-Exupéry called 'the slope of events'.[45] That is, by factors that lay beyond the immediate reason for the reforms; for example, in 1908 by anxieties about the damaging effect of a 'degenerating' population upon the nation's military and economic power, in 1948 by the changes in attitudes and expectations that war had produced and, in 1989, by a powerful media keen to report on 'cases' that exposed human tragedies and the shortcomings of the services that were expected to prevent them.

More specifically, however, it is striking how important the convergence of evidence was in the evolution of all three Acts. In each case there was evidence that matters could no longer be left as they were. This emanated from several sources: from the activities of pressure groups, from the work of committees of inquiry, from telling statistics, from the results of research and from the processes of consultation, albeit that their relative importance varied. These emerging facts shared several notable features. One was that they had been accumulating for some time but waited upon what might be regarded as a catalyst before they were brought into play politically. A second was that there was little dispute about their validity, not something that is common in debates about the direction of social policy. Third, the 'facts' began to be quantified, not always correctly, but again without substantial challenge. Last, the information came mostly from what were regarded as 'reliable' sources – from well-regarded pressure groups, from distinguished researchers (such as Booth and Rowntree) or from official or semi-official sources. In particular, it was when that information demonstrated a worsening, or predicted worsening, of what was widely considered to be a problem that it gathered political momentum.

As well as convincing information about problems there was, of course, that which addressed the solutions. In the case of our three examples this provided the detail around which the impending legislation could be shaped; for example, the clauses suggested by the National Society for the Prevention of Cruelty to Children (NSPCC) for the Bill of 1908 or the draft Bill that the Law Commission team drew up prior to 1989. Likewise, the reports of the committees of inquiry that preceded the Acts of 1948 and 1989 certainly suggested what should be incorporated in fresh legislation.

Many accounts of the reasons for reforms are couched in terms of the influence exercised by particular individuals. In 1908 the decisions taken by Herbert Samuel are often cited, together with the intervention of the shadowy figure of Mrs Inglis. No account of the genesis of the 1948 legislation is usually complete without a glowing reference to the role played by Lady Allen of Hurtwood[46] and to the contribution of Myra Curtis. In the case of the 1989 legislation accounts draw attention to Renée Short's influence as well as to that of Brenda Hoggett. There is no doubt that all these individuals were important in their different ways; but there were many others, some of whom were civil servants, such as the group of chief clerks in 1908 (to whom Samuel paid particular tribute), the more senior officers (up to permanent secretary level) in 1948 as well as people like Sir Arthur Rucker who, as Deputy Secretary at the Ministry of Health, wrote the key paper on how the break-up of the poor law should be achieved. In 1989 the ability of Rupert Hughes to secure the productive outcome of the working party that he chaired needs to be recognised. Yet, even when the roll call of those involved is lengthened it was still the context and the events that enabled them, at different times, to make their mark. However, let us consider another potentially important factor in the evolution of our three examples: differences between the political parties.

If one looked only at the events preceding the Act of 1908 it might be concluded that the election of the Liberal government was decisive and therefore that party politics have played an important part in the evolution of child welfare legislation. Of course, we do not know what might have happened had a Conservative administration been returned to power in 1906, but it seems possible that it too would have made some response to the events that have been described. And, of course, steps towards realising something like the Act of 1948 had already been taken by the Coalition government well before the Labour party's election victory in 1945. In both cases the political imperatives were sufficiently strong to ensure that *some* kind of reform would be introduced, although they would not have determined exactly what. Furthermore, some would argue that when proposed reforms concern the welfare of children there is usually a measure of cross–party agreement, or at least acquiescence. This seems to have been evident prior to each of our three Acts but particularly before 1908 and 1989 when steps were taken to avoid the possibility of damaging disputes between the political parties about what was intended. For example, with respect to the 1989 Act Harris has argued that this potentiality was avoided because of the way in which 'the exercise' was handled,[47] and part of that 'handling' reflected the fact that David Mellor, Minister of State for Health in the Conservative government, took steps to reduce the possibility of later disagreements by granting the Opposition and MPs access to the officials involved and it was he who introduced the Bill and saw it through the Commons. Nonetheless, there were low level disputes about the extent to which the State should intervene in family life; but although these reservations were expressed in, for example, parliamentary debates they did not necessarily follow party lines and failed to derail what was intended.

Nevertheless, consensus cannot be taken as a general rule and although not fiercely opposed certain child welfare legislation has been promoted or favoured by one party or another. Indeed, several commentators have argued that the ideological differences between those who favour 'interventionism' and those who stress the importance of respecting families' autonomy, except in exceptional circumstances, have followed party lines, the left being associated with the former and the right with the latter.[48] That was not clear cut in 1908, with the new Labour MPs and certain Conservatives expressing misgivings about the intrusion of the State in family life; nor was it in 1948, partly because of the existence of a coalition government during the war years. The 1989 Act (that tended towards non-interventionism) may have been different, but it is worth recalling that Renée Short, for example, was a fairly radical Labour MP and that neither she nor her party opposed the Bill in Parliament. This is not to say that ideological distinctions were absent from the politics surrounding our three enactments but that these did not accord nicely with presumptions about party differences.

That may be becoming less true as private for-profit enterprises assume an increasingly significant role in the provision of children's services (a development that is discussed in later chapters). Even though the left and the right of the present political system may not differ greatly in their attitudes towards the contracting out of these services, public and professional disquiet about the consequences may gather sufficient force to oblige parties (whether national or local) to reassess and make clear their positions on the matter.

Although, however, party political disputes were not a prominent feature in the progress of the three Acts that have been discussed, departmental rivalry was, in both 1908 and 1948. This was not solely a matter of ministers endeavouring to protect or enhance their domains. Civil servants too had a strong attachment to 'their' department and to its particular emphases and perspectives. For reasons like these it has mattered which arm of central government held the principal responsibility for children's services, whether the Local Government Board, the Home Office, the Department of Health or, now, Education.

The reader will doubtless have been struck by the long-drawn-out preludes to these three Acts. It is as if they waited upon some kind of critical mass to be reached, whether that was of information, outrage, negotiation or the accumulation of so much partial or amending legislation that the call for its consolidation became irresistible. But these delays also owed something to political caution, particularly when competing ideas or claims were in play. There were also practical matters that slowed progress; for example, crowded parliamentary schedules and, in both 1908 and 1989, the delayed availability of a parliamentary draftsman.

Finally, a word about the enduring nature of the problems that the legislation in question sought to address and resolve. A century ago the 1908 Act tried to grapple with the problem of how best to deal with juvenile offenders. It secured a more humane approach: but the dilemmas remain. The Act also included provisions that it was hoped would reduce the amount of juvenile smoking, a problem that remains with us. The 1948 legislation endeavoured to improve the way in which children in care were looked after and, certainly, it shifted the balance away from institutional care towards boarding-out. Nonetheless, we still struggle in practice, as well as in principle, with how best to safeguard children and provide for those who are separated from their families. The manifestation of the problems and the priority attached to them may have changed, as we see reflected in the 1989 Act, but they still revolve around the challenges of forestalling or offsetting the complex deprivations that are still suffered by too many children.

CHAPTER 5

Getting started with the Children Act 1948: what do we learn?*

Having read Judith Niechcial's biography of Lucy Faithfull[1] I became curious about others of her generation who also entered the reconstructed children's services at a senior level in the wake of the Children Act 1948. The new children's officers whom the local authorities were obliged to appoint, together with their committees, were expected to implement the substantial reforms that the Act required. How did they get started and what difficulties did they have to confront? What qualities did they require and how successful were they? Are there still conclusions to be drawn about such reforms that are useful in today's world of regular administrative upheavals?

Of course, Lucy Faithfull (later Baroness Faithfull) was not one of these initial appointees but she was, at the time, one of the Home Office inspectors who, with their colleagues, endeavoured to oversee and guide what was happening at the local level. However, she did move to become the children's officer for Oxford city in 1958. In tracing her career Niechcial has provided us with a window onto the broad sweep of events that unfolded in the children's service after 1948 and, indeed, up to Lucy's death in 1996.

I A starting point

The Children Act 1948 established separate children's committees in all county councils and county borough councils in Great Britain. These were to be responsible for a more integrated service for children in need of care and for a service that was to raise the standard of the care that was provided. Children's officers were to be appointed to see these reforms realised and were to have no other responsibilities. We shall come to the question of how standards were to be raised later, but first it is important to appreciate the scale of the integration that was put

*First published in *Adoption & Fostering*, 2011, 3 (5), an article that benefited from Bob Holman's work and also from Kenneth Brill's unpublished thesis that he completed just before his death in 1991: my thanks to them both.

in train because it was this that presented the children's officers with their initial practical and political challenges.

Before 1948 the public care of children deprived of a normal home life was divided locally between the public assistance committees, education and public health departments. The first of these was responsible for administering the poor law, one part of which concerned the 'relief' of children through their admission to care on a voluntary basis, although it was possible, in certain circumstances, for the local authority to assume the rights and duties of parents. The reasons for these children's initial admission included parental incapacity, desertion and orphanhood. In 1946 there were 33,000 such children in care in England and Wales, of whom, as we have seen already, just 15% were boarded-out.[2] In Scotland there were 7,000, 76% of whom were in foster homes.[3]

Local education departments became involved when it was considered necessary for a court to make a 'fit person order' removing a child from home in order to ensure their adequate care or protection. The 'fit person', almost always the local authority, then assumed the powers and duties of the parents until the child was 18 or until the order was discharged. However, the Children and Young Persons Act 1933 specified that a local authority should discharge these responsibilities through its education committee; they could not be exercised by a public assistance committee.[4] It was because of this that, before 1948, there were staff in education departments engaged in the supervision of committed children, whether they were placed in foster homes or in residential care. In England and Wales in 1945 about 10,000 children were subject to these fit person orders, 60% of whom were boarded-out.[5] In Scotland there were 1,500, 72% with foster parents.[6]

The third arm of local government that was concerned with children's services prior to 1948 was public health. These departments were responsible for supervising (usually through their health visitors) those children who were subject to the child life protection provisions of various public health acts. Children under nine years of age who were not in care but who were 'taken for reward' in private foster homes, in nurseries run for profit, in a few unregistered voluntary homes or who were placed privately for adoption had to be visited and their well-being checked. In 1944 14,200 children fell into these categories.[7] However, the 1948 Act raised the age below which such children had to be visited to 15 and to 18 if they remained in education. This immediately boosted the number to 34,800, an increase of 41%; but that now included 25,000 children who were in independent boarding schools.[8] However, in 1954 the Chancery Court ruled that these 'boarders' were not 'living apart' from their parents and therefore were not subject to the child life protection legislation.[9] Children's officers must have breathed a sigh of relief.

Thus, the new children's officers became responsible for a disparate body of children transferred from three different departments operating different systems, keeping different records and with different policies.[10] Furthermore, as the Curtis committee that reported in 1946 on the care of children pointed out, there had been a history of tension between them and inadequate co-ordination.[11] There had also been a history of uneasy relations between the three central government departments involved; namely, the Ministry of Health, the Ministry of Education and the Home Office. As we have seen in the previous chapter, during the negotiations prior to the 1948 Act each had contended for the overall control of the children's services, a contest eventually won by the Home Office.[12]

II The lucky dip

The report of the Curtis committee had placed considerable importance on the need for each county and county borough council to appoint a separate children's committee, but also for there to be a children's officer answerable to it. Indeed, the Curtis committee maintained that in the new organisation that was recommended these chief officers would be 'its pivot'.[13] Yet it went further, offering a rather detailed specification of the qualities that were required in such officers who, it expected, were likely to be women. They would need to have 'marked administrative capacity', be able to work well with their committees, have a good grasp of local government procedures and have 'enough faith and enthusiasm to try methods old and new'.[14] Ideally, these paragons would also be graduates with a social science diploma and have had experience of work with children. It needs to be borne in mind, however, that the parallel committee of inquiry in Scotland, led by Lord Clyde, although largely mirroring the recommendations of Curtis, made no suggestions whatsoever about the qualities that were to be sought in the new children's officers,[15] nor did the subsequent Act or its accompanying circular.[16]

Although the Curtis requirements may have been desirable it was always going to be difficult to find enough candidates who fulfilled them. Indeed, in the 1951 report of the work of its children's department the Home Office acknowledged that it was 'unrealistic to suggest that all children's officers appointed possessed...the high qualities specified by the [Curtis]...committee'.[17] In the first place there were 129 children's authorities in England, 17 in Wales and 55 in Scotland and although two or more could jointly appoint a children's officer, few did. Where were so many competent officials to be found over a matter of months? A few authorities (such as Essex) had made their appointments earlier, foreseeing the competition that was likely to arise. Many moved quickly after the 'appointed day' but others did not, sometimes from indecision, sometimes from a lack of suitable candidates, sometimes because of unresolved issues within the authority and sometimes because of differences with the Home Office whose Secretary of State had to be consulted about all proposed appointments and who was able to veto those that were considered to be unsuitable.

Some years later the Home Office characterised these initial appointments as 'a lucky dip' that had influenced the success or otherwise of the new services.[18] Who, in the event, was appointed? Although the information is limited we do have two sources upon which to draw. In 1963 Clare Winnicott compiled details of the first 146 appointees in England and Wales. These showed that overall there were 93 women (64%) and 53 (36%) men.[19] Later, Kenneth Brill assembled somewhat fuller details about 119 of those appointed. He found almost the same division between women and men but was able to add that in the counties 79% of those appointed were women, whereas in the boroughs it was 63%.[20]

Both of these sources provided information about the children's officers' previous occupations. Winnicott found that in the 83 county boroughs 67% of those appointed came from education departments and the rest from broadly defined 'social work'. By contrast, in the counties she classed 71% as previously employed in social work and with almost all the rest coming from education. Brill did not give these details separately for the boroughs and the counties. Overall, however, he classified 41% as having been 'social workers' and 37% as having been drawn from 'education'. He allocated the rest to miscellaneous backgrounds, although hardly any had anything to do with health; for instance, only one assistant medical officer of health was appointed and one health visitor.[21] This may seem surprising but, as Brill pointed out, the salaries being offered to the children's officers were low compared with those being paid in the health field or, indeed, elsewhere in local government.[22]

As we have seen those children's officers who had been employed in education would have been mainly concerned with the placement and supervision of children committed to their departments on fit person orders. Some would have been involved in issues of school attendance and some with special education. Only two had been teachers. The 'social workers' were a much more mixed bag, but almost all came from the voluntary sector. Few were professionally qualified[23] and few had any experience of working in local government. Whereas Curtis had recommended that most of those appointed should be graduates, in the event only 37% were, and fewer still combined this with a social science diploma.[24] Of course, many university careers had been forestalled or cut short by the war, with the result that there were fewer graduates than might have been expected. On the other hand, many who were appointed had been in the armed forces during the war or had worked in the United Nations' relief and rehabilitation organisations, people accustomed to bearing a measure of responsibility, often at a young age. In addition, some of the women who became children's officers had been concerned with the wartime fostering of evacuees.

III Women in higher places

One claim made about the consequences of the 1948 reforms in children's services has been that they opened the way for able women to occupy senior posts in local government. Certainly, some of them proved to be exceptional and it has tended to be their names that are remembered and for whom obituaries have been written: women like Joan Cooper in East Sussex who rose to be the chief inspector at the Home Office and then Director of the Social Work Service at the Department of Health.[25] However, it should not be overlooked that some very able men were appointed as well and that even in the early years after 1948 a good deal of reshuffling took place. In Middlesex, for example, the children's officer (Mr Ainscow) moved almost at once to the London County Council as its chief officer, creating an interregnum before another appointment was made.[26]

Nonetheless, the introduction of women into chief officer posts in local government was new and significant. For example, in the 1938 edition of the *Municipal Yearbook*[27] no women were listed as occupying the posts of county or town clerk, medical officer of health, director of education, housing manager or chief welfare officer anywhere in Great Britain. The only female chief officers were five librarians, three museum curators and a registrar of births and deaths. However, there was a sprinkling of deputies, particularly in health and education. Of course, it was up to each authority to decide whether certain posts were accorded the title of 'chief officer' but it is reasonable to conclude that before the war there were no women in the top positions of local government. However, in one fell swoop the Children Act brought in around 125 (throughout Great Britain) and it should be noted that there were now more women in the inspectorate of the Children's Department of the Home Office. In 1946 nine of these 17 inspectors were women. However, by 1954 there were 31 out of a total of 74. Furthermore, they now occupied more senior posts: one (Miss Rosling, who had been joint secretary of the Curtis committee) was an assistant secretary, one the chief inspector (Miss Scorrer), one the senior medical inspector, another the supervising inspector together with seven grade I inspectors, one of whom was Lucy Faithfull. Previously no women had occupied the rather fewer senior positions in what had been called the Home Office Children's Branch.[28] Inspectors in that branch had been concerned chiefly with approved schools, remand homes and hundreds of voluntary children's homes.[29]

It is interesting to bring the story forward. In 1970, the last year of separate children's departments, the proportion of children's officers who were women had fallen to 46% (England and Wales) from its level of 66% at the beginning.[30] However, by 2011 52% of the directors of children's services were women and this virtual parity now exists irrespective of the type of authority.[31]

IV Getting established

By 1949 it might have been expected that that year's *Municipal Yearbook* would see children's officers numbered among the chief officers; but they appear in only 38 of the authorities' entries, none of which was Scottish.[32] The significance of so many omissions should not be overlooked, for they offer a glimpse of the difficulty that many of the new children's officers had in establishing themselves in the top tier of their local authorities and in having the services for children for which they were responsible given the priority that was required.

What, then, were the principal difficulties that challenged those who were to lead the newly created children's services? Inevitably, as we have seen on many occasions since, administrative reform is not trouble-free. It causes upheavals. Establishing a new service is a demanding task at the best of times, but for the new children's officers there were problems over and above those generally associated with rearranging who does what, changing priorities and introducing new policies.

In the first place there were the consequences of the war. There were the disruptions to family life, the effects of which were still being felt in 1948. Services had been run down. Shortages abounded. Austerity was the order of the day. In these conditions competition for almost all resources was intense. If they were to win a sufficient share to enable standards to be raised children's officers needed both determination and political skill. Some rose to the occasion; others struggled. Nevertheless, the challenges were by no means the same everywhere. The standard of the children's services that were inherited varied considerably, as did information about them. Furthermore, the contexts within which problems had to be confronted were different from place to place. There were, for example, eight authorities in England and Wales with populations of over a million (all of which appointed men), while at the other extreme 37 had populations of less than 50,000; and even in between there was a wide variation. Similarly, 12 authorities had more than 1,000 children in care at the time (accounting for 41% of the total) but 23 had fewer than 100.[33] In Scotland only Glasgow had more than 1,000 children in care while 18 authorities had fewer than 50, doubtless the reason why many of them felt that a separate appointment was unnecessary.[34] What was demanded of a children's officer in a large authority was not the same as what was asked of them in a small one, or in a sprawling county rather than a compact urban area; and these differences were often accompanied by different political cultures.

Nonetheless, in whatever kind of authority, children's services could only prosper once their standing had been established. Several factors made this more difficult for the first children's officers. One, as we have seen, was that the majority of them were women who found themselves in organisations that were unaccustomed to having women in senior positions. As Dorothy Watkins (children's officer in Cornwall) rather forcefully put it 'the prospect of a woman chief officer appalled most local authorities'.[35] Moreover, many of these women were young (Barbara Kahan in Dudley and Frances Drake in Northamptonshire were both 28 when appointed)[36] and, as we have seen, many had no experience of working in local government. Moreover, their 'departments' were small by comparison with other arms of local government. They commanded few resources and were paid relatively low salaries. It was not surprising therefore that they found themselves occupying the lower ranks of the council hierarchy.

These, however, were not the only matters that made it difficult to gain an acceptance of the status of the children's services and of those associated with them. Although often referred to as children's departments the 1948 Act did not make this a requirement. A separate department was not obligatory and in some areas, as in Kent for example, the children's officers found themselves located, at least for a time, in the clerk's department and regarded as one of its 'sections'. Then there were the ever-important symbols of status, particularly accommodation and whether or not the new posts warranted the use of a local authority car. In the early post-war years accommodation was at a premium and fitting in one more separate enterprise posed real problems. By and large children's officers had to make do with what they were handed and then fight for something better. Even so, there were some outlandish examples. Brill recounts that in one case the new appointee was given a chair and a table in the macebearer's office[37] and Watkins recalls how her first accommodation was a hut in the County Hall car park.[38]

One important difference between the authorities in which the new officers found themselves was the composition and leadership of the new children's committees. Some included members who understood and were sympathetic to what had to be done in order to improve children's services and who were in a position to influence the authority as a whole. Other committees were less supportive, while some children's officers, unfamiliar with working to an elected committee, failed to use them to best advantage. Furthermore, there were committees that contained disgruntled members because they disliked the reforms. For example, Brill makes the point that 'on the whole the councillors and officers connected with education thought that the child care service could well be done by the education service.'[39] In some cases a local authority's wish to make the director of education or the chief welfare officer responsible for the new children's services (alongside their other responsibilities) had been blocked by the Home Office, creating a simmering discontent that could dog the efforts of the 'imposed' children's officer who would not necessarily have known of this history before they were appointed.[40] Hence, as in all administrative reform, there were elements of dissatisfaction, if not outright opposition, with which children's officers had to contend, albeit that they were not as prevalent everywhere.

As well as all of this there was the question of the staff that were made available. In some places there were none. In others some officers who had been involved in boarding-out were moved across from education or public assistance departments and where this happened it could be a matter of rather delicate negotiation, both during the transfer and after. In Berkshire the Home Office inspector reported that the children's officer could not 'deal with' three such women who were accustomed to working independently of any authority and whose records they kept close to themselves.[41] Likewise, children's officers inherited staff in residential homes, many of whom were fearful of what the changes might portend. Some of these people were unsatisfactory but difficult to dismiss because of their long service, because of the support of elected members or because the children's officer could not face the ensuing confrontation. And, in any case, it was difficult to find good enough replacements.

It was not only these staffing problems, however, that had to be faced but also, in many places, a dearth of secretarial help. Some children's officers began with none. Yet the establishment of the new organisation called for much assistance of this kind. As we have seen, cases were inherited from other departments, together with all the paperwork that went with them, some of which, the inspectors reported, was not up to date, was missing or in a chaotic state. All this had to be sorted out. Without adequate help children's officers could find themselves having to do things that were certainly not what might have been expected. Many worked long hours in order to find out what had to be done and then cope with it. Furthermore, it needs to be remembered that much was, or had to be, handwritten and that typing (together with making corrections and carbon copies) was often a laborious and time-consuming business.

Given the circumstances surrounding the newness and standing of the children's officers in the early years, as well as the fact that many had no experience of working in local government, it is not difficult to imagine that they were liable to feel rather isolated, if not at sea. They needed both support and advice. There were several possible sources, but five were most common.

In 1949 the Association of Children's Officers was formed in order to provide a network within which members could find mutual support, reassurance and information. From the start a Bulletin (of which Kenneth Brill was editor for many years) was distributed ten times a year. Conferences and meetings were held, both nationally and regionally, a sub-committee was established to give advice on legal matters, working groups were set up and evidence submitted to various inquiries. Indeed, the Association came to exercise considerably more political influence than might have been expected, often with the aid of the Home Office inspectorate.

Some children's officers obtained help and advice from the Home Office inspectors directly; but this could not be available on a day-to-day basis, and much depended on the relationship that was established between particular individuals. In some cases this was warm and collaborative; in others it was decidedly frosty.[42] In the larger authorities children's officers may also have been able to call upon the advice of experienced staff who had been transferred from other departments. However, this again depended upon the kinds of relationships that emerged and, of course, these could go either way.

This was equally true of the potential allies who might have been available elsewhere in the authority, particularly directors of education, medical officers of health, chief welfare officers, chief constables, clerks or treasurers. However, they could be indifferent or frankly obstructive if they were unsympathetic to the new arrangements. For example, in Bob Holman's interview with Rosalie Treece (formerly Spence) who became children's officer in Nottinghamshire in 1948 she explained that 'the medical officer of health, the director of education and the public assistance [sic] people didn't want to give up any of their responsibilities, particularly to a woman chief officer', adding that she 'was 34, very young'.[43] But there were certainly exceptions. In her first report, published in 1950, Elizabeth Harvie, the children's officer in Kent, expressed her 'sincere thanks' to the 'generous co-operation' that she had received from the former public assistance officer, from the county education officer and from the medical officer of health.[44] It might be noted that the first of these was John Moss who had been a member of the Curtis committee and a willing signatory. Likewise, several children's officers paid tribute to the support that they had received from the clerks of their authorities, sometimes because they had been placed in those departments as one of their 'sections' and, in a sense, sheltered within a powerful department of local government.

Children's officers certainly depended upon their committees for the support without which little progress could be made. Although the pattern was undoubtedly uneven the available evidence suggests that committees were generally sympathetic to what needed to be done. In Glamorgan, for example, Beti Jones recounted that as children's officer she 'could not have had a better authority' and this she attributed to her committee members having 'a warm instinct towards children and a passion to see that their potential was fulfilled'.[45] However, much turned on who was selected to serve on these committees. For example, in his study of the Manchester children's department, Holman found that Ian Brown, the children's officer, considered himself fortunate in that the woman who first chaired his committee was a strong personality with enough allies to 'put the children's department on the map'.[46] But Brown was doubly fortunate in that he also had the support of Philip Dingle, the town clerk, who became one of the first members of the central Advisory Council on Child Care. He probably also had the advantage of having worked for Manchester as an assistant education officer and of being, at 45, one of the oldest children's officers appointed after 1948. The Manchester case exemplifies the fact that although single sources of support, such as the committees, were important, even more important was the existence of several such sources and, of course, the ability to nurture them and draw upon them with skill and discrimination.

Nonetheless, it was, first and foremost, the committees (and sub-committees) with which the new officers had to establish a working relationship. Sometimes there were members who entertained old poor law attitudes about the limits that should be placed on what was done for children in care, attitudes that could frustrate efforts to secure more benign conditions in residential homes or greater flexibility in supporting foster parents. There were also committees (particularly sub-committees) that were reluctant to allow children's officers sufficient discretion on day-to-day matters or which became over-involved in the running of particular homes. In time, however, these issues began to be ironed out as the membership of committees changed and as mutual confidence was established; but much still turned on how well children's officers played their hand.

As we saw, the Home Office later termed the choice of children's officers as something of a 'lucky dip'; but this could equally well have been said of the authorities to which they were appointed. Only gradually did many of them discover how lucky or unlucky they had been, the most able building on their luck or working to overcome their lack of it. Some were able, some very able, but others were not and it is to these distinctions that we now turn.

V Assessing performance

With so many children's officers it is, of course, impossible to make an overall assessment of their ability, even more so after nearly 70 years. Nonetheless, Brill was able to examine 97 of the assessments of the officers' performance made by the Home Office at the time.[47] These were grouped into five categories. Ten per cent were classed as very good, 40% as good, 26% as satisfactory, 16% as less than satisfactory and 7% as poor.[48] In the 12 largest authorities nine children's officers were reckoned to be less than satisfactory.[49] There was no difference between the counties and the county boroughs or between those who held an academic qualification and those who did not.[50] The one in four officers who were considered below average probably reflected the fact that in 1948 there were just not enough good applicants to go round. Furthermore, although the Home Office could veto some appointments that were considered unsuitable there was no comparable power for them to have a children's officer dismissed. For example, in Berkshire the Home Office inspector considered the children's officer 'weak', unable to get her department organised, 'dilatory in…

instituting the necessary statutory records' and 'incapable of planning' and although comments like these continued to be recorded no further action was taken.[51]

Twenty years after the 'appointed day' the Home Office submitted evidence to the Royal Commission on Local Government in which it set out another assessment of 121 children's departments (not quite the same as the children's officers). Nine per cent were considered to be 'very good', 25% 'good', 39% 'acceptable', 22% 'below acceptable' and 8% 'weak'.[52] Compared with the earlier figures this would suggest some deterioration, although the assessments may have become more rigorous and the challenges more demanding.

Along with their assessments of the children's officers in the early 1950s the Home Office inspectors also gave their views about the children's committees. Twenty-three per cent were considered to be good or very good, 43% satisfactory and 34% less than satisfactory, but only 3% were regarded as 'weak'.[52] What we don't know is how this grading related to that made of the children's officers which would have been interesting – as would the answer to the same question today. For example, although we know that there was a preponderance of women councillors on children's committees we do not know how that affected, if at all, the manner in which they worked with their children's officers, whether men or women.

VI Improving the services

This account of the appointment of the first children's officers and the establishment of a reformed children's service might have been expected to have begun with an overview of the service problems that had to be tackled; but that was not its main purpose. Nevertheless, the performance of these officers cannot be considered without describing the most pressing issues that they faced, apart from their immediate administrative and political challenges.

If improvements were to be made the children's officers had to recruit more trained staff. Yet, as the Home Office pointed out in 1951, 'provision for training was…totally inadequate'.[53] Indeed, prior to 1948 there was no national qualification in child care and, as a matter of urgency, the Central Training Council in Child Care was established in 1947 in order to promote training courses for boarding-out officers and residential care staff. By 1949 there were six rather prestigious courses for the former based in universities and, by 1950, 19 for the latter organised by local authorities; but the output was small. Two hundred and sixteen students had qualified as boarding-out officers by 1950, only four of whom were men.[54] By the same year 355 students had successfully completed residential care courses, 55 of whom were men.[55] It took many years, therefore, before there was anything like an adequate supply. Even by 1964 (the first survey) only 27% of the field staff of English and Welsh children's departments were recognised as qualified by the Home Office and a comparable figure for residential staff still awaited publication.[56] Furthermore, it was the best-led departments which tended to attract the qualified staff so that their distribution became somewhat skewed.

A second major problem was how to shift care from residential establishments to foster homes. That, again, depended on what field staff could be recruited. However, the starting point was different in different authorities. Although, as we have seen, the overall rate of boarding-out in England and Wales in 1949 was 35%, among the different authorities it ranged from 68% to 9%.[57] In Scotland rates were already high, averaging 61% and remained at that level throughout the 1950s.[58] Nonetheless, high proportions did not necessarily mean that there were no problems. In Scotland, for example, many children were placed with families in remote areas of the Highlands and Islands and rarely visited. In England and Wales in 1949 a quarter of the children in foster homes had been placed in another authority's area. Apart from everything else this could create problems of co-ordination, a shortcoming tragically exemplified by the death of Dennis O'Neill from Newport in his foster home in rural Shropshire in 1945.[59] It could not be assumed, therefore, that inheriting a high rate of boarding-out meant that all was well; and many foster homes meant many visits, making it that much more difficult to find new ones.

Caseloads were heavy. In an undated but early report to her committee the Essex children's officer (Miss Wansbrough-Jones) explained that her ten visitors had to supervise the existing foster homes, find new ones, investigate all applications, visit the homes of children in care in order to see if they could return and also attend juvenile courts. On top of these demands there were the children in notified private foster homes to be visited.[60]

As well as the development and improvement of foster care many children's officers were faced with a poor legacy of residential care. Even by 1953 there were some 15,000 children living in large local authority homes in England and Wales and another 6,000 who had been placed in voluntary homes. Perhaps of greatest concern were the residential nurseries. In 1949 some 5,000 babies and infants were being looked after in residential nurseries,[61] some of which were still located in former poor law institutions. Foster care was arranged for some and a few were adopted; but the other solution was the creation of more separate and up-to-date residential nurseries. Between the appointed day in 1948 and February 1951 49 new such nurseries were provided, but 74 still remained in the old institutions.[62]

Thus, many children's officers had to decide how best to deal with deplorable institutional legacies and then win the resources to do what was needed. This was a challenge. As well as the staffing issue the upgrading of residential establishments had to compete for building materials, building labour and win the co-operation of the local authority's hard-pressed architect's department while at the same time satisfying the Home Office's exacting requirements and those of local fire officers.

These various problems in improving the services had to be grappled with at the same time that the number of children in care was rising rapidly. In England and Wales at the end of November 1949 the figure stood at 55,255,[63] but by the same month in 1952 it had grown to 64,682, an increase of 17%.[64] There is, of course, the interesting question of why this happened. Among the reasons offered have been: the aftermath of war and evacuation, much homelessness and a greater willingness on the part of other agencies to refer children to the new children's departments now that there was no longer an association with the poor law. Certainly, there were more and more referrals but not always the time to decide which of them did *not* warrant admission. Whatever the reasons these rising numbers undoubtedly exacerbated the many other problems that had to be faced.

VII Lessons?

A frequent reaction to an historical exploration is to ask what lessons can be learned. Sometimes there are such lessons and sometimes there are not. Sometimes what a study tells us is glaringly obvious and sometimes remarkably surprising. In this account of the early days of the Children Act of 1948 there is a mixture. There are a few conclusions that may still be worth bearing in mind today. Most are about the process of administrative reform.

As remarked earlier, such reforms create upheavals, the consequences of which are not always foreseen and therefore tend to create new problems. In the first place the inauguration of substantial changes on an 'appointed day' and without much preparation take time to 'settle', particularly when they are accompanied by major shifts in policy. One of the obvious reasons is that even when the changes are advocated on the grounds of economy there are always unforeseen costs. For example, foster care was to be advanced because it was considered better for the children but also because the unit costs were less than residential care. There was, it seemed, the marvellous coincidence that what was best was also the cheapest. Yet in order to develop foster care, children's officers needed the necessary staff as well as a range of other resources the costs of which were not always reflected in the accounting process. Furthermore, as we have seen, reforms that are viewed as improvements are liable to increase demand or, at least, to alter its pattern; and this is not always predictable.

Administrative systems generate sets of interests and when these systems are changed there are both winners and losers. Certainly, many children in care were to benefit from the creation of the children's departments and, organisationally, the cause of professional women took a step forward. On the other hand education and public health departments saw their influence being reduced. Likewise, in a number of areas children's officers had to contend with a measure of discontent among the heads of the residential homes that they had inherited, some of whom saw their status and autonomy threatened. Although children's committees were not responsible for the approved schools they were responsible for any children in care who had been placed in them and some children's officers, such as Barbara Kahan in Oxfordshire, were particularly anxious to avoid this. For both reasons negotiations with the often-powerful heads of these institutions could be difficult. And then there were the voluntary children's organisations that foresaw that much of their work would come to be taken over by the local authorities and were understandably apprehensive. In 1949 11% of the children in local authority care were still being looked after by these organisations.[65]

On all these counts the new heads of children's departments had to deal with fears and disaffections, both within their authorities and beyond, disaffections that were likely to make essential collaboration that much more hazardous. Such problems are the common accompaniment of structural reform, but their extent and consequences are not always evident beforehand. Yet their impact will affect the subsequent course of events. It is sensible therefore to assess what they might be and to consider how their perverse effects might be offset, not least by negotiation before rather than after the event.

All this calls for considerable sagacity on the part of those charged with the implementation of significant reforms, and that was undoubtedly true in 1948: hence the importance of these early appointments. However, how was this ability to be determined by appointing committees and in different local contexts? In any case, was it a single attribute? As Brill pointed out, the children's officers might be full of passion and determination but be sadly lacking in political skill. Yet the one without the other will rarely be enough. So, what is the nature of political skill? It varies, but rests upon the possession of vision combined with information and the associated foresight. That is to say the ability to understand the terrain, to appreciate the character of the obstacles ahead and the pattern of potential alliances. Yet, even then, the manner in which this skill is exercised will vary. There is a good example in Judith Niechcial's biography of Lucy Faithfull in which she contrasts Lucy's 'style' as children's officer in Oxford city with that of her neighbour, Barbara Kahan, in the surrounding county. Barbara, she writes, 'made a conscious decision to be a "battleaxe" rather than a "nice girl"...Lucy used quite other tactics. She was the "nice girl" personified, who used her charm, diplomacy and "people skills" to get her way.'[66] Both seem to have been successful although working in somewhat different settings. The lesson might be that appointing committees have to know what will be needed and, for that, they too have to have good local information together with a vision of the future. Only then, and only with difficulty, will they be able to pick the right candidate. In 1948 it was understandable that some committees did not understand what was going to be wanted of their new chief officers and what might have to be faced in the years to come, most notably the emergence of child abuse as a prominent issue and the quest for prevention.

Though inspiring, the prescription for the new children's officers that the Curtis committee laid out was too general to be easily applied and some committees, as well as their appointees, held too closely to one of its main recommendations; namely, that the children's officer should have a personal relationship with the children for whom she (usually she) was responsible as well as with her staff. This could lead to unreasonable centralisation, to a reluctance to delegate and to a preoccupation with detail at the expense of the broader issues. Nevertheless, it is fitting to end on a note of approbation for what many children's officers and their staff achieved between 1948 and 1970. Partly by their individual and collective efforts and partly through the work of the Association of Children's Officers and of its companion group the Association of Child Care Officers,[67] as well as other pressure groups and an emerging body of research,[68] services for children and their families were transformed, the extent of which is still not always appreciated. Much was achieved against the odds.

CHAPTER 6

Child care in the melting pot in the 1980s[*]

As explained in the preface, this chapter is my view of the state of the child care services in 1984. It has not been brought up to date and the use of the present tense refers to that time. This was deliberate because, standing largely as written, it provides an historical benchmark. It focuses mainly on what questions needed to be addressed in order to improve the standard of these services. In the light of subsequent events the reader might like to judge the accuracy of my analysis as well as the kind of progress that has been made since, perhaps with the help of subsequent chapters.

Our child care system has been shaped and sustained by powerful and persistent perceptions. These images have become so much a part of the way in which questions of policy and practice are approached that they generally pass unnoticed. Even when they are recognised they tend to be taken for granted. That is not surprising, for some of these images trace their origins back at least as far as the spate of child and family legislation of the 1880s. Yet we have reached a point where a reconsideration of these dominant perceptions is needed if improvements are to be made. Admittedly, many issues are being reassessed and important new developments are being introduced. But the framework of perceptions within which they occur remains much as it always has been; and that constrains the scope for imaginative reform. It is also liable to distort the way in which problems are defined. Both constraints and distortions arise because the conventional perspectives of child care are: (1) narrow, (2) undifferentiated, (3) static and (4) imitative.

[*]Based upon a lecture delivered in Edinburgh at the 1984 AGM and Study Conference of the Scottish Child and Family Alliance and published in the conference papers under the title of *Child Care in Perspective: Kilbrandon Twenty Years On* (1984).

I Narrowness

The debate about child care usually revolves around children for whom local authorities are more or less responsible. They owe their separate enumeration to the existence of the legal and administrative categories into which they fall. The problems that face these children and their families then come to be seen as of a different order (rather than of a different degree) from those that face many others as well. As a result policies are rarely located in the wider context of family and child policy. This becomes a hindrance to the energetic pursuit of prevention, integration and the alleviation of some of the serious disadvantages to which children are exposed.

The child care system is even separated from other forms of substitute care, although it is increasingly clear that some of these are inter-changeable and inter-dependent. For instance, it is hardly a matter for congratulation if we reduce the number of children in care by deflecting more of them to the penal system. Boarding schools offer another form of substitute care. There are, indeed, more children in private boarding schools than there are in local authority care, and they may well stay longer. Some children who are deemed to be physically or mentally disabled come to the attention of health and education authorities rather than to the social services and may then be placed in special boarding schools. Although the overall number of children in such schools is falling, the number is rising in schools (especially private schools) for the 'maladjusted'.[1] Whereas there is a growing concern about children in care who remain in a state of limbo waiting for firm decisions to be made about their futures, less disquiet is expressed about other children who languish in special schools or certain hospitals.

Furthermore, some forms of substitute care are viewed in a distinctly more favourable light than others partly, but not wholly, because they are used by a different class. When middle-class divorcing parents tell the judge that they intend to send their young children to a boarding school he will almost certainly accept that as a 'satisfactory' arrangement.[2] By contrast the children of less well-off or less well-organised parents may be made the subject of a matrimonial care order and placed in the local authority system, possibly until they are 18.[3]

In this and in other circumstances the relationship between private and public systems of care needs to be taken into account in the policy debates; but it rarely is. Take for instance private and public foster care. In the last ten years the number of children in local authority foster homes has risen by about as much as the number in private foster homes has fallen. The overall number of children in foster homes of both kinds has remained remarkably steady.[4] It is always noteworthy that while publicly supported foster care by strangers has grown, publicly supported foster care by relatives has fallen even though several recent studies (including one in Scotland) offer evidence that the placement of children in care with their relatives is one of the more successful arrangements.[5]

In the light of considerations like these, why should there be such a narrowly conceived debate about substitute care? There are at least three reasons. First, responsibility for each of the different varieties of care is compartmentalised and divided between different organisations or social and economical sectors. Each administration stoutly defends its separate budget as well as its jurisdiction. Second (except in the penal system), it is only in the public child care sector that coercion is employed to secure the separation of children and parents. That tends to set it apart. Third, in continuing to approach the issue of substitute care in a tightly-defined way the level of public expenditure can be more readily controlled. Thus, there is a range of complicated interests in viewing substitute child care narrowly rather than broadly.

Nonetheless, there are signs that modifications are occurring to our traditionally limited conception of child care. One of these is the blurring of the sharp distinction between a child being in care or out of care. For example, in England and Wales at the end of March 1982 17,200 of the 44,000 children who had been committed to care by a court order were allowed to be 'under the charge of parent, guardian or friend'; that is 39%.[6] Although there is no evidence that this was a deliberate policy it has altered the profile of the manner in which children who are subject to care orders are looked after. Whether the practice of allowing such children 'home on trial' will continue at its current level is another matter.

Even children who are in residential homes seem increasingly to spend weekends or longer periods at home. Doubtless fewer live-in staff, the difficulties of weekend coverage and the more extensive unionisation of residential employees have played their part in these changes. However, the point remains: regular periods at home contribute to the breakdown of the practical, if not the legal, distinction between being 'in care' (away from parents) and 'out of care' (with parents). This process probably has much further to go, encouraged, for example, by the more flexible and informal use of residential resources as family centres and by the growing number of queries about whether we need to have a specially devised legal category for voluntary admission to care. Certainly, this is one of the questions that, following the report of the Short committee for England and Wales,[7] one might expect the working party on the review of child care law to be considering.[8]

The narrowness of the conventional image of child care may also be undermined by reforms in another quarter. As well as the review of child care law, the Lord Chancellor's department and the Home Office in England have set up a working party on family courts. A renewed impetus has been imparted to ideas first aired in the 1960s.[9] Many organisations are busy formulating views and submitting evidence. Exactly what will emerge from these deliberations is difficult to predict; but even a partial integration of the various family and child jurisdictions that now exist will break down some of the insulation around conventional child care. Questions of custody and access, for instance, that have been dealt with quite separately in the two areas of divorce and child care, will more clearly be seen for the common issues of principle that they are. Indeed, one might argue that the increase in divorce followed by family reformulation that has occurred in the last decade or so has made it increasingly difficult to regard key issues in child care concerning the relationships between parents, children and others as being of a quite different order to those which arise elsewhere.

These are some of the opportunities that are now available for broadening our perceptions and conceptions of our children's services. There are three reasons above all others why such opportunities should be seized. First, the existence of a special class ('moral category' would not be too strong a term) to which seven children in every thousand and their parents find themselves consigned heightens the likelihood of stigmatism and detracts from an *overall* approach to child care issues. As the Short report was at pains to point out, the very existence of their special committee on children in local authority care 'unwittingly reinforced the popular assumption that children in care constitute a group apart'; but, they went on to insist, 'they do not'.[10] The second reason why any opportunities for dispelling the image of a segregated and special class of children must be grasped is that unless we do, it is exceedingly difficult to plan for such children, both individually and collectively. Once the children and their parents are separately classed so too are the resources available to them. Ironically, admission to care may then close off some options rather than opening others. The third and final reason for taking seriously the chances that we now have of merging a narrowly conceived child care system with child welfare issues more generally is that only in this way will the often repeated aspiration for 'prevention' stand any hope of realisation. Effective prevention relies upon the promotion of *general policies* – about child and family health, educational opportunity, adolescent employment, day care and so on. These are matters well beyond the scope of narrowly conceived child care services.

II The lack of differentiation

Paradoxically, not only are perceptions of substitute care too narrow but, at a different level, they are not specific enough. There is a strong tendency to regard children in corporate public care as a homogeneous group, even though that is immediately belied by a moment's thought or a brief glance at the statistics. Yet again, the legal and administrative categories that we employ encourage the idea that children in care are a largely undifferentiated group. Beyond that, however, other longstanding influences have played their part.

Historically, the parents of the children for whom the state or charitable organisations have assumed responsibility have been looked upon as feckless, immoral, irresponsible or vicious. They have been held in low esteem as individuals and considered to be unworthy or undeserving as a group. Children had to be saved from their undesirable influences or from their inability to exercise sufficient or acceptable control. In many ways this view still survives. Since the parents of the children who become the responsibility of the state were assumed to share the same faults there was little difficulty in concluding that their children also shared a common condition.

Later, the view that children in state care could be thought of as an undifferentiated group was reinforced by the influences of two theoretical formulations. The first, the Bowlby[11] proposition, emphasised the adverse effects of separation upon young children. One of the consequences of applying that conclusion was that most children in care could be considered to suffer from the common adversity of separation that, in turn, created similar problems. The second theoretical influence that encouraged the view that children in care formed a largely undifferentiated group explained juvenile delinquency as but a variation in the response that children made to deprivation. It was then only a short step to believing that the neglected child of four could be placed in the same category as the young offender of 14. The roots of both problems were assumed to lie within the family.

The assumption that all children who were placed in public care shared common characteristics has also been fostered more recently by the understandable desire to stress the structural explanations for their disadvantaged position. They come disproportionately from poverty-stricken backgrounds, from single-parent families and from deprived areas. Although an emphasis upon these undoubted features of their origins is crucial for the development of *general* policies of prevention and in the campaign for social equality, it is also liable to lead to a lack of differentiation in the policies that are adopted once a child has passed into public care. They are all regarded as sharing a structurally determined and common adversity.

The convention of homogeneity has to be abandoned once and for all. While it remains it encourages blanket policies about, for example, forms of substitute care, rather than a much needed range of policies that are sensitive to differences in age, ethnicity, family circumstances and a host of other variations. It simply will not do to have blanket policies for children in care, convenient or fashionable though they may be.

This is not to deny that social workers strive to respond as best they can to the unique circumstances of each child and each family. The existence of observation and assessment centres was justified on just these grounds, as has been the need for regular reviews; but the aspirations that these examples portray are not reflected in the organisation of resources. Policies pay lip service to individualisation but are relentlessly drawn towards generalisations. Of course, that is the nature of policy. Policies have to deal with whole categories or classes; the question at issue is their definition and *refinement*. But such sharpening of blunt policies depends a lot upon how much reliable and detailed information is available about vulnerable children and their families.

Nevertheless, there are encouraging signs that the perception of children in care is becoming more differentiated. Three examples will serve as illustrations. First, there is the growing impact of the children's and parents' rights movements: the 'Who Cares?' groups, the Voice of the Child in Care, Parents' Aid and similar initiatives. Although they express general views they are also well placed to raise particular issues from their first-hand experiences. In a similar way the legal developments in respect of the separate representation of children in court proceedings – through the curators and guardians ad litem – draw increasing attention to individual variations. Likewise, the new requirements about what local authorities must do when they wish to curtail parental access will tend to have the same effect.

The second encouraging sign that across-the-board policies for children in care are being challenged is to be found in the particular attention being paid to the needs of children from minority ethnic groups – particularly the black community. Until comparatively recently the question of the placement of black children has not been openly and publicly confronted. Indeed, some local authorities have refused to enumerate the black children in their care, maintaining that were they to do so it would amount to discrimination. But highly charged issues of trans-racial adoption and foster care have made such positions increasingly untenable.[12] It is no longer politically feasible for governments, both central and local, to shut their eyes to matters of ethnicity in child care.

A third and important example of a shift towards the greater recognition of diversity among children who are on the threshold of admission to care is to be found in Scotland. The children's hearings provide an excellent opportunity to take account of individual differences. Nevertheless, that opportunity may be seriously limited to the *procedure* for making decisions, rather than the particular outcomes. These still appear to be narrowly circumscribed, just as they are in England and Wales, by the range of options available.[13] The pressure then remains to treat children in care as more homogeneous than they really are in order to fit them into the provisions available.

III Static images

Much of what we know about the children and families who become involved in the child care system is derived from information that is collected at particular points of time. As a result we sometimes fail to appreciate the extent to which circumstances change, to remember that what is recorded is true of but one stage or juncture in child and family careers. Furthermore, the time at which the assembly of information occurs is likely to be unusual, surrounded as it often is by crises of one kind or another. For instance, in my Dartington colleagues' study they found that 35% of their large sample of children in care had been referred and then admitted on the same day.[14] Place of safety orders are becoming more numerous; there were some 6,300 in England and Wales in 1981–82.[15] The climate of urgency and crisis that such facts suggest is likely to produce rather unrepresentative information.

Not only is the information upon which the images of child care are built liable to reflect a time of particular upheaval for families and children, but also to be discontinuous. In England and Wales, for instance, about a fifth of all admissions to local authority care are second or subsequent admissions.[16] What happened in between? The information about those periods is often vague; certainly it is uneven. Yet for children like these, and others as well, periods of publicly provided substitute care are episodes in their life. The collection of the information that shapes perceptions of child care is unduly concentrated at particular points, points that are influenced by administrative and legal responses.

Similarly, when we describe what provision is made for children in care we do so by saying that such-and-such a percentage are in foster homes or in certain kinds of residential care; but during their time in care we know that many children experience several different kinds of placement. For instance, the already mentioned Dartington study found that although around 40% of children were in residential homes on a particular day, some 80% of the boys and 70% of the girls had experienced residential care at some time. Without information like this the policy debate is liable to be conducted by reference to still rather than to moving pictures; and that may lead to serious errors. For example, the amount of residential care required will be differently calculated depending upon which kind of picture is considered; that is, by whether planning is based upon a 'stock' or a 'flow' view of the issue.

Many of the questions concerning substitute care about which there is most dispute might be more easily resolved if we had more accurate and up-to-date accounts of the circumstances of children's families. Relying upon what was known about them when a child was removed is often misleading. The fact that authorities appear to lose touch with many families means that the crucial updating is simply not done. That makes it virtually impossible to assess the prospects of a child being restored to his or her family unless, that is, the loss of contact is itself taken as evidence that restoration is not possible. Yet a number of studies, such as Fanshell's in the United States,[17] have demonstrated that, by more diligent searching, parents who were presumed to be 'lost' could be located and, in some cases, found to be in circumstances where, with help, they could resume the care of their child.

Hence, it is not only our images of children in care that stand in danger of petrifaction as a result of the patterns of collecting information, but also our images of their families. Of course, regular reviews are an important means of keeping up-to-date. Yet this must be done for both the child *and* the family; and that is one good reason for seeking parental participation in such procedures.

There is another sense in which popular images of child care tend to reflect past rather than present circumstances. The danger partly arises because of the time lag in the collection and publication of national statistics, but also because, in aggregate, year-to-year changes are small. Significant trends are only discernible over much longer periods. During the last 25 years the proportion of children coming into care who were under five has fallen from 55% to 31% and as a proportion of those in care at any one time from 20% to 10%.[18] Nowadays young people of 16 and 17 make up a quarter of the total; two-and-a-half times the number who are under five. Slowly, yet surely, the age structure of the group of children in question has been changing. Nonetheless, many of the images (particularly those held by the public) stem from an earlier time when the age structure was significantly different.

It seems difficult to catch up with new realities or, indeed, to foresee those that might lie ahead. The Registrar-General, for instance, forecasts a 20% increase in the number of children under five by the end of the twentieth century and a reduction in the number over school age.[19] If the overall demographic structure of the child population has any effect upon the number in public care (a question still to be resolved) the need for another adjustment to our perceptions may be required before too long.

Clearly, for our images of child care to be accurate they have to be based upon a dynamic perspective. Images that are transfixed, whether in general or for particular children and families, foreshadow poor planning and poor decisions. There are few certainties. Mostly we rely upon the estimation of probabilities: what are the likelihoods? What is best on balance? Is this the best that can be done in the circumstances? Decisions are often rather fine and quite small reinterpretations of information or changes may lead to different assessments. The best interests of children who are at risk of coming into care or who are already in care are by no means so self-evident that a *somewhat* different perception makes no difference: it often does. Beyond that there is one other good reason for emphasising the need to develop the moving pictures of child care; that is, in order to prevent an undue pessimism arising from moments of crisis and upheaval.

Admittedly, there are considerable obstacles to overcome. Updating is costly. Key decisions are often seen as resolving a problem rather than ushering in a new episode. And there remains the inclination to fall back upon both established records and 'authoritative' accounts. Both tend to contribute to the fixity of our images. Nonetheless, there are promising signs. Much may be achieved by the government's response to the Short committee's conclusion that, 'If drift and indecision are to be prevented, and if the concept of planning for a child's future with some degree of permanence is to have any meaning, the review process must be tightened up.'[20] Likewise, the possibility that England and Wales will move towards time-limited care orders, as in Scotland, may help to focus attention upon reassessment and reconsideration. Furthermore, it seems likely that the new unit returns about children in care that have to be submitted to central government will offer a better basis for the longitudinal study of child care careers than those that have been collected in the past. Their continued development may well help to obtain a running revision of ideas about both the nature and potentialities of child care.

IV Imitation

Most children are looked after by one or both of their parents. The crucial characteristics of that relationship are threefold. They are: the unity of care and responsibility, permanence and partisan commitment – love. These are the cornerstones upon which the care of dependent children has been built. Kinship supplies the rationale. Of course, variations occur in the mixture of these three characteristics of parental care; but admission to public care changes each of them in a decisive fashion. This is because a shift occurs from personal responsibility for the child to corporate responsibility.[21]

This has three consequences. First, day-to-day care is usually separated from an ultimate responsibility for the child. Second, both the personnel who carry the responsibility on behalf of the corporation and those who look after the children frequently change. Third, special commitments to each child are exceedingly hard to maintain. On the face of it foster homes appear to overcome this difficulty. Yet there is evidence that foster parents may face taxing conflicts of loyalty as between their own children and foster children.[22] Moreover, a foster parent's strong partisan commitment to a child may only be achieved at the expense of reducing the chances of that child's return to his or her own family. Finding a balance between the need to hold a child's family in trust for his or her eventual return and the need for the formation of new attachments to those who look after them in the meantime remains a problem.

Despite these and other ways in which corporate care differs so significantly from parental care, corporate bodies have sought to secure the advantages of parental care by endeavouring to replicate family care. By adopting the terminology of the family and by selecting settings that more or less resemble the family it was but a short step to believing that corporate care could be provided as if it were parental care. That attractive but dubious assumption has tended to hinder the development of a critical analysis of just what can and should be done to provide good care for the separated child. To that end 'ordinary' parenting should probably not be taken as the prototype for corporate care, even though the aim is to secure as many of the benefits that parental care confers as possible.

In any case, it is necessary to ask just what kind of image of the family forms the prototype for substitute care policies. All manner of changes are occurring in the structure and composition of families. Single-parenthood, step-relatives, serial partnerships and so on are not peculiar to the families of separated children although, as Jean Packman points out, they do offer 'a vivid and exaggerated example of recent social trends'.[23] These changes in the social structure may well provide an important stimulus for reconsidering exactly how the benefits of parenting can be achieved without striving to provide parental replicas, especially where adolescents are concerned. The forthcoming revision of the 1955 boarding-out regulations should also offer an opportunity to reconsider assumptions, such as that embedded in the present requirement for foster parents 'to bring up foster children as if they were their own'. Likewise, the recognition that special skills (not to be found among 'ordinary' parents) are needed to care for disturbed and separated children is a further step down the same path.

None of this, of course, is to deny that a new family is appropriate for some children; but the number is relatively small and even adoption, which has traditionally meant the complete replacement of one set of parents by another, is not quite as complete as it was. Courts are beginning to add provisions for parental contact and, in a small way, the opportunity for adopted children to learn more about their origins when they reach 18 has had the effect of making adoption somewhat more open.

In short, the uncritical resort to certain family models as the basis for child care should be avoided and the problem of how best to secure the undoubted benefits of good parenting for separated children squarely confronted.

V So, what's to be done?

I have already suggested some of the opportunities that exist to break down these historically dominant perceptions of the child care system. How might they be best exploited? There are at least three requirements. They are: information, integration and imagination.

Information

Better and more up-to-date information provides no guarantee that perceptions of the issues in child care will be modified in the directions that have been suggested; but without it little progress is possible. Obviously, selection in what is collected is essential. Given a commitment to improving the availability of data the key question then becomes, 'What do we collect?' What is it that we must know before informed policies can be fashioned? Where are the major gaps?

The child care services have, understandably, tended to be child-centred and so has the kind of information that is gathered. Yet the pressing issues, such as prevention and firm planning, actually require us to know much more about the significant adults in a child's life and about how their trials and tribulations, opportunities and aspirations or circumstances affect future likelihoods. We also know disgracefully little about children's grandparents or brothers and sisters. In the Dartington study 45% of the sample were admitted to care with siblings but 90% had them, albeit some were half or step. In Scotland in 1980 nearly three-quarters of those in care on a voluntary basis had siblings as had 56% of those subject to residential supervision orders;[24] but we need more sophisticated information than this in order to plan for each individual child with reference to his or her brothers and sisters and if such considerations are also to be taken into account in the formation of policy.

Simply considering what information is *not* regularly available offers one way of checking how matters stand. Furthermore, some of the categories that we use in making 'returns' are outmoded and unhelpful. The same information might be processed differently and give much more illumination. For example, in the statistics of 'reasons for admissions to care' that are produced annually the single largest classification in England and Wales – accounting for almost a third – is now 'other',[25] partly because the categories according to which the returns have to be made have remained largely unchanged since 1948. The same goes for children's ages. For years only three groupings were used: under school age, of school age and over school age. Now there are two extra divisions, but that is still not enough for us to be able to calculate age-specific rates of admission to care, although it seems highly likely that the distribution of risk by age describes a U-shaped curve, with high risks in the first year of life and again at 14 or 15. The lowest rates appear to prevail during the years of primary schooling. If that is the case it may have rather important implications for preventive policies and for the distribution of scarce resources.

Although it goes without saying that the evaluation of different policies is important the first priority is to obtain and distribute basic descriptive information about what is happening. There is so much we do not know. The new unit returns should provide the opportunity for linkage over time, storage and recall. Yet despite the wizardry of micro-technology their usefulness still turns upon what is collected in the first place, and that is determined by the prevailing perceptions that are held about the nature of the child care system and the problems that it confronts.

It may also be extremely fruitful were the 'children in care' statistics to be published together with other data about children in general; perhaps in an annual abstract or an occasional audit. The appearance of the promising publication *Children and Parliament*[26] might be taken as a model.

Integration

Of course, there is widespread agreement that services should provide a wide range of options in order to meet the different needs of children and families. Nonetheless, the possibility of adjusting services in imaginative ways depends a good deal upon what the range of appropriate services is assumed to be. But the processes whereby children become the responsibility of local authorities tend to compress further a range of options that is already delimited by the administrative boundaries that exist between social security, housing services, health, education and the personal social services, as well as by those separating the private and public systems and by those between the rich and the poor. It is often suggested that the one way to overcome such difficulties is to draw new boundaries, albeit around larger jurisdictions. That can help, but it tends to change the composition of the bundle of options rather than enlarging it. Administrative reform goes only so far. Three other things might take us further.

First, there is the now familiar plea for social work to become more 'integrationist'. The model is the better-off and knowledgeable family that, when faced with problems, shops around and puts together solutions, often with the help of sympathetic professionals, some of whom they pay to act on their behalf. The solutions they contrive are not necessarily constrained by administrative demarcations and, if these do stand in the way, they are often swept aside by a vigorous, forceful and skilful assault. Disadvantaged families and children in care are in no position to do these things and when they are assertive or argumentative they are liable to be classed as simply troublesome, obstructive or unreasonable. A widely accepted integrationist role for social work (advocacy that is not limited to welfare rights alone or to the mobilisation of informal community resources) could provide a countervailing pressure to those that conspire to keep some options permanently closed.

A second change that might achieve a greater measure of integration concerns classification. Since the administrative and legal categorisation of children and their families tends to restrict the range of available options it is worth considering whether (and if so how) such classification can be avoided or deferred. Once set along a particular track – whether it be health, education, social work or the penal system – children tend to remain on it. Crossing points seem few and far between. Those practices that do *not* require categorisation may actually be preferable to those that do. This, of course, runs counter to ideas about the value of early identification, early diagnosis and clear-cut decisions, but it may nevertheless warrant careful consideration. We should be sure that classification is actually necessary in the interests of children and families.

Third, the problem of inflexible and limited service options is not only a matter of how social work is organised or how needs and circumstances get classed. It is also the outcome of the resources available. One reason why access to a multiplicity of services is applauded in principle but unrealised in practice is that limited access (together with close classification) fulfils an important rationing function. More open and across-the-board access makes it difficult to regulate demand. There are, therefore, obvious interests in *not* pursuing it as a goal of practical policy. Paradoxically, although better integration is often advanced as a means of economising (through greater efficiency) the very pressures on resources that it creates increasingly strain resources which then make integration less possible in both practice and policy. A more desperate defence of boundaries and budgets then follows.

Imagination

If we are to grasp the opportunities that exist to refashion our children's services it is essential that we have a reasonably clear idea of what it is that needs to be achieved. What is often lacking in today's social planning is the idea of a visionary future. Yet without it we constantly start from where we are and then have to stumble forward by small and detached increments. We do not think backwards, as it were, from a visionary future.[27] Of course, it is usually claimed that visionary planning is impractical, contentious or naïve; but unless there is a broad conception of this kind (which includes how the community will cherish children and support their parents) then it is impossible to know whether even the modest changes that we are able to make are steps in the right direction.

Admittedly, imagination about what might be does not come easily: it requires to be stimulated and kept in good repair. One of the ways in which it can be cultivated and encouraged is by the intervention of those whom Colin Wilson called the 'outsiders' in his book of that title.[28] Historically, it has been outsiders who have provided much imaginative genius. By listening to the views of outsiders we may be helped to free ourselves from the straitjacket of our conventional images. Who are the outsiders in child care? In terms of policy formation they are first and foremost the children themselves; but there are other outsiders as well whose views should be canvassed if we are not to remain unimaginatively hide-bound by our historical legacies and our comfortable assumptions. The knack is to identify who these outsiders might be. Who don't we consult?

My final point is that imagination is so important because it inspires optimism. The disadvantaged children and their families with whom child care policies and practice are so much concerned are frequently and understandably also the victims of fatalism and despair. Not only must our social policies aim to eradicate their causes but also incorporate approaches that are themselves essentially hopeful, encouraging and positive; and in that quest imagination can prove a valuable ally.

CHAPTER 7

Trends, transitions and tensions: children's services since the 1980s[*]

Each period has witnessed changes in the manner in which our children's services have been organised. The legislation to which they are subject changes, different problems become more or less pressing, policies are re-thought and practices modified. However, over the last 30 years many such changes have been more pronounced: legislative activity has intensified, there have been numerous inquiries into child deaths that have led to more procedural guidance and new issues have arisen, all within the context of a notable increase in information. Nonetheless, certain issues and tensions have persisted, as have significant gaps in our understanding.

I Looking at some statistics[1]

Statistics tend to be treated with a measure of scepticism. Undoubtedly they have their shortcomings, but they provide a means of detecting or illustrating trends that might otherwise be overlooked. Many changes happen gradually and are hardly discernible in the short term; but where we have a sufficiently long run of data it becomes possible to see what is changing, what is not and what is subject to the ebb and flow of events. However, we have to be careful that definitions (and their interpretation) have not changed and that there is a consistency in what is recorded. In short, we have to do the best we can with what we have and, as far as the children's services are concerned, what we have is as good as most other social statistics and better than many. Let us look at some of the more significant trends over the last 30 years or so.

The number of children in care has fluctuated considerably. For example, in England at the end of March 1980 the figure stood at 95,300; in 1994 at 49,000 and in 2013 at 68,110.[2] How are these variations to be explained? The answers (and there are several) will depend partly upon whether we seek to account for the increases or the

---

[*] First published as 'Change and Continuity' in *Adoption & Fostering*, 2010, 34 (3), but here with some revisions and material brought up to date.

reductions and, of course, we have to bear in mind the *rates* per 1,000 of the population under 18 that these figures reflect. Furthermore, of course, the count on one particular day (which these figures are) does not tell us how many children entered or left the care system during the preceding year.

The number of children in care at the end of March each year had begun to increase in the early 1970s partly, as we have seen, because of the inclusion of the approved schools' population at the beginning of 1971 (adding about an extra 12,000), then boosted by the increase in the number of committal orders as a result of changes brought about by the Divorce Law Reform Act of 1969[3] and by 'the rediscovery of abuse'.

Although 1977 was the peak year, with 96,234 children in care, the highest *rate*, of 7.8 per 1,000 of the population under 18, was reached in 1980. Thereafter both the number and the rate declined quite rapidly, the number falling to 74,845 and the rate to 6.5 by 1984. The subsequent further reduction of the number in care was probably attributable to a greater emphasis being placed on prevention and, after the Children Act 1989, to the fact that young offenders and those failing to go to school could no longer be committed to care by the courts on these grounds alone. The rate mirrored this, falling steadily until it reached its lowest point of 4.5 per 1,000 in the years 1994–95. After that there was another upward movement until it levelled out at around 5.5 between 2003 and 2009. In 2010 the rate rose to 5.9 and remained there during the next two years. In 2013 it stood at 6.0. However, despite these latest increases in both the number and the rate of children looked after the levels are still lower than in the period before the early 1980s and indeed lower than in the years between 1952 (6.9) and 1973 (6.7).[4]

It should be borne in mind, however, that there are local variations, although in most cases local trends have mirrored what was happening nationally. For instance, I compared the number of looked-after children in each local authority at the end of March 1988 with the number at the same date in 1995. This period was chosen because it witnessed a marked reduction in both the number and rate of children being looked after. Among the 98 authorities in England for which there was complete information only 12 deviated from the downward trend and almost half reduced the number in their care by more than 20%. Of course, different authorities lowered their numbers from different starting points and the relative position of these points showed little change. Where marked contrasts to the downward trend occurred they were usually explicable; for example, much of the 70% *increase* in Hillingdon in London, with Heathrow airport on its doorstep, was attributable to the arrival of young asylum seekers.

A detailed explanation of the long-term ups and downs in the number and rates of looked-after children requires a fuller exploration than can be offered here and would have to take account of material on the pattern of admissions to and discharges from care as well as information on the duration of the care episodes. These data began to be available from 1977 when the new method of collecting statistics from local authorities was introduced based on an individual record for each child. Since then further information has been collected, although not necessarily on a regular basis. Even so, it remains a complicated exercise to explain the variability in the size of the 'in care' population and an uncertain undertaking to predict what it is likely to be, other than in the short term. Furthermore, even when the overall size of the looked-after population does not change much, its detailed characteristics and what happens to the children may alter considerably. We have already seen examples of this in earlier chapters but their numerical scale warrants a little elaboration.

Both the proportion and the number of children in foster homes have witnessed a considerable increase since 1980. In England the proportion rose from 37% in that year to 75% in 2013 and the number by 14,700, or by 42%.[5] Although the proportion of all looked-after children in foster homes rose considerably this was partly accounted for by the decline in the overall number in care. Nonetheless, both the increase in the proportion and in the number of children in foster homes reflected a marked change, driven largely by the quest to reduce reliance on residential care but also by a mixture of other factors. It may be that a wider pool of foster carers began to be tapped, that more marginal foster parents were being used, that better payments had an effect as well as more determined foster family finding. In addition, there were fewer residential places available as an alternative. Indeed, whereas 34% of children in care in England at the end of March 1980 were living in children's homes or hostels, in 2013 the proportion had fallen to 10%. This was an even more dramatic change than the growth of foster care; indeed, it amounted to 30,000 fewer children being cared for residentially.[6] As has been pointed out already one important contributory factor has been the steady reduction in the use of observation and assessment centres to which many children were allocated on admission and before their next placement was decided.

Another notable change in the years since 1980 has been in the adoption of children from care. During 1980 there were 1,500 (3% of all discharges from care) but the number had risen to 3,980 by 2013

(14% of those leaving care). The age of those adopted has also altered. In 1978 (England and Wales) 23% were under one year of age[7] but by 2013 only 2% were that young. In part this reflected the disappearance of the stigma associated with illegitimacy and thus to few unmarried mothers relinquishing their babies for adoption. Nevertheless, 74% of the children adopted from care in 2013 were between the ages of one and four: only 2% were more than nine years old.

The increase in 'adoption from care' was largely attributable to its vigorous encouragement (both legislative and otherwise) by central government from the late 1990s onwards, an encouragement that was closely associated with the conviction that more permanent solutions had to be found for children whose families were no longer able or were unfit to care for them.[8] The Children and Families Act 2014 includes further changes that aim to simplify and accelerate the adoption process.

Legal changes have also modified the in-care 'profile' considerably. For example, as we have seen, since the Children Act 1989 children are no longer committed to care as offenders; at the end of March 1980 they comprised 14,700 of the total, or 15%. Likewise, children are no longer committed to care for not attending school; but in 1980 4,500 were recorded as being in care for this reason, or some 5% of the total. Although these changes help to explain the declining number of children being 'looked after' they also reflect changed attitudes towards the treatment of these problems as well as the re-classification of 'reasons for being in care'. Some who fell into in these former groups (offenders and those failing to attend school) will now be classed as being looked after because of their 'abuse or neglect', a designation that at the end of March 2013 covered 61% of looked-after children, up from 18% in 1980.[9]

Such statistics emphasise the emerging prominence of 'abuse or neglect' as problems with which the children's services have to grapple. Of course, we cannot be sure whether there has been a real increase in these phenomena. Nevertheless, they now dominate the scene in most children's services as well as finding a prominent place in the media. Both facts have contributed to an intensification of the tension between striving to keep child and family together (or achieving their re-unification) and the need to protect children from actual or potential harm through their commitment to care. Furthermore, the uneasy balance that has to be found between these two objectives, both in policy and in practice, can be quickly disturbed by a child's tragic death at the hands of their parents or by what appears to be their precipitate and apparently unwarranted removal.

The 'abuse or neglect' of children has not been the only 'new' issue to be reflected in the statistics however. For example, in 1980 there were no figures about the ethnicity or education of children in care. The 2013 returns cover both issues. They tell us that 78% of the looked-after population was classified as 'white', 9% as 'mixed race' and 7% as 'black or black British' (an over-representation of both these latter groups). Those with Asian backgrounds accounted for 4%. As well as this information about ethnicity we now know the educational attainments of children in care at Years 2, 6, 9 and 11 as well as the gap between their achievements and those of other children. Further additional statistics have also made an appearance; for example, the number of young mothers of 12 years old or more who are looked after (340 in 2013) and information on 'outcome indicators', again reflecting a considerable change since 1980 when little attention was paid to the assessment and measurement of outcomes.[10] Such changes in what is enumerated reflect the rise and fall of the issues of the day, but because of this data are liable to be discontinuous, making comparisons over time that much more difficult.

Even though the statistical coverage of the children's services is much greater than in the 1980s, there are still matters about which there is less numerical data. It will not have escaped the readers' notice that most of the statistical information that has been discussed concerns looked-after children. Yet much of the work of the children's services takes place with families whose children are not looked-after. Indeed, child protection and other support and rehabilitative endeavours constitute a substantial part of the work. The child 'in care' or discharged from care represents just one consequence of what is being done, the scale and nature of which has been more readily discerned since the inauguration of the annual children in need census that were required under the Children Act 1989. For example, in the year ending March 2013 in England there were 593,500 referrals of children potentially in need of social care services. These had to be investigated, leading to 441,500 'initial' assessments of which 232,700 then required a 'core' assessment to be made. All this demanded the collection of information and many meetings. There were, for instance, 60,100 child protection conferences. Although these are the briefest of figures they do illustrate the magnitude of what is *not* reflected in the 'looked-after children' statistics.[11] Work to protect children from harm has increased considerably. For example, whereas there were 38,600 children on the child protection registers at the end of March 1992 there were 52,700, subject to a child protection plan in 2013.[12]

II Policies and politics

There have been major transformations in the social, economic and political conditions of the country since 1980. Some of the repercussions will have affected the children's services, although it is not altogether clear which, to what extent, or how. There has been the increase in divorce, the growth in the number of step-parent families, more one-parent families, youth unemployment, growing inequality, the arrival of young asylum seekers and so the list might be continued. However, apart from such changes there have been other important alterations in the 'climate' in which these services have operated. At least five have been significant: the rise of pressure groups, the proliferation of research, the firmer establishment of children's rights, the quest for prevention and the rapid expansion of private sector provisions.

Pressure group activity

By 1980 there had been a discernable increase in pressure group activity. For example, the Family Rights Group had been set up in 1974, the National Association for Young People in Care a year later and the Children's Legal Centre in 1981. Other new groups followed. Associated journals began to appear, such as the *Who Cares?* magazine in 1985. The rights issue continued to gain in significance, both for children and for their parents (including fathers) as well as for carers, much of it exemplified in the changes introduce in the Children Act 1989.

Inquiries into the deaths of children in care or of children for whom social services carried some responsibility proliferated. Criticism abounded, much of it heightened by an increasingly robust media. In 1983 the House of Commons Social Services Committee chose to inquire into the state of the child care services and published its telling report a year later.[13] In 2003 a Children's Commissioner (Ombudsman) was appointed, partly in response to the report of the inquiry into abuses in children's homes in North Wales,[14] but also as a result of pressure from several groups concerned with children's rights. Such developments have meant that children's services have become exposed to closer public scrutiny and to influences that pull them in many directions. The work has become more complicated and more demanding. Expectations are raised and calls increase for governments to respond to each new disquieting event, and often more rapidly than before. New policies and procedural directives emerge, making it hard for practitioners to keep up.

The growth of research

In the last 35 years research has come to play its part in both policy and practice. In many ways Jane Rowe set the ball rolling with her study of 'Children who Wait' in 1973[15] but the establishment of the National Children's Bureau two years later was also significant, as was the decision of the Department of Health to sponsor a programme of research into children's services. Although the influence of research has waxed and waned there is certainly much more of it. Its findings appear in a growing number of journals, material is to be found on the internet and organisations like Research in Practice and Making Research Count have sought to make studies more readily available to practitioners. In short, we have had a cascade of research since 1980 although there has been little detailed monitoring of child well-being and few randomised controlled trials of particular programmes.[16] The quality of the research has also varied, posing problems of selection for those who seek to use it. Furthermore, of course, research is liable to create new doubts and pose fresh problems as well as providing helpful guidance. It tends to be most readily used by those who see its results as confirmation of what they believe or as support for the changes that they seek to make.

Children's rights

An increasing emphasis has been placed upon what children have to say: about their feelings, their experiences and their aspirations. This, of course, is related to the rights of the child that have been incorporated in legislation, in particular in the Children Act 1989 that requires both courts and local authorities to ascertain 'the wishes and feelings' of children and to 'take them into consideration' when decisions are made.[17] In the same year the United Nations adopted the Convention on the Rights of the Child and one of these was the child's right to be heard. Even though difficulties remain, not least when it comes to young children and in moving from what individual children tell us to generalising for the many, the very fact of expecting children to be listened to marks a laudable and important break with the past. This is illustrated in the information that is now collected about looked-after children's participation in their statutory reviews. Excluding the under fours and those in care for fewer than 28 days 45% of those required to have a review were reported to be present and to have spoken for themselves in 2013, 13% had made their views known through a 'facilitative medium' and 15%, although not present, had their views conveyed by someone who was. Only 3% did not speak for themselves or have someone contributing on their behalf.[18] However, we do not know the extent to which the children's views were reflected in what was decided or whether there were discernible patterns in what they had to say that could be translated into policy or practice.

Pursuing prevention

An important 'policy direction' has been the growing emphasis placed upon 'prevention'. This has developed from its narrow codification in the Children Act 1948 that obliged local authorities to take steps to prevent children having to stay in care unnecessarily to its wider formulation in the 1963 Act in which a duty was placed upon local authorities 'to promote the welfare of children by diminishing the need for them to be received into care, to be kept in care, or to be brought to court'. Although the requirements of the 1948 and 1963 Acts have remained intact a broader interpretation has emerged. This stressed the need to develop interventions that would reduce the disadvantages that blighted the lives of many children and not just those who were considered to be at risk of having to be admitted or committed to care. Particular attention was to be paid to children's early years. Naomi Eisenstadt has provided an excellent account of why and how this happened during the years of New Labour, emphasising the importance of the rift between Tony Blair and Gordon Brown and the latter's desire to see the Treasury (and he at its head) make its mark in shaping social policy and in developing new ways in which that could be done.[19] One result of this was the comprehensive spending review of services for young children undertaken by the Treasury in 1997; a second was the 1999 white paper *Modernising Government* which, among other things, pointed out that services for children under four were uneven and fragmented and that 'early intervention and support is important in reducing family breakdown; in strengthening children's readiness for school; and in preventing social exclusion and crime'.[20]

One of the first fruits of these convictions was the Sure Start programme that was launched in 1998, locally based, integrated and with parental involvement. The broad aim was that the centres would support parents, provide various services to improve health, enhance educational opportunity and lead to less stressful and therefore better parenting. Furthermore, as Michael Little pointed out, Sure Start offered a 'platform for better prevention'.[21] By 2010 there were 3,632 designated Sure Start Children's Centres (re-named in 2004) scattered through every local authority in England,[22] but by 2013 the number had fallen to 3,116 (a reduction of 14%).[23]

Retracing our steps to the New Labour period, however, we find many policy initiatives that bore upon the condition of children.[24] One was the considerable importance attached to improving educational opportunity. Another was based upon the conviction that a better integration of education and children's services was needed, exemplified by the transfer of central responsibility for the latter from the Department of Health to the Department for Education in 2004. A third feature of New Labour's policy agenda was the ambition to move people from 'welfare to work'.[25] Among other things, that required an improved provision of day care, especially in order to get 'welfare-dependent mothers' into the paid labour force. For example, since 1998 all four-year-olds have been entitled to a funded early education place and in 2004 this was extended to three-year-olds. By 2013 the take-up was 96% of the relevant population, but not necessarily full-time and with local variations.[26] Other developments followed.

Under the Childcare Act of 2006 specific responsibilities were placed upon English local authorities to 'secure, so far as is reasonably practical...the provision of child care...sufficient to meet the requirements of parents in their area' so that they could 'take up, or remain in work' or 'undertake education or training' that would help them to obtain work. However, in 2011 a Department for Education memorandum concluded that the Act had had mixed success and had had only a limited effect on the wider child care market.[27]

In these and other initiatives that were launched by New Labour one sees a fusion of prevention and promotion. In a sense prevention became incorporated in promotional exercises and in the process it became less specific to 'at risk' groups. This was partly because child welfare and family support became more closely associated with 'welfare to work' policies. Nonetheless, the emphasis continued to be placed upon young children, especially the 'early years', partly because it was their day care that released mothers to take up paid work and partly because early intervention was regarded as the cornerstone of prevention.

These twin objectives continued to be pursued (albeit somewhat differently) by the in-coming Conservative–Liberal coalition government of 2010. Indeed, in its first year the Prime Minister invited the Labour MP Graham Allen to undertake a review of 'early intervention', especially as it applied to the youngest children. Allen delivered his report and recommendations to David Cameron at the start of 2011.[28] Six months later a second report was produced that dealt with the financing of early intervention. It argued that such a programme was the best 'sustainable structural deficit programme' and that the costs could be met by the better use of existing monies and by attracting outside funds.[29] Allen had also recommended that an Early Intervention Foundation should be established to monitor and encourage preventive schemes and this materialised in 2013.

The expansion of the private sector

The most notable shift in the direction of policy in the children's services has been the rapidly growing involvement of the private sector, particularly in the provision of foster care and residential care for looked-after children. In 2001 in England 12% of looked-after children who were in foster homes (other than with relatives or friends) had been placed and then supervised by 'independent agencies' (that is, by private or voluntary organisations) on behalf of local authorities.[30] By 2013 that proportion had risen to 36%,[31] almost all the placements having been arranged by private for-profit enterprises.

This development has been mirrored in the residential field. In 2000 there were 256 private children's homes in England. By 2013 the number had risen to 1,347 provided by 407 agencies. The independent sector is now dominant, providing 78% of all registered children's homes and 72% of the available places.[32] However, looked-after children are also placed in residential schools and residential care homes and here too there is significant private provision. In 2013 there were 930 looked-after children living in residential schools, 76% of whom were in places provided by the private sector and 13% in those supplied by voluntary agencies. Although there were fewer (670) in residential care homes (mainly children with the severer disabilities) the pattern was much the same; 70% were in places offered by private organisations and 3% in those provided by the voluntary sector.[33]

Several aspects of these data about foster care and residential care are notable. The most obvious is the rapidity with which the private sector expanded from about 2000 onwards. Another is the comparatively small part being played by voluntary agencies in the so-called 'independent sector'. However, there are other important features of the new pattern, in particular the diverse nature of the market. In 2012, for example, local authorities were purchasing fostering services from some 250 private agencies, most of which were relatively small enterprises.[34] The picture is much the same in residential care. That market also comprises mainly small providers: in 2013 64% owning just one or two homes. However, the nine largest private owners accounted for 22% of the homes (the largest, the Advanced Childcare Group had

133 in 43 local authority areas). The financial structure of the sector is mixed, 'including private equity and venture capital as well as family owned companies and individual social entrepreneurs'.[35]

So, why have local authorities turned to the independent sector for the care services that they require? Doubtless the answer varies from one to another, but at least four explanations (probably in combination) are the most common. First, there is the matter of availability; for instance, 52 authorities (just over a third of those in England) had no children's homes of their own in 2013.[36] Others may have lacked the specialised services needed in the homes that they did have. In these circumstances some have looked to other authorities with the appropriate vacancies but most have contracted with private providers. However, in the case of foster care a local authority's lack of sufficient places may have more to do with not having enough staff engaged in finding foster homes, notwithstanding the existence of 'fostering teams'. In England in 2014, for instance, the vacancy rate among the relevant social workers was 14% and as high as 50% in a few authorities. Likewise, turnover is considerable. In England as a whole it stood at 15% in 2014 but was as high as 82% in one authority.[37] It is as true now as it was after 1948 that the satisfactory development of local authority foster care depends upon there being enough trained staff available to do the work.

A second explanation for local authorities' use of the independent sector may lie in cost differentials. For example, in 2013 the average weekly cost per child in local authority homes was £4,135. The comparable figure in private and voluntary homes was £3,860, a difference of £275. It seems unlikely, however, that this order of saving would have been the most important consideration in the shift to independent providers, but it may well be a contributory factor, especially in times of tight budgets. The difference between the two average costs, however, has been narrowing: it had been just over £400 two years earlier in 2011.[38]

A third reason for local authorities' growing use of private (and to a much lesser extent voluntary) provisions probably springs from the needs conundrum. The better assessment of children's needs means that more diverse services are required, which is something that the independent sector may offer. For example, unlike the longstanding pattern of foster care (described in Chapter 3) boys outnumbered girls among those who were placed in foster homes by independent agencies.[39] Overall 59% were boys. However, there was little explicit specialisation although there was in the private and voluntary residential care. If, for instance, one looks at the *Commissioners' Handbook* of the Independent Children's Homes Association one sees that almost all of its 95 member agencies describe themselves as offering specialised services, primarily for children with 'emotional and behavioural problems' and mainly for adolescents.[40]

One further explanation for the remarkable growth of the private sector in particular is to be found in a mixture of political convictions in both central and local government. There have been various components. One has been linked to the belief that non-governmental provision is more efficient (value for money). Another, springing from somewhat different roots, has stressed its capacity to increase diversity and thereby 'consumer choice'. Yet the underlying theme has been (albeit with more or less emphasis) a desire to see 'welfare' shifted towards a market system facilitated by the customer–contractor principle. There has been no mandatory requirement but firm encouragement. In 1991, for example, the Department of Health, through its inspectorate, 'encouraged authorities to be active in stimulating a mixed economy of care',[41] an encouragement that has continued.

One of the confusing aspects of this movement away from public service provision has been (deliberately or otherwise) the use of the term 'the independent sector' to cover both private and voluntary provision. In reality these are two separate systems based upon different philosophies and with different characteristics. One reason for them being presented as if they were the same may lie in political apprehension that, standing alone, the private-for-profit sector's involvement in the provision of children's services is liable to attract unwelcome criticism. Voluntary initiatives largely escape criticism, generally being seen in a favourable light by the public.

III And some continuities

Co-operation

One of the notable features of the various inquiries into child deaths or other tragedies has been the exposure of failures of co-ordination within and between different services. This has been a constant refrain, at least since the inauguration of children's departments in 1948. In spite of much exhortation and the establishment of a range of local and central committees to improve matters the problem endures. Progress has been made but failures still occur. What has been missing from the accounts of 'what went wrong' has been an analysis of the structural reasons that have made it difficult to ensure the protection of vulnerable children. The fragmentation of administrative systems is called into question but a division, and therefore a limitation, of responsibilities cannot be avoided, however widely these are cast. Furthermore, responsibilities are not always clearly demarcated, especially when situations arise that are complicated and where information is incomplete, added to which co-operation between agencies is likely to require the diversion of scarce resources from other activities.

Although the favoured remedies have changed the problem remains. One reason may be that these remedies have concentrated on co-ordination and integration, assuming that co-operation would follow. It is all well and good to have co-ordinated policies and procedures but co-operation between workers in the field depends on much more: upon the pressures that they are under, upon the similarity of the information to hand, upon a common language and upon the existence of trusting personal relationships. It is a complicated picture made more complicated when there are many agencies involved, when there is a high turnover of staff, when there are agency staff who come and go and when communications are difficult or misunderstood.

There have been numerous recent attempts to address these problems through detailed official guidance. In 1999 there was *Working Together to Safeguard Children: A Guide to Inter-agency Working*;[42] a year later the *Framework for the Assessment of Children in Need and their Families*[43] that led on to the *Common Assessment Framework* in 2006. Since then *Working Together to Safeguard Children* has been revised twice, in 2010 and in 2013.[44] Although the Coalition government has sought to reduce 'central prescription' the statutory guidance of 2013 still runs to nearly 100 pages and is expected to be followed by a score of organisations. Nonetheless, funding for the Children's Workforce Development Council (that had been responsible for professional 'toolkits and guidance') is being withdrawn and there is no longer to be a national IT records system to assist 'working together'. This does not suggest that the core problem of co-operation has been resolved, although it may have been ameliorated. Even though we may understand better why there are failures of co-operation it remains difficult for that understanding to be translated into solutions at the field level.

Leaving care

Despite considerable efforts and specific legislation such as the Children (Leaving Care) Act of 2000 (and the up-dated regulations of 2013) children who leave care at 18 still face many of the same problems that they did in the past. In 2013 the largest proportion (37%) of 19-year-olds who had been in care in England at least since they were 16 were classified as being in 'independent living' while the next highest proportion (13%) were living with parents or relatives. Eight per cent had been lost to view and 3% were in custody. On a different analysis one finds that 29% were not in education, training or employment and a further 5% fell into that category because they were ill or disabled. The picture has remained much the same since 2009, except that between 2009 and 2012 the number not in education, training or employment rose from 1,610 to 2,020, that is by 25%.[45] The transition from being 'looked after' to various forms of independence remains hazardous for many young people.

Few (5% in 2013) continue to live with their foster parents. Whether they go back to be with parents or relatives, move into some form of independent living ('how independent?', one asks) or find themselves in bed and breakfast accommodation, they experience discontinuity. Furthermore, the figures that have been quoted only relate to those who were 19 years old and not to those beyond that age. Do their problems ease as they get older, remain much the same or worsen? And what makes the difference?

Disruption and instability

Although its scale has been reduced there remains the problem of 'disruption'; that is, of a child having a sequence of placements. Thirty-four per cent of the children who were looked after during the year ending March 2013 had had three or more placements.[46] But there are other sources of instability as well. Many of the children's families are unstable and, as we have seen, there continues to be a considerable turnover of staff, especially in certain areas, often associated with a persistence of unfilled posts, factors that are likely to have a deleterious effect upon the quality of the services.

A form of instability also arises from uncertainty. Although a child may be 'settled' in the care arrangements being provided their future may often seem to them to be uncertain, more uncertain indeed than that of most other children who can rely upon a long-lasting anchorage in family relationships. Even short-term futures may seem to be worryingly unreliable, especially if neither further education nor regular employment is in prospect.

Local variation

At the end of the 1970s there were marked differences on many matters between the local authorities responsible for the provision of children's services. For instance, in 1978 the number of children in care per 1,000 of the population under 18 ranged from 27.2 to 3.6.[47] In 2012 the variation was from 15.0 to 1.9.[48] Differences still exist, albeit that they have become less pronounced. Similarly, the rates of foster care continue to vary. In 1980 the range was from 70% to 24%;[49] in 2012 it spread from 86% in 57%.[50] Thus, although there has been a lessening in disparities on both these measures there continue to be notable differences between authorities, doubtless reflecting the different problems they face.

This is illustrated by figures from the children in need surveys. For example, in 2012 the rates of referral per 10,000 children under 18 varied from 1,542.4 in East Sussex to 185.3 in Shropshire. The next two highest rates were in Torbay (1,296.0) and Bournemouth (1,123.8) and the next two lowest in Richmond-on-Thames (208.5) and Worcestershire (248.4). Similar differences existed with respect to the rates of children in need. These ranged from 1,378.3 in East Sussex to 320.1 in Harrow.[51] Many more differences exist between local authority children's services and although they may not be quite the same as 30 years ago they continue to pose problems when it comes to the implementation of national policies. There is some recognition of different local challenges in the annual grants that central government provide and in special grants such as the pupil premium plus that is calculated on the number of looked-after children in particular schools. Even so, the criteria upon which these adjustments are made remain relatively crude: significant local differences persist in both the problems that have to be faced and in the services that seek to address them.

Gender

Unlike the continuities discussed so far some attract little attention. One is the ratio of boys to girls being looked after. In 1952 55% of the children in care were boys and 45% girls. The proportions were exactly the same in 2013. Throughout the life of the former children's departments the ratio never deviated from those proportions. In the 1970s it widened to 60/40% in favour of boys due to the inclusion of the approved school population, 85% of whom were boys in 1968.[52] They gradually 'aged out' of the system so that, by the mid-1980s, the boy/girl ratio had resumed its historic balance.

Furthermore, with the exception of a few years in the adolescent range the preponderance of boys prevailed at all ages and in almost all local authorities. For instance, in only four of the 152 English local authorities in 2013 were more girls than boys being looked after.[53]

The explanations for this persistent difference are not as straightforward as might appear. Before the approved school population was added to the 'in care' figures in 1971 the large number of boys in that system (not all of whom were offenders) might have been expected to *reduce* their number in the care system relative to the girls. Furthermore, given the presumption that girls are especially vulnerable to sexual abuse this might have been expected to narrow the gap between the number of boys and girls who were looked after. Indeed, until the Children Act of 1989 one of the specific grounds upon which a care order could be made was that a child was exposed to moral danger and 80% of those subject to such orders were girls.[54]

The most obvious explanation for the difference between the number of boys and girls being looked after is that more boys start to be looked after each year; but that does not answer the question of why.[55] Is it because of differences in the behavioural manifestations of distress, by different thresholds of risk being applied by social workers or by more boys being re-admitted to care? Doubtless, there is a combination of reasons, but these have hardly begun to be identified, let alone untangled.

Public perceptions

One thing that seems to have changed little since 1980 is the public perception of the children's services. Considerable opprobrium continues to be heaped upon social workers and upon those with whom they work. In terms of the politics of these services this is a significant problem and one that may intensify in the atmosphere of 'welfare cuts'. Among the many steps that the improvement of children's services calls for must be an improvement in their public image through a determined effort to convey a sense of the difficulties that they face as well as by giving an account of the progress that has been made. A more extensive engagement of the agencies and the professional bodies with the media would help but the manner in which this is done needs to take account of the fast-moving developments that are occurring within it. 'Letters to *The Times*' are no longer sufficient.

CHAPTER 8

Reflections on the assessment of outcomes in child care[*]

The Department of Health working party that I chaired, and whose report *Assessing Outcomes in Child Care* appeared in 1991, led to the 'Looking After Children' scheme. This provided a means of assessing the outcomes for children who were, or had been, in local authority care.[1] Since then I have reflected upon some of the issues with which we grappled and upon others that emerged later. Although significant progress has been made in monitoring outcomes tantalising questions remain.

I The stability of outcomes over time

Taxing problems surround deciding when an outcome should be assessed. At certain times there may be a temporary improvement or an uncharacteristic deterioration. What we observe may be an enduring condition, but it may also be no more than a transitional stage. If the latter there could be subsequent reversals, further advances or eventual stabilisation. A few examples will illustrate how careful one needs to be in deciding just when a course of events has reached the point of being appropriately regarded as an outcome.

A report on Jewish children saved from the concentration camps and brought to Britain in 1945 described their profoundly disturbed emotional state but also the apparently miraculous rate of their psychological recovery.[2] However, as time passed this recovery often failed to be sustained, although exactly when the setbacks occurred and how serious or lasting they were was found to be hard to predict; and no long-term follow-up was undertaken. Other studies, such as that of Cornish and Clarke,[3] also drew attention to the fact that although disturbing behaviour could be modified while youngsters remained in controlled residential settings the changes did not usually survive once

---

[*] Based upon a paper given at the third international conference on Assessing Outcomes in Child Care; Worcester College, Oxford, 1997 and published in *Children and Society*, 1998, 12.

they left and the control disappeared. Likewise, Bartak and Rutter[4] showed what progress could be made with autistic children given favourable staff ratios and a well-controlled classroom; but they also noted how difficult it was to maintain the educational improvements when the children returned home unless there was good collaboration between parents and school.

Such examples serve to remind us of the fragile and unstable nature of certain kinds of 'progress'; but unexpected improvements may follow changes in context, especially when these occur in the realm of personal relationships. This was demonstrated in Quinton and Rutter's study of young mothers who had spent considerable periods in children's homes.[5] In spite of this, the majority were providing satisfactory care for their toddlers. What, above all, distinguished these mothers from those who fell short in their child care was the kind of partner that they had acquired; ideally someone who was supportive and not a social casualty.

A similar set of issues surrounds what might be called the 'delayed effects' of various types of organisational intervention. In my first research on the success and failure of long-term foster care I found that the peak time for placements to 'fail' was 17 months after the child's arrival, with a rapid increase of such risk from about a year and a steady decline after two.[6] In another study of children who had been committed to care for their protection, but who were allowed home without the court order having expired or having been discharged, Elaine Farmer and I found a 25% rate of re-abuse or neglect. This occurred over a period of two years but did not happen at once, or even during the first year. As we pointed out, the risk to a child may seem to have diminished but may increase again later given new circumstances, new stresses or changed behaviour.[7] Outcomes may be mistakenly considered to be favourable (and then services perhaps withdrawn or wound down) if the assessment is made too soon or, of course, some valuable short-term benefits may be overlooked if it is made too late.

One of the most telling examples of the way in which outcomes may be differently interpreted with the passage of time is provided by the Head-Start initiative in the United States. Significant gains in the IQ scores of the disadvantaged children in the scheme were achieved by the time that they entered mainstream schooling; but these gains were subsequently lost and the programme cut. However, in their late teens the children in the experimental group were found to have fewer difficulties than the controls; but these benefits had occurred in spheres other than their measured intelligence.[8]

My purpose in offering these few illustrations is to emphasise that a good deal of instability is likely to be found in 'outcomes'. It is important, therefore, to know what prevails at a number of stages in a child's career; hence the value of continuing *re*-views that are truly *re*-assessments.

It is also prudent to avoid determining an outcome at points of particular stress or crisis for a child, such as starting or changing school, moving home or when a new baby is born into the family. Similarly, the special nature of 'honeymoon' or 'testing-out' periods has been recognised for a long time. Over and above such considerations there are also those that take account of ages and stages in child development. For instance, in her study of the consequences of physical abuse Gibbons noted the increased vulnerability of one to two-year olds, suggesting that 'this age might represent a period of particular stress in child rearing' and adding that it was also a time when support from health services declined and when other services were usually not yet in place.[9]

II The relationship between individual and aggregate outcomes

Our working party identified five perspectives of child care outcomes: public, service, professional, family and that for the child. Although appreciating the importance of each we concentrated upon outcomes from the child's point of view. Since then the assessment of agency performance (that is, service outcomes) has become an increasingly important activity, both routinely and in response to scandals and tragedies. Organisations are anxious to monitor their own performance as well as that of other bodies from whom they may be commissioning services. They are also subject to various kinds of external scrutiny.

These developments raise the question of the relationship between the way in which organisational performance is assessed and the manner in which the assessment of outcomes for individual children is approached. There are notable differences. In the first place different amounts and types of information are likely to be used. Both an organisation's performance targets as well as the indicators employed to monitor their realisation are strongly influenced by the data that are considered to be relevant and, indeed, obtainable. Above all, of course, there has been the constant reference to details of expenditure and cost. Coupled with this is the fact that when it comes to the interpretation of this type of performance data (how good or bad are we?) considerable reliance is placed upon comparisons with similar organisations as well as with previous performance. These are the conventional benchmarks.

By contrast, the assessment of outcomes for vulnerable children involves a great deal more information, and information of a personalised nature. Furthermore, until recently there has been little systematic comparison with other children,[10] either with those who have been exposed to similar misfortunes or with 'control' groups of one kind or another. Indeed, there is a common conviction that the children with whom social workers are engaged (especially those with the most complex problems) defy the broad classifications that the aggregation of data entails.

The 'Looking After Children' project offered an opportunity to build a bridge between the assessment of individual and organisational outcomes. The information that it generated could be assembled to provide more sensitive indicators of how well an authority was attending to the welfare of those children for whom it carried some responsibility. Certainly it was still necessary to take account of the kinds of items (such as unit costs, the rates of provision of this or that service or social workers' caseloads) that were to be found in the Department of Health's 1994 list of 'key indicators'[11] or in the Audit Commission's review of services for children;[12] but these were essentially input variables and were not based upon what was actually achieved (or not achieved) in promoting children's well-being.

The statistics about outcomes that have been gathered and published by the Department for Education in the last few years are an important step forward to a different style of social accountancy and one that offers a more realistic picture of an authority's performance on behalf of those children for whom it carries a responsibility. This is because it is based upon a summation of information about individual children, information such as the state of their health, their educational achievement, their emotional and behavioural problems and so on.

Even so, there are two important drawbacks. One is that the performance of authorities is being assessed on 'outcome' information about children who are at different stages of their care careers. Some will have been 'looked after' for several years, others for only a short time. Although, therefore, it may be appropriate to regard some children as being at a point where it is reasonable to consider that an 'outcome' has been reached, this would not be true for others. The second concern about the current collection of outcomes data is that it does not (and perhaps cannot) combine the different indicators in order to provide something that might be regarded as an overall 'score', a conundrum that is discussed next.

III How comprehensive should selected outcomes be?

The 'Looking After Children' project identified seven dimensions upon which outcomes for children should be considered: health, education, emotional and behavioural development, family and peer relationships, self-care and competence, identity, and social presentation. It was agreed that this reflected the need to disaggregate the notion of 'an' outcome, since progress was likely to be different in different components of a child's life. However, it was not proposed that outcomes in these separate areas should be re-assembled into an overall score. This was partly because such a process of homogenisation was likely to mask potentially important variations (for instance, that between an improvement in education and a persistence in confusion about identity) but also because of the practical problems of deciding what weight should be attached to outcomes on one dimension in comparison with those on another. Furthermore, how was any cancelling-out effect of combining the positives with the negatives to be taken into account?

Despite our decision not to try to resolve these difficulties the concept of different dimensions of outcome seemed a useful advance from the one-dimensional approach. Indeed, that is now recognised in the assessment of outcomes for looked-after children that are conducted by the Department for Education, although the dimensions being used are somewhat different from those that our working party proposed.[13]

Whatever 'dimensions' are chosen and whatever indicators are used to monitor them, however, it hardly needs to be said that there are many types of outcomes in many spheres and that these are associated with a variety of interventions and life events. But how do these combine and to what effect and, in any case, are they actually as mixed (in terms of the good and the bad) as our working party was pleased to assume? One example will serve to emphasise the complexity of the issue. In our study of children returned home from care 'on trial' Elaine Farmer and I found that 44% of the teenage girls became pregnant over the two years of the study, as against a national rate for the 16 to 19 age group of 3%: indisputably, a poor outcome some would conclude. Yet only one of their babies was taken into care in that period and their relations with their families (especially with their mothers) appeared to improve.[14]

Just how specific should we be in the outcomes that we choose to assess? If the kind of disaggregation that is to be found in the 'Looking After Children' scheme is the preferred pattern, then there is still a case for making some *general* assessment of how a child's welfare has improved or deteriorated. Life satisfaction scales might help, as might the exercise of informed judgement or autobiographical reflection.

Although both adults and children do differentiate between outcomes ('he's doing well at school but I'm worried about…') they also weigh up the pros and cons to convey a view of their lives overall. I was struck by this in reading Albert Facey's moving autobiography *A Fortunate Life*.[15] After an Australian childhood of harsh treatment and emotional deprivation, erratic schooling, exploitative employment and suffering serious wounds at Gallipoli, he concluded his story by writing: 'I have lived a very good life, it has been very rich and full. I have been very fortunate and I am thrilled by it when I look back.' By contrast, one of the men quoted in Phyllis Harrison's collection of the life stories of people sent to Canada as children by Barnardos tells her that he wonders, 'What might have been if I had had a normal childhood. Actually I ceased to be a child at the age of ten. No one can understand my feelings of loneliness and despair.'[16] The message from these two extracts is not only that different people view the quality of their lives in different ways and for different reasons, but that what happens later (in Facey's case his marriage in particular) can offset the effect of what occurred earlier or simply confirm it. Yet we are still uncertain how the multiplicity and succession of 'intermediate' outcomes are or should be assembled in order to provide the more comprehensive assessment that, in the end, will most accurately reflect children's sense of their own well-being.[17]

IV The categories of children for whom outcomes are assessed

The 'Looking After Children' scheme of outcome assessment was conceived mainly in relationship to 'looked-after' children; that is, children living away from home for whom a local authority was acting in loco parentis. However, since the working party was engaged in its deliberations the work of children's services has become more diverse and more complicated. Fewer children are being looked after in ways that impose parent-like responsibilities upon authorities and more are being sustained in situations in which there is a mixed pattern of responsibility, and hence of accountability.

We adopted a straightforward criterion for what an authority should do in order to give the best chance of favourable outcomes for the look-after children for whom it was directly responsible; namely, they should ensure that those matters were attended to which it could reasonably be expected would be the concern of most parents. There is no similar criterion that helps to decide what an authority should be expected to do when working 'in partnership' with parents in order to promote the well-being of children in their own homes. Is their degree of responsibility for what happens or does not happens in these situations different from that which they carry for looked-after children? In any case, are the same indicators of outcomes appropriate in both circumstances?

V The evaluation of outcomes

Most research that seeks to identify the influences that bear upon outcomes also endeavours to evaluate them, often by incorporating at the outset a definition of what will be regarded as a good or a bad result. Yet the favourable or unfavourable nature of many outcomes is actually quite hard to decide except, of course, in extreme cases. This is true for both individual outcomes and organisational performance. The point may be illustrated by drawing yet another example from our 'home on trial' study. We employed an essentially 'overall' assessment of outcomes, constructed in part from our own judgements and in part from those of a mixed panel of professionals, children who had been in care, parents of children in care and a grandparent. On this basis the placements of 30% of the children over the age of criminal responsibility who offended during the two years of the research were actually classed as 'positive'. Similarly, once returned home the school attendance of nearly three-fifths of the older children who should have been at school was poor; even so, a quarter of their placements at home were judged to have been positive.

Had special significance been attached to offending or to the failure to attend school the overall rate of successful placements would have been considerably lower; and there were grounds for according these factors greater prominence since many of the offenders had originally been committed to care on the grounds of their offences and many of those not going to school had been committed for non-attendance (both possibilities having been grounds for a care order prior to the changes introduced under the Children Act 1989). Had we evaluated the outcomes against the ostensible reason for these children's removal from home (certainly a defensible position) a rather disheartening picture of their return home would have had to be reported.

Indeed, one of the problems of evaluating outcomes lies in knowing what 'levels' are to be regarded as good, good enough, indifferent, or quite unsatisfactory. Again, in the same study, as noted earlier, a quarter of the younger children were abused or neglected while back at home; but three-quarters were not, despite the fact that the reasons for many of them being committed to care sprang from their previous abuse or neglect. How is such an aggregate outcome to be evaluated, and against what criteria? Should evaluations reflect 'relative' progress rather than the achievement of a prescribed standard?

Do we too often pitch our expectations at an unreasonably high level and hence virtually ensure poor rates of success? Or, on the other hand, do we set them too low, thereby being content with mediocre or even unacceptable outcomes? The lesson may be that more attention needs to be paid to what would constitute a good outcome (or indeed a poor one) on a child-by-child basis rather than by the application of blanket formulae. Again, the 'Looking After Children' approach went some way to making this possible, although it may be necessary to give rather more emphasis to the children's evaluation of the services that they have received. Several studies (for example those of June Thorburn[18] and of John Triseliotis[19] and his colleagues) have discovered that the recipients' views of the help that they have been offered tend to be more favourable than those of the social workers who were responsible for providing it. For example, the latter study found that two-thirds of the young people thought that their lives were better at the end than at the start of the one-year inquiry, although not always as a result of social work help. Nevertheless, nearly half said that their expectations of such help had been met. By contrast, only 30% of the social workers were equally satisfied with what had been achieved and parents were less likely than their children to consider the interventions to have been helpful. Results such as these underline the fact that even those closely involved can reach different conclusions about the value of the same intervention or about whether things have got better, worse or stayed the same. There is a danger in attaching undue importance to any one view of an outcome.

VI Attribution, prediction and explanation

It goes without saying that many factors contribute to shaping an 'outcome'. Sophisticated statistical techniques and the power of computing allow us to identify significant associations, take account of overlapping influences and different combinations, as well as discern those sets of factors that best discriminate between one outcome and another. But the scope of such analyses is circumscribed by the extent and nature of the data to which they are applied and these data, in their turn, are largely the product of what is already believed to be important, together with what it is considered possible to collect.

Although it is necessary to be aware of such limitations and difficulties we should not be deterred from trying to sift out what has contributed to a particular outcome and then using the results to inform practice and policy. Even with 'gold standard' research employing randomised controlled trials we are unlikely to be able to say with confidence that a particular outcome is attributable to this or that form of intervention or set of factors. However, with aggregate data about enough cases it is feasible to establish the *chances* of an outcome being realised (or not being realised) given the existence or absence of certain intervening variables. In short, the prediction of outcomes from known past regularities can furnish the kind of informed guidance that is often lacking in children's services and for which practitioners are often heard to ask.

Of course, none of this removes the need for the exercise of judgement (a matter discussed further in Chapter 10). Even if it is established that there is, say, an 80% probability of a successful outcome with these kinds of children, in these circumstances and with this type of intervention it remains to be decided whether the case in question is one of the majority or whether it promises to be one of the exceptions. There are, indeed, certain intangible aspects of any social situation that are not amenable to statistical treatment but which may nevertheless need to be taken into account. Likewise, knowing that there is an 80% chance of 'success' if certain steps are taken cannot indicate what is an acceptable level of risk. This will be determined by considerations of policy, prevailing expectations and aspirations, the availability of alternatives and *their* presumed risk.

Hence, well-founded prediction, based upon the examination and recording of past outcomes, offers relevant information in a condensed and useable form. It also serves to broaden the range of experience upon which practitioners can call as well as providing them with a yardstick against which they can reflect upon their own assessments. In these ways such an approach can counteract or compensate for the uniqueness of each worker's experience.

Over and above these benefits, the prediction of outcomes may have an important contribution to make to the more appropriate deployment of scarce resources. For instance, if, having made a decision, we know that the likelihood of success is fairly low, more attention and support may be required or special precautions taken. Similarly, knowledge of prevailing probabilities may assist in the conservation of resources. There are key decisions in social work that, if inappropriately made, commit the agency to years of expensive and unrewarding work. Just how much of this work social services agencies create for themselves in this way is hard to tell, but if well-calculated probabilities can forewarn of such risks they may decide not to commit extensive resources in ways that show little evidence of making a difference.

Thus, I would argue that the use of statistical prediction, based upon good initial data, is one important means of dealing with the complicated business of sorting out just which factors contribute just how much to identified outcomes. Even so, however well we untangle the problem of attributing outcomes to key influences we do not necessarily *explain* what we discover. What exactly are the processes involved? The point is that attribution should not be confused with explanation, although the one may take us a good way towards understanding the other; and it is undoubtedly helpful to know what 'works' or does not work even though the precise reasons remain unclear.

CHAPTER 9

The role and function of inquiries*

There is such a variety of inquiries (together with reviews, inquests, tribunals and inspectors' reports) that they do not lend themselves to easy generalisation. However, for the most part they are political instruments. They may be set up to advance particular policies, as a defence against unwanted pressure, as an expedient response to a public outcry, to sound out influential opinion prior to the introduction of a new policy or new legislation, to establish the facts of a disturbing case or to challenge prevailing assumptions: and so the list could be continued. Thus, although inquiries share a political *character* their *functions* are varied; and a single inquiry may well serve several purposes, not least because the interested parties seek different outcomes.

If one accepts that inquiries are essentially political (in the broadest sense) then it becomes important to appreciate why they are initiated, by whom, the timing, the form that they take, the interests that are reflected in their deliberations, the consequences of the conclusions that are reached and, of course, the relationship between these various matters. Let us consider a few features of each, having in mind their frequency in the field of child welfare.

I Variety, scope and classification

The initiation of an inquiry usually follows an event, often one that is vivid enough (or is made vivid enough) to speak for similar issues. Nevertheless, those events can be of two kinds: the general and the particular. The general might be exemplified by the health select committee's inquiry into the welfare of former British child migrants that reported in 1997[1] or by the royal commission on the funding of long-term care for the elderly that reported two years later.[2] Just when and how such concerns gain enough momentum to prompt an inquiry is, of course, of considerable significance; but two factors are

---

[9] This chapter has been developed from an unpublished paper prepared for the Sequali programme of training events for members of inquiries in 2011 and organised by King's College, London and the Garden Court Family Law Chambers, London.

noteworthy. One is the availability of statistical evidence, especially about trends that show a worsening situation. The other is the role played by interest groups, and sometimes by research, in creating a sufficient groundswell of disquiet to make a political response necessary.

Particular events may also lead to an inquiry, serious case reviews offering a prime example;[3] but there are many others in the field of children's services that go back many years, such as the inquiry into the death of Dennis O'Neill in his foster home in 1945[4] or the investigation into the administration of punishment at Court Lees approved school in 1967.[5] What is of interest is which particular events result in an inquiry and which do not, and in this the role of investigative journalism should not be discounted nor the eagerness of the media to attach their stories to individual 'cases'.

Of course, inquiries may be set up by many different bodies, the main distinction being between those initiated by official action, whether national or local, and those established by non-governmental organisations. Yet even within each there is a wide variety in terms of their standing, independence, accountability or ability to require witnesses to give evidence. Consider, for example, the difference between a royal commission and a parliamentary select committee.[6] The former will have been a government initiative with carefully framed terms of reference. The latter will have a cross-party membership and some scope for choosing the issues it addresses. Or, take the difference between an inquiry launched by a Royal College and one begun by a vociferous user group. Indeed, there is such a variety that some kind of classification seems to be called for. In the case of officially promoted inquiries Wheare offered such a scheme as far back as 1955[7] as did Rhodes 20 years later, providing a list of all such committees of inquiry between 1959 and 1968, there having been 174 (excluding the standing committees).[8] Yet both commentators chose to group inquiries by their subject; they might equally well have been arranged, say, by sponsorship, by membership, by their outcomes or by their political purpose. Corby and his colleagues proposed a different classification in 2001 based principally on the purpose of inquiries: that is, whether they were administrative, fact-finding or investigative.[9]

II Inauguration, form and procedure

The timing of the inauguration of an inquiry is often important. For example, a general issue or problem does not suddenly arise and demand investigation. Most will have been evident for years and a good deal of background information will have accumulated. What is it *now* that seems to call for investigation? Has the matter, as it were, reached a critical mass?[10] Have the interest groups around it changed? Has more telling information appeared? And what, therefore, are the implications of the particular timing of its establishment as to how the deliberations unfold? Furthermore, as we shall see, just when an inquiry completes its report may affect its reception and what follows. Sometimes there are pressures for an inquiry to be completed quickly in order to catch the moment, while at other times there are powerful interests that are happy to see it long drawn out and then for its report to be consigned to the shelves. Indeed, some never do report, an eventuality mocked by A.P. Herbert in his satirical poem *Sad Fate of a Royal Commission*.[11] An inquiry's political purpose may already have been fulfilled simply by its establishment; for example, by deferring or avoiding the need to take immediate action.

The form in which an inquiry is set up can be a contentious matter. To start with there is the question of its terms of reference. Sometimes these are so general that they set few limitations, while on other occasions they impose tight constraints; and sometimes terms of reference are subsequently altered. Those who frame them clearly exercise a measure of control over the scope of what is done. For example, terms of reference may include a requirement that any recommendations be accompanied by an estimate of the cost of implementing them, or they may impose a time limit.[12] In particular, it is always worth noting what is left out of terms of reference. Furthermore, committees may be informally instructed that their terms of reference do not extend to the investigation of certain matters or to making recommendations about particularly sensitive (usually political) issues. For example, the Wagner committee, which was set up by the Secretary of State for Social Services in 1985 to review the state of residential care, was told that their brief did not include any boarding schools, although representations were made that these should be included.[13]

Next there is the question of who should conduct an inquiry and how. Again the variety is considerable but not random. Where speed and close control are required a single individual is often chosen. When the issue touches upon a national interest, but one that demands strong legitimacy for its findings, a royal commission may be established (although now less often than in the past). Does the topic or event call for experts to undertake the inquiry or to be included? For example, where there are likely to be legal issues a QC is often appointed, sometimes to work single-handedly or with one or two others. This was the case in the committee that investigated the death of Maria Colwell in 1974,[14] in the panel of inquiry into the circumstances surrounding the death of Jasmine Beckford in 1984[15] and in the inquiry into the pindown practices in a residential home that reported in 1991.[16] Yet inquiries into similar tragedies have been constituted differently; for example, Lord Laming, a former head of the social services inspectorate, was chosen by the Minister of Health and the Home Secretary to conduct the inquiry into the death of Victoria Climbié and he, in turn, was able to appoint four experts to assist him.[17] Since the early 1990s, however, serious case reviews, organised by local area child protection boards, have become the most frequently adopted means for investigating child deaths or other suffering that may have befallen children. Indeed, in England and Wales there were 268 such reviews between 2007 and 2009.[18] Not only are they numerous but also more informal, not required to apportion blame, always public and, of course, they tend to have a local orientation. They are probably cheaper to conduct than other forms of inquiry and usually take less time. The emphasis is upon the lessons that can be learnt for future practice.

Depending on the topic and the issues surrounding it, however, the membership of an investigating committee (whatever its form) may call less for experts but more for a selection that reflects key interest groups, not least in order to avoid their subsequent opposition to what the inquiry might recommend. Nonetheless, the difference between expert and non-expert is something of a false distinction: experts have interests or affiliations that go beyond their expertise while non-expert representatives may have valuable first-hand experience and contribute more, much as a witness might. Even so, the choice of 'representatives' can be a hazardous business. It exposes itself to the criticism that this or that group or interest has been favoured or has been passed over. Such accusations are likely to have particular force if it has been claimed that the membership *is* representative.

The composition of inquiry or review teams usually reflects the choices of the individuals or bodies that set them up, and this in itself is a political process that is influenced both by how the 'problem' is seen and by what purpose the investigation is intended to serve. In particular the choice of who is to chair the undertaking is likely to be significant. We have already noted the frequency with which QCs have been recruited; but the range is considerable. Is a notable public figure needed in order to emphasise an inquiry's importance: a noble lord, a business leader or a retired but eminent politician for instance? If, as is often the case, an inquiry is claimed to be independent (independent of which interests?) how will this be achieved through the choice of those called upon to conduct it? Indeed, the independence of an inquiry may be challenged on various grounds, most often that all or some of its members cannot be dispassionate, particularly when the investigation is an 'in house' exercise. For example, many inquiries have been conducted by the inspectorates of different government departments or by inter-departmental groups of civil servants. Local authorities, health or police authorities too may decide to mount an inquiry (individually or collectively) without the involvement of central government, albeit sometimes pressed to do so by it. Indeed, central government may be pleased to leave it at this level in order to imply where responsibility lies, or will lie.

In addition to these considerations there is the matter of evidence. What kind of evidence is to be gathered, from whom and how? Will evidence be invited and, if so, which individuals or bodies will be chosen to do so orally and why? Will visits be made and, if so, where and to whom? When will it be considered necessary to find out what happens in other countries? If so, which are selected and why?[19] Are they really necessary or only included in order to meet the criticism that an inquiry has failed to look beyond the domestic situation? In any case, how far will it be expected to go in assembling evidence? Will it take what it can get or what is offered; or commission its own research? What weight will be given to different kinds of evidence? Will legal or scientific submissions trump all others or will more attention be paid to statements of position in order to be able to judge the climate surrounding the issue? When they report some inquiries hold firmly to what the evidence indicates while others go beyond it.[20] These are all issues that have a political connotation which is liable to affect the fate of the eventual report.

One aspect of the production of a report that is rarely mentioned is how it comes to be written. How is all the material that is assembled sorted out, cut down to size and then brought together? It is hardly practical for a whole committee to do it. So, who undertakes the difficult sifting and editorial tasks? Sometimes the answer will be found in the acknowledgements, where it will be discovered that the secretary (if there was one) shouldered the burden, or maybe some other relatively inconspicuous individual. On other occasions the person in the chair may assume the responsibility (and, in any case, they will usually lend their name to the ensuing report). Particular members of an inquiry may write certain sections. When it comes to serious case reviews someone will be commissioned or appointed to sieve through the evidence and produce a draft report, although it has not always been clear who that was and how and why they were chosen.[21] Even though what is eventually written will have been vetted by the whole committee (and sometimes by those who set it up) some members will be more scrupulous in examining drafts than others and thereby exercise more influence over what emerges. Indeed, those who do not agree with the general view may feel obliged to produce a minority report or a note of dissent about certain issues. In short, it is certainly worth asking *how* a report got written and how its *format* was determined. Will it be slanted towards a particular readership; indeed, will it *be* readable? Will it be cut to the bone or comprehensive (the Climbié report ran to 400 pages)? Will it eschew statistics or depend upon them to reinforce its conclusions? Will most of the evidence be published, just a selection of it or none at all? And what extra will be available on line?

III So, what next?

What happens once an inquiry is completed? Do its findings affect policy or practice, or are they largely ignored? In short, what determines the impact that it makes? The timing of a report's appearance can be as significant as the timing of its inauguration. Have the circumstances changed in such a way that the inquiry's brief has been overtaken by events; or is the issue still topical? Have the media lost interest or is the matter still newsworthy? A skilfully managed inquiry will release its conclusions when conditions are most favourable to a sympathetic and telling reception. Sometimes that will call for acceleration (through, for example, an interim report or a carefully contrived leak) and sometimes, as we have already noted, a deliberate delay will be engineered. Of course, none of this will affect the outcome if, say, there has been a change of government and the inquiry had been a creature of the outgoing administration from which the new government is keen to disassociate itself.

Where an inquiry involves a committee or working party it will be important whether or not it has been able to reach a unanimous conclusion. Examples of minority reports and dissenting appendices are plentiful.[22] In general they tend to weaken the impact of an inquiry; for example, by giving a government or other authority that is unenthusiastic about its recommendations the opportunity to claim that too many uncertainties exist for action to be taken. Whether unanimity is achieved or not will largely reflect the composition of a committee but also the extent to which, beyond the committee, a more general consensus already exists. That notwithstanding, if it had been felt necessary to include members with opposing views or competing constituencies in order to demonstrate an inquiry's representativeness, that may make it harder to secure a consensus later or delay the work unduly.

Then there is the question of what it might cost (or save) to implement an inquiry's proposals. As we have seen some committees are required to provide such calculations. Others may trim their recommendations to what is thought likely to pass financial scrutiny. Some, such as the Seebohm committee on the reorganisation of the personal social services, tactically chose not to offer any view on costs.[23] Of course, it does much to help if what is being suggested can be shown to save money; indeed, some inquiries are set up specifically to explore how this might be done, to examine financial estimates[24] or to scrutinise what has been spent.[25]

All inquiries have their constituencies. There are those who decided that they should be established in the first place, there are those who meet the costs, there are the interests of those who pressed for there to be an inquiry (not forgetting those who wanted no such thing), there are those who give evidence and those whose views have been ignored. There are, of course, also those whose lives may be affected by an inquiry's findings, either favourably or unfavourably. An inquiry that is alive to this mixture of interests and takes them into account (without being hamstrung by them) has a better chance of making an eventual impact than one that is not.

Are there individuals or groups ready to campaign for what an inquiry recommends? If not, a report may lie where it falls. On the other hand governments, whether central or local, may already be prepared to act upon the findings. Or, it may be that the members of an inquiry team take it upon themselves to keep the report in the public and political eye. Sometimes there are lobby groups ready and willing to do so. Depending on the subject the media may be keen to keep the issue going. There may be parliamentarians, indeed particular ministers, anxious to do so as well. Keith Joseph, the then Secretary of State for Social Services, explained this when he addressed the annual conference of the Association for Mental Health in 1971, saying that 'the sudden revelation of conditions well known to the expert of which the public is unaware gives Ministers the chance to galvanise their colleagues and *to get the resources* to improve things. Heaven help any government from revelations, but when they come they often serve a high purpose' (emphasis added).[26]

The point is that the findings of an inquiry can shift the prevailing balance of political influence; for example, in the light of Joseph's observation the opportunity to prise more money from the Treasury for this or that department's favoured scheme. Indeed, he appears to have been successful in doing so, certainly with respect to the re-organised personal social services that saw an annual rate of growth in expenditure of 17% between 1970 and 1973.[27]

The discussion so far has rather assumed that inquiries make recommendations; but that is not always so. Some are required simply to establish the facts (as was the case in the Court Lees Approved School inquiry), to collect information or test out counter claims. Nevertheless, the impact that such explorations make will also depend upon who is ready and able to use what they provide as well, of course, upon the quality of what is produced: will it stand up to further scrutiny? Then there are disciplinary committees, such as the General Medical Council and the Law Society, that are not only charged to determine the facts of a case but then to make binding decisions

IV The call for lessons to be learned

Most committees of inquiry or review are exhorted to make clear what lessons need to be learned from what they have unravelled, and most members will wish to do so. Even so, that is far from a straightforward matter. This is evident if we return to the division that was suggested earlier; namely, that between general and particular issues as the impulse for an inquiry's establishment. In the case of the former it seems quite reasonable that general conclusions should be drawn, since they will concern the broad thrust of policy. However, when it comes to the latter (the inquiries prompted by a specific event) it is less certain that general conclusions should follow without a clear examination of the uniqueness of the event in question, or at least of the probabilities of it happening again. There appears to be a strong temptation to urge that 'lessons be learned' without an assessment of the event's singularity or of the structural (including political) reasons that stand in the way. Take, for example, the predictable finding that the tragedies befalling certain children might have been forestalled by better collaboration between the agencies concerned. Inquiry after inquiry draw the lesson that this must be improved and suggestions about how it might be done usually follow. Yet little attention is paid to trying to *explain* why this lack of collaboration persists although there are theoretical formulations that could be helpful.[28] Likewise, there are theories about why those responsible for child protection make 'common errors of reasoning' as Munro puts it.[29] In short, an undue preoccupation with the fallibility of 'procedures' may detract from the opportunities that inquiries offer to understand better why procedural reform has limited scope to rectify persistent problems, not all of which are organisational.

There is also the question of who it is who is supposed to learn which lessons. The answer is usually to be found in the reforms that are suggested; but these may be so narrowly cast (especially when culpability is an issue, or is made an issue) that they obscure or overlook how much further afield 'lessons should be learned'; perhaps by those who determine the conduct of inquiries or by the research community? Finally, of course, one has to ask whether it is actually possible for a lesson to be converted into appropriate remedial action.

The fact that the plea that 'lessons must be learned' is so often heard following tragedies of all kinds suggests that it fulfils certain psychological functions over and above the need to avoid a repetition. There appears to be a strong feeling that the terrible things that happen to people, especially to children, should not have happened in vain. Both the establishment of an inquiry and the insistence that lessons must be learned from its deliberations can be, in Reder and Duncan's words, 'cathartic', marking 'the life of the child who has died, recording their suffering and giving meaning to their life and death'.[30] Symbolically, an inquiry proclaims that a child will not be forgotten; that *something* will be taken from a tragedy that will help to safeguard other children in the future. If this is the common emotional response to terrible events, especially those that befall children, it helps to explain the need for inquiries as well as what happens once they have run their course.

Given the emotional, and therefore political, overtones that inquiries into tragic events engender it is not surprising that they are likely to shift priorities. Indeed, several commentators have maintained that child abuse inquiries have propelled child protection to the top of the children's services' agenda at the expense of other aspects of this work.[31] In short, that they have led to a rearrangement of resources. That, of course, is liable to happen after any disturbing inquiry report, but it does beg the question of whether the 'best' balance of resources has thereby been achieved. This consideration reminds us that there may well be additional lessons to be learned from the *consequences* of the implementation or rejection of what an inquiry has recommended.

V Inquiries: change or continuity?

So, what has changed since, say, the mid-nineteenth century with respect to inquiries? It is, of course, not easy to generalise, but several points are worth bearing in mind. First, although the nature of inquiries has altered, their functions have not; at least in their political significance. All the purposes that have been noted may be found in earlier investigations; and there are plenty of examples. Second, the changes that *are* apparent concern such things as the pattern of membership of committees (today more representative), the frequency with which inquiries are set in train (certainly more concerning children than in the past), the quality of the reports that are produced (better in the nineteenth century than later), the amount of evidence that is published (less nowadays), a marked shift in the balance between inquiries about general topics and those concerned with individual cases (fewer of the former, particularly since the Thatcher years) and the role of the media which has become more notable in shaping both the initiation of inquiries (through, for example, telling investigative journalism) and the reception of their findings. The media have become less restrained than, say, before the 1970s; and the impact of social media may become increasingly significant, almost as an independent running inquiry.

These changes reflect shifts in social patterns and social expectations. In particular, the human rights agenda has contributed to the growing number of 'case' inquiries. Likewise, the assumption that organisations should be, and can be, held to account for what they do or fail to do, means that the close examination of their performance is more likely than before, not least because of the establishment of many more complaints procedures over the last 20 years or so. What has most changed the character and frequency of inquiries might be summarised therefore, as the greater exposure of organisations to public scrutiny.

CHAPTER 10

Evidence, judgement, values and engagement[*]

Relevant and reliable research should inform both policy and practice. Nevertheless, the use of evidence remains decidedly patchy: serious obstacles remain that arise from the nature of the evidence at issue, from the unavoidable need for judgement, from the underlying values involved and, finally, from the vicissitudes of 'political will'.

I Evidence

How confident should we be in what research concludes? Rather crudely one might begin by identifying three levels: evidence that is fairly conclusive, evidence that is indicative and evidence that is tentative. Of course, all kinds of scales can be used to make such distinctions. Quite simple devices could serve reasonably well. However, the problem is that the evidence is never complete. It is never wholly satisfactory; there are always deficiencies and there are always gaps.

Nonetheless, there is at least one test that can be applied: that of convergence. Do the results in question confirm the conclusions of other similar studies? Indeed, *are* there comparable studies against which they can be assessed? Furthermore, has this or that study been designed and reported in such a way that it could be replicated? If one looks back to Bowlby's influential report to the World Health Organisation on maternal deprivation in the early 1950s[1] one sees that not only was he drawing upon his own research but upon other studies that went back to the 1920s. Most of that research pointed in the same direction as his, and that was partly the reason why his report made the impact that it did. My early research on foster care provides another example.[2] One of the most important findings (as explained in Chapter 3) was that foster homes where there were 'own' children of about the same age as the placed child were significantly more likely

---

[*] First published in Tunnard, J. (1998) *Commissioning and Managing External Research*. Dartington: Research in Practice, but here with various revisions.

than others to disrupt. Indeed, that one single factor – the presence or absence of own children around the same age – accounted for a large proportion of the variation between those placements that were successful and those that were not. Somewhat earlier, Trasler[3] had arrived at a similar conclusion from his study, and many of those that followed produced the same finding.[4] Nevertheless, when an apparent convergence of results is discovered it is always wise to check that they are indeed reasonably comparable; for example, with respect to ages, cultures, the nature of the questions at the heart of the studies or the period that is covered.

The convergence of results from different studies should not be regarded as a conclusive way of deciding how much confidence should be placed in research findings however. Studies that are at odds with previous results should not be dismissed. They may reflect the consequences of a more sophisticated approach, changes in contexts or the effect of a different disciplinary perspective. They may be significant in raising doubts about hitherto uncritically accepted assumptions. How seriously such challenges should be taken will depend on the quality of the evidence but also upon the quality of the studies (if there were any) that have given rise to the accepted wisdom.

How searching should one be when it comes to assessing a study? One of the pitfalls is that when the results reinforce our convictions we tend to lower our critical threshold and are then unduly willing to accept its conclusions. This is also liable to happen when research concerns matters about which practitioners feel uncertain, undecided or at sea, tempting them to grasp at whatever seems to offer guidance. On the other hand, when the findings are contrary to what we believe or to our experience we tend to raise our critical threshold and to look for what in the results can be explained away or found wanting. It is far from easy to be consistent in how we assess the merits of different studies.

Of course, there is always the possibility that certain research produces good quality evidence but evidence that is not actually relevant to the issue in hand. Attempts to apply it inappropriately will almost certainly be misleading. For example, if one takes Martin Knapp's work on the costing of the personal social service[5] (and children's services in particular) one learns that the analysis of unit costs may not be an appropriate basis for drawing conclusions about the economics of policy development. For certain purposes marginal costs provide better guidance. So, although the result of studies of unit costs are correct as far as they go they may not be an appropriate basis for determining the relative costs of different options.

The evidence derived from research is not only uneven in its quality but also in its coverage. It rarely proceeds at the same pace or to the same depth on all fronts, even when these are closely related. Typically, it makes spearhead advances or conducts exploratory probes. One of the difficulties, therefore, is that there is liable to be better data about some problems or proposed solutions than about others. It follows that those who carry the responsibility for deciding what should be done have to make choices between options that are unevenly informed by research evidence. This may lead to an unduly optimistic or to an unduly pessimistic view of the case for one course of action rather than another. Therefore, it is crucial for it to be known that there *is* an unevenness of evidence when different policies or practices are being contemplated and for that to be taken into account or rectified if the time and the means allow.

As well as questions about the quality of evidence it is important to consider the categories (or types) that are available as aids to decision. Let me offer three examples. First, there is evaluative research; that is, research which looks at what works and what does not. There is, for example, the Barnardo's *What Works?* child care series.[6] Often, however, we have more information about what does not work than about what does. If we are armed with mainly negative evidence it is tempting to assume that the positive factors are simply the absence of the negative ones. That may or may not be the case.

There is another kind of research that is concerned with patterns of distribution. A study about disabled children with which I was involved was based on the data obtained by the Office for Population Censuses and Surveys (OPCS) in its surveys of the late 1980s.[7] One of the results that emerged from the closer analysis of these data was that two parents with only one child received disproportionately more services than one-parent families and larger families, irrespective of the nature and severity of the child's disability. This seemed to fly in the face of what one might reasonably have expected had the services been distributed in a way that reflected the social as well as the disability needs of the family. Likewise, significantly fewer services were received by the poorest fifth of the families than by the other four-fifths. Such evidence is clearly relevant to service planning and to day-to-day practice.

There is a third type of evidence (of which there are many examples) derived from research that deals specifically with needs. Much of this quantifies, identifies or redefines a 'problem', sometimes highlighting some that are new or unacknowledged. Another example, taken from our research on children with disabilities, will serve to illustrate the point. We found that, at the end of the 1980s, only 5% of the families looking after disabled children were receiving any kind of respite care. When the OPCS had asked families what additional help they wanted only 1% had mentioned respite care. However, subsequent research undertaken by the Norah Fry Centre at Bristol made it clear that the demand for the service had grown considerably.[8] If one had taken the late 1980s data as a measure of the 'need' for respite care it would have been quite misleading some years later. Knowledge of the service had widened, the services on offer had changed and attitudes towards the use of respite care had become more favourable. The point is that if the same questions are asked five or ten years later rather different answers may be obtained.

The results of research need to be interpreted in order for their meaning to be discerned. Sometimes researchers explore these matters and offer interpretations. Sometimes they do not venture beyond an account of what they have discovered, leaving it to others to reach conclusions about meaning and explanation. Of course, some evidence is useful and useable in the absence of a proper understanding of exactly what it is that has made it significant. Even so, it is important to keep in mind the distinction between evidence and explanation. Sometimes we are offered evidence without explanation, sometimes (worryingly) explanation without evidence. However, the relationship between evidence and its explanatory interpretation needs to be mediated by theory. A good theory should be a concise and elegant way of summarising observations in the pursuit of explanation. Nevertheless, a theory should always be regarded as provisional and, in principle, capable of being refuted by new or better evidence.

II Judgement

Many of the results that research provides are actually (or implicitly) expressed in terms of probabilities; probabilities such as that for this group of children, or these types of families in these situations, there is, let us say, a 75% chance that this will happen. Of course, that means that in 25% of the cases something else will happen; a minority will not conform to the most likely outcome. Unfortunately, because probabilities are statements about aggregate categories they do not indicate which particular case will conform to the general pattern and which will not. That being so, an important role is left for the exercise of judgement.[9] However, one of the interesting and unresolved questions concerns the nature of such judgement. How are good and bad judgements to be distinguished? And how best is good judgement to be nurtured? Experience is clearly an important factor; but it has to be experience that is cumulative, organised, assessed critically and therefore progressive. One way of ensuring that experience does not become stultified is by its exposure to evidence that is derived from other sources, from citizens whose lives are or will be affected, from colleagues, from research and from adjacent disciplines. For experience to bolster good judgement it has to be set within a framework of critical and thoughtful learning.

There is, of course, a fair sprinkling of poor judgment in all professional fields. All kinds of decisions can masquerade as good judgement although being little more than a reflection of fashion, prejudice, predilection or undue haste. It is always worth asking what it is that is generally taken for granted, not questioned or not even seen as a matter for debate. One of the values of research is that it can challenge such prevailing wisdom. An example from the history of child placement will serve to illustrate the point. One of the supposedly common sense assumptions to be found in the foster placement literature before the 1950s was that homes should be found that provided 'playmates', either for the fostered child, for the children already in the family or for both. As pointed out, by the 1960s the risks of such placements had begun to be exposed by research; 'common sense' had to be reconsidered. Or, to take another example, there is the common assumption that there are generational continuities in child abuse; that is, that the abused child becomes the abusive parent. Admittedly, parents who abuse their children have often suffered abuse themselves, but not all children who are abused go on to become abusing parents. In fact several pieces of research now indicate that it is a minority.[10] The statement that abusive parents are likely to have been abused as children is not the same as saying that abused children become abusive parents.

III Values

One of the reasons for gathering evidence through research, whether in social work, in physics, in engineering, in medicine or whatever, is in order to reach certain objectives more successfully. However, questions then arise as to whether these ends are generally approved (and by whom) or morally justified. Although such questions have not always loomed as large in social work as they have, say, in the fields of genetic engineering, chemical warfare or the exploitation of natural resources, they do exist and should not be ignored. For example, the ability to tap childhood memories about sexual abuse may be powerfully and appropriately applied, but the process may also encourage damaging false memories. The fact that we become better able to achieve certain ends with the aid of better evidence does not relieve us of the responsibility for checking that both the ends and the means are indeed justifiable.

It is always possible that values may collide with the evidence obtained from research. Deeply held values, whether they be political, religious or ethical, may be at odds with what research has to tell us, not least about the deficiencies of policies and practices that have been guided by strong convictions. Indeed, there is a long history in child welfare of values driving action, a good example being the child rescue movement of the nineteenth century that was often based upon the belief that the welfare of certain children could be best safeguarded by their complete severance from their families. The fact that, in some cases, strong convictions have been the motive force for improving the lives of children should not encourage the assumption that conviction always leads to children's betterment. Convincing evidence is also needed.

A good illustration of the moral dilemmas that research could create was offered by Leslie Wilkins (former head of the Home Office Research Unit) in his book *Social Deviance*.[11] 'It may be believed', he wrote, 'that it is wrong to flog offenders, but it is difficult to make such a claim unless it is known whether or not those flogged tend afterwards to commit more or fewer offences than those not flogged.' Even if, he went on to argue, it were demonstrated that 'flogging resulted in fewer reconvictions...it may still be held that it would be wrong to flog'. Later, he gives another example: 'If it was self-evident from research that capital punishment did prevent murder, would we feel the same about our ethical stand on attitudes towards capital punishment?' Well, would we? These are, of course, hypothetical questions drawn from rather extreme examples. Nonetheless, they are the kinds of ethical questions that research findings might expose, but which are not always acknowledged for what they are.

IV Engagement

Given that well-founded evidence about the issues with which practitioners and politicians grapple exists much then turns upon their willingness to use it. The record has not been encouraging. It is therefore important to consider why. Some of the reasons are to be found in what has been discussed already, particularly uncertainty about the quality of the evidence or about the disturbing implications of applying it; but other explanations also need to be taken into account, three of which are among the most common: attitudes towards what social science has to offer, the pressures of time and the lack of adequate communication between those offering evidence and those for whom it could be useful.

Especially in the field of social policy there has been, and in some circles remains, a scepticism about the scientific credentials of the 'social sciences'. This was sharply illustrated in 1981 when Keith Joseph, the Minister of Education, insisted that if the Social Science Research Council (SSRC) was to continue, its title had to be changed to the Economic and Social Research Council. The word 'science' had to be dropped.[12] In fact, the Council narrowly avoided being disbanded. Furthermore, any research that was supported by government was to deal with practical problems as formulated by the respective departments. The customer–contractor principle emerged, although the customers were not always clear what questions (if any) they wanted investigated.

However, over and above these misgivings lay the fact that the SSRC, created in 1965, was the suspect child of Harold Wilson's Labour government. For those on the political right the social sciences were heavily tainted by left-wing sympathies. It is less clear that the same assumptions existed in Conservative-controlled local governments where, indeed, some on the traditional left have been as sceptical about the value of social research as the Thatcher government.

This little history serves to make the point that social science in Britain has not been regarded as politically neutral and is, therefore, held at arm's length by those who suspected its leftish affiliations. There is an interesting contrast to be drawn with the situation in the US where, for example, an independent non-profit-making Social Science Research Council has existed since 1923, funded by grants from large corporations (such as Ford) and, in some cases, from government. The social sciences there appear not have the same political associations as they are assumed to have here.

Politicians and practitioners have to get on with what they have to do. They have to devise some kinds of solutions to the problems with which they are obliged to deal, however rough and ready these might be. In short, in most cases there are already 'solutions' (policies and practices) in place and which may have taken considerable political negotiation to achieve. As one senior administrator put it at a conference on the uses of research: 'Yes, but you researchers don't understand that what you come up with are problems for all our solutions.' If taken seriously, new evidence is liable to require changes, the repercussions of which are likely to spread and lead to new negotiations that may be difficult and time-consuming.

Yet, sometimes solutions have to be found for problems, especially those that have gained sharp public prominence; and often they have to be found rather promptly. What do the social sciences have to offer? There may already be relevant evidence to hand, but when none is available inquiries will need to be undertaken; and that will take time. When something has to be done quickly the political and practice 'customers' will want results sooner than a two- or three-year project can provide them. Even 'quick and dirty' exercises often take longer than those in the political, administrative or professional systems feel able to wait. So, one reason for an unwillingness to seek the help of research is that it is not there when it is wanted.

Such problems are more likely to be lessened when a regular dialogue exists between the research community and the potential users of their studies. That seems to be encouraged when each has had some experience of the others' worlds. David Donnison has pointed out, for example, that 'government departments and major local authorities cannot be expected to make good use of independent research unless they first have research units of their own and employ staff capable of communicating on equal terms with their colleagues in the universities'[13] and, one might add, in other research enterprises outside the universities. Of course, the other side of the coin is that if research teams wish to see the fruits of their studies being utilised they need to have some staff capable of making and sustaining links with the potential users. However, it has to be recognised that having good links with one type of user (for instance, a campaigning pressure group or the media) may make it more difficult to achieve them with another.

Thus, political scepticism, the pressures of time and the lack of adequate communication are three of the barriers to getting good research evidence accepted as useful by those who are capable of applying it. Yet there remain sources of evidence that lie outside the kinds of conventional research that this analysis implies, evidence of a kind that *forces* its attention on governments or other organisations in such a way that it *demands* a response. Donnison sums it up in the concluding paragraph of a recent essay, reminding us

> that however good our academic research and however effectively it is communicated, we shall still need investigators prepared to go undercover with cameras and recording equipment in hospitals, old people's homes, prisons and other places where our most vulnerable citizens are subject to unaccountable power; investigators who will find out what really goes on...and communicate what

they learn to *Panorama* programmes or the columns of *The Sunday Times* or *Daily Mail*; working in ways that would not be permitted by ... ethics committees.[14]

CHAPTER 11

Emerging issues: looking ahead

It's hard to say how the children's services might develop in the future, particularly the more distant future. New problems will arise, different policies will emerge and social trends may take us by surprise. Despite welcome advances in our understanding and in the amount of data that is available, prediction still remains hazardous.[1] Nevertheless, there are several ways in which we can anticipate what may lie ahead, at least in the fairly short term.

One way is to see what significant changes are already discernible and then to consider how they might develop and what new issues that might provoke. The use of private for-profit children's services by local authorities is one such an example. An examination of statistical trends may offer another way of looking into the future of the children's services. There are numerous examples, but three offer useful illustrations as well as being important in their own right: children's ethnic origins, their disabilities and their gender. Yet another way of considering how the children's services may develop is to consider whether certain longstanding problems may be able to be moderated, problems such as how best to prevent the grave misfortunes that befall too many children. Each of these approaches is explored in what follows.

I The private provision of services

The rapid increase in local authority commissioning of private for-profit children's services in the last two decades was discussed in Chapter 7. Nevertheless, a brief recapitulation of the salient points will serve to introduce a consideration of the issues that are evident now and of others that may arise.

Foster care

Before 2001 statistics about private foster care related to the informal and unorganised service that was provided for parents who were unable to look after their children themselves. Those who took in children on this basis and were paid were required to notify the local authority and were then subject to inspection. In England in 2012 there were

1,780 such 'notifications'.[2] However, 2002 saw the publication of an additional set of statistics that recorded the number of children who were looked after by local authorities but who were living in foster homes arranged and supervised by 'independent agencies', mainly private for-profit but also voluntary.[3]

In 2001 there were 3,670 such children, or 12% of all looked-after children who were in foster homes in England (excluding those placed with relatives or friends). By 2013 this had risen to 15,800 children, almost all of whom (97%) had been placed by some 230 private agencies, the remainder by voluntary bodies.[4] This amounted to 36% of all looked-after children who were in foster care.

The surveys undertaken by the Office for Standards in Education, Children's Services and Skills (OFSTED) provide a certain amount of information about these independent agencies and their services.[5] For example, 27% of the 21,912 approved placements were vacant at the end of March 2011; 2% of the children who had been placed were classed as 'disabled' and there had been 1,039 'unplanned endings' among all the placements over a three-month period, suggesting perhaps 4,000 a year. Of the approved foster carers, 74% were 'white British', followed by 8% who were African-Caribbean, 4% who were Pakistani, 3% who were African, 2% who were Indian and another 2% who were of mixed marriages. This was broadly in line with the ethnic backgrounds of the children who had been placed, except that there were substantially more children of mixed parentage (1,243) than there were similar foster parents (332). Unlike the longstanding pattern of foster care (described in Chapter 3) the independent sector placed more boys than girls at a ratio of three to two.

We learn more about the pattern of placements made by these agencies from the Department for Education's annual statistics. Whereas 22% of the children who the local authorities had placed were in foster homes beyond their boundaries in 2013, the figure for the private agencies was 65%. These statistics also tell us that the placement of children with 'relatives or friends' (14% overall) was arranged in almost all cases (96%) by local authorities themselves.[6] These and other differences between the practices of the private sector and the local authorities may have important implications for the emerging pattern of foster care; for example, with respect to the work of securing a child's restoration to their family.

The Nationwide Association of Fostering Providers (NAFP) is another source of information about the independent fostering agencies. In 2012 it had 62 members (of which six were voluntary bodies) but these appear to be among the largest enterprises since they were providing foster homes for 80% of the looked-after children placed by the independent sector.[7] A few offered a nationwide service; some operated regionally, the great majority in England. Most had been set up during the last 20 years, often by social workers and managers drawn from the public sector. There is comparatively little indication of specialisation, although there was some, particularly for children with behaviour problems, those with complex health needs and, in one case, placements just for siblings. A few offered additional services like supported living and residential care. Their various web sites emphasise their wish to recruit more social workers and more foster carers as well as giving information about how foster parents could transfer between agencies, including from local authorities.[8] This suggests that they are competing for foster parents as well as for staff. Both processes are likely to make it more difficult for local authorities to maintain and develop their own provision of foster care.

Thus, although the term 'private fostering' is still employed with reference to the traditional arrangements it now refers to a quite different institution as well, an institution about which we are just beginning to discern the details, not least those that provide some indication of the likelihood of further expansion or contraction and what each of these developments may portend. Much remains to be done if the impact of private agency fostering is to be understood, particularly its impact on the well-being of looked-after children.

Residential care

Local authorities have also been commissioning services for their looked-after children from the independent providers of residential care. In Chapter 2 it was explained that in England between 1995 and 2000 the number of private children's homes increased from 182 to 256; that is, by 40%.[9] By 2013 there were 1,347, a further fivefold increase.[10] However, one should be cautious in interpreting these data given that the residential market appears to be in a state of flux. Nevertheless, the independent sector is now dominant, providing 78% of all registered homes and 72% of the available places, not all of which are occupied.[11]

In both the local authority and independent sectors the number of registered places in each residential 'unit' is remarkably small: in 2013 the former had an average of 5.8 and the latter 4.0. Only four out of 1,718 were registered for more than 20 places, all of which were in the private sector.[12] The question arises, therefore, in what way the many small homes (20% were registered for only one or two places) differ from foster homes, some of which would be looking after three of four children. One answer might be that they offer more specialised services; but, increasingly, so do some foster parents.

Some general issues

Services that are provided directly by local authorities are clearly accountable to them and they to their electorate. These lines of accountability are less evident once the responsibility for providing a service has been delegated to a third party and possibly by them to yet another. Certainly there are arrangements for ensuring that such third parties are accountable to the commissioners (through inspection, auditing and reporting) but these may not be familiar to the users, especially when they seek to lodge a complaint. Furthermore, where a local authority is contracting with numerous service providers it can be difficult for them to have enough detailed information to impose a proper accountability.

Clearly, the growth of the independent sector has resulted in a wider dispersion of looked-after children. The Department for Education has highlighted some of the questions that this raises.[13] For instance, how will local authorities support the children placed away from their local communities and ensure that relevant services are provided? Will parents be discouraged from keeping contact with their children by having to make lengthy journeys in order to do so? And how much more difficult will it be to achieve the restoration of a child to their family if that is the plan?

Another issue concerns the 'durability' of these private for-profit initiatives. What happens if they cease trading, go into receivership or are closed down by OFSTED because of deficiencies? The fostering regulations, but not those for the residential homes, do set out how the work is to be transferred to another agency if that happens and both regulations contain sections that relate to the appointment of liquidators.[14] However, none deal with the steps that need to be taken to minimise the disruptive effect of a change of service provider upon the children involved.

Serious financial matters also arise from the widespread commissioning of services by local authorities, the implications of which are still not entirely clear. To start with there are the considerable administrative costs (for all parties) that are generated by the commissioning process.[15] Although this is important in its own right it has added to the financial stresses that have followed reductions in local authority budgets, reductions that may lead to (or have already led to) a greater emphasis being placed upon 'best price' rather than upon children's needs.

Furthermore, the commissioning process has created a range of financial uncertainties for the independent providers. 'Spot purchase' (that is the purchase of a service for a particular child) only provides small increments of income that vary according to how long they are required. Even standing contracts (which are not common) are usually for no more than a year, although with provision for renewal. It becomes difficult for the independent agencies to know what their future financial standing is likely to be, not least because many have to deal with a variety of local authorities with different fee structures.

What are, or will be, the consequences of tight margins and financial uncertainty for the independent services? Will they be able to make the regular re-investments that are required; for example, in staff training and re-training? How long will they be able to carry deficits? Of course, such uncertainties are exacerbated by the economic stringencies that face the local authorities whose procurement policies may change with the economic tide or with a shift in political representation.

As well as these financial issues the children's services still face the longstanding problem of how best to ensure the co-ordination of the diverse provisions that are required if a child's needs are to be adequately met. It seems likely that this problem will become more difficult to resolve the more widespread and fragmented the 'market' becomes, prompting calls for the better integration of policies and practices in both the private and the public sectors – and between them. In 2013, as already noted, there were 407 private and voluntary providers of children's homes (45% owning just one establishment)[16] and 230 independent fostering agencies.[17] Add to these figures the 152 local authorities and we find 789 agencies directly involved in the provision of care services for looked-after children in England. Furthermore, much of the work of the children's services involves obtaining the co-operation of agencies over which they have no formal control, especially those in the fields of health and education. Yet here too a fragmentation is occurring, adding to the difficulties of securing across-the-board agreements (and their realisation) about how the co-ordination of services is to be achieved. This may become easier when the organisations representing the independent providers of foster and residential care increase their membership. At the moment the Nationwide Association of Fostering Providers has 27% of the independent agencies in membership and the Independent Children's Homes Association 23%.

In addition to these matters there is the important question of how appropriate a commissioned service is to each child's needs. That turns on how well local authorities know the 'market' upon which they might (or do) call. The more dispersed and fragmented this becomes the greater the difficulty there is likely to be for commissioners in choosing the most appropriate service. Do they have sufficient accurate information? There are, of course, the OFSTED inspectors' reports, but they may not have been drawn up recently and, in any case, they provide a general view of the quality of a service. Then there is what the providers say that they offer; but they have an understandable interest in describing their service in the best possible light. Choices may not be as carefully made where local authorities are anxious to make a placement and the independent services to secure one. How often, one wonders, do the independent services decline to accept a child because they feel that it is an inappropriate referral? Of course, all these possibilities can apply when local authorities use their own services; but now they have more options to consider.

There is at least one more important matter to be noted. Part one of the Children and Young Persons Act 2008 (introduced by New Labour) allows local authorities in England to delegate their functions with respect to looked-after children to a 'third party provider'. However, this part of the legislation was not implemented until 2013 by the succeeding Coalition government which also wished to go further and to include most other children's social care services in this arrangement.[18] Regulations to that end were drafted and a process of consultation set in train. This revealed considerable opposition.[19] Indeed, of 1,300 responses to the consultation only 2% supported the proposal. In the light of this the government is to amend the draft regulations to exclude the possibility of local authorities contracting with private for-profit organisations to manage its child protection services.[20] However, they will still be allowed to commission non profit-making agencies to do this work, underlining the different degree of public support and confidence that the two components of the 'independent sector' evoke.

Even with the back-tracking over the latest proposed change, the various issues that have been highlighted in regard to the provision of care services by private and voluntary agencies still apply. In particular, questions about the increase in fragmentation, about accountability, about durability, about finance and about standards of performance. Delegation on the proposed scale also raises questions about the relationship between the market and local government, about its impact on the viability of public provision and, indeed, on the existing independent sector. And there are also the symbolic aspects to be borne in mind.

The post-war welfare state was widely regarded as an expression of social solidarity, of a compassionate society concerned about the condition and rights of its citizens. The reality limped along somewhat behind these fine ideals; but they were important as touchstones against which what was done could be judged. As our social services are increasingly transformed into market services we stand in danger of losing an important manifestation of collective responsibility.

II Emerging trends

As suggested at the start of this chapter one way of anticipating developments in the children's services is by examining existing trends with the help of statistical data; but there are drawbacks. The statistics may not be comparable over time, the definitions upon which they are based may change or not be well chosen, they may be misinterpreted and, inevitably, they will be selective. Even so, with due caution, they can alert us to patterns of change and continuity. It will be recalled that three aspects of the profiles of looked-after children have been chosen as illustration: ethnicity, disability and gender.

Ethnicity and culture

Information about the ethnic backgrounds of looked-after children was not collected and officially published until 2002. Since then the proportion classed as 'white' has hovered around 78%, with 'mixed' and 'black or black British' constituting the next largest groups. However, several points about the more detailed figures concerning 'ethnic origins' are noteworthy.

Of the 68,110 children who were being 'looked-after' at the end of March 2013 there were 7,110 (10%) who had been assigned to various 'any other [ethnic] background' categories.[21] This suggests a widening of ethnic origins among looked-after children. Whether or not that continues will depend upon several factors, not least upon the extent and character of immigration. This, in its turn, could be influenced by how many unaccompanied older children arrive in Britain seeking asylum and whose ethnic backgrounds are likely to reflect the prevailing locations and intensity of armed conflict. However, it was not until 2002 that statistics showing how many young asylum seekers were being 'looked after' were assembled and published. By then the figure stood at 2,200.[22] A peak of 3,890 was reached in 2009, and that was the first year in which the ethnic origins of these children were collected. By 2013 their number had dipped to 1,860.[23] However, the origins of 67%

of these young people were classed as 'any other', again emphasising a growing diversity.

Further diversity stems from the fact that some looked-after children have mixed parentage. In 2002 4,400 (7%) were classified in that way.[24] At the end of March 2013 the figure stood at 6,090 (9%), suggesting another source of spreading diversity.[25] The most common parentage among these looked-after children was 'white and black Caribbean' (37% of the 'mixed origins' group in 2013), followed by 'any other mixed background' (32%) and then 'white and Asian' (19%). Given these variations one should be cautious in generalising about how children, particularly looked-after children, incorporate their mixed parentage into their sense of identity. Moreover, these 'parentages' seem likely to become increasingly varied. If so, the injunction that social workers should take account of the ethnic and cultural backgrounds of the children for whom they plan will pose even more of a challenge than it does now.

It is also notable that there was a considerable variation between local authorities. For example, in 2012 in the London borough of Lambeth 76% of looked-after children were classified as 'non-white', among whom 41% were described as 'black or black British'. Although a similar proportion was classed as 'non-white' in Tower Hamlets the majority (35%) were 'Asian or Asian British'.[26] As noted already, in 2012 the second largest group after 'white' was 'mixed'. However, as with all the 'non-white' groups they were not distributed evenly across the country. For example, they constituted between 20% and 30% of the looked-after children in 16 authorities, albeit mainly in London, but also in places like Reading and Bedford.[27]

Clearly, different authorities face different issues in taking account of children's ethnic and cultural backgrounds – as they are required to do. Furthermore, the ethnic composition of the population served by one area office in a local authority may be different from that served by another. Hence the classification of children by their 'ethnic origin' can do no more than provide a general picture, even for a particular authority. Moreover, the 'origins' being listed, and often used in practice, may not reflect the reality of children's lives, especially the lives of those born in Britain. In that respect although employing skin colour, race, religion or nationality as a basis for classification is a convenient simplification it is liable to be misleading; and that matters when it comes to deciding upon children's placements and in working with their parents or carers. Furthermore, it cannot be assumed that parents and children share the same feeling (or intensity of feeling) about their ethnic or cultural identities; or that children will have the same sense of their identity at 18 as they did, say, when they were 10.

Issues surrounding the difficult concept of ethnicity are not confined to work with looked-after children however; they also arise in supportive and preventive work with families and in this too it seems likely that diversity will spread, increasing the tasks of understanding, comprehension and judgement. Yet we know comparatively little about the ethnic profiles of the families of children at risk, what the trends are or are likely to be and what implications these might have for the organisation of effective preventive services and, in particular, for child protection. Not only are there practice issues but also those that demand delicate policy decisions, both locally and nationally.

In all of this there is a danger that assumptions are made about the significance of ethnicity to the children and the families with whom the children's services work. For them other concerns may predominate: poverty, unemployment, security or obtaining adequate accommodation. Furthermore, their various *cultural* backgrounds may be of greater importance than their 'ethnic origins'. Children are exposed to many cultural influences – the school, the street, the media and social networks. Any of these, singly or in combination, may transcend ethnic identities.

Of course, the recognition and better understanding of these various diversities does not automatically provide a guide to what should be done, whether that be in the formulation of policy or in work with individual children and families. Indeed, sorting out the relationship between understanding and action is a challenge that threads its way through the history of children's services. Nevertheless, when it comes to questions of ethnicity and culture, that challenge is likely to intensify, not least because of its strong political overtones.

Disability

Issues surrounding the promotion of the well-being of disabled children may also become more prominent in the years to come. The number of children being looked after at the end of March 2013 where the 'need category' was given as 'disability' stood at 2,260,[28] a figure that had not changed much since 2002. However, it is important to look at the provision of 'respite care' by the children's services. In the Children Act 1989 and in the accompanying guidance this is described as 'a series of agreed short-term placements'.[29] Although such respite care is not provided exclusively for disabled children and their families 84% of the children for whom it was provided in 2012 were disabled. What is noteworthy is that between 2008 and 2012 the number of these agreed series of short placements fell from 8,120 to 1,928.[30] If we assume that respite care serves, at least in part, serve to prevent admission to longer periods of care then its reduction might lead to more disabled children having to be 'looked after'. Of course, one would have to see what happens over the next few years. Furthermore, since the majority of the children whose families are provided with short-term respite care stay in residential establishments and are likely to be adolescents it seems possible that this has been, and will be, a factor in the greater use of private and voluntary homes, especially those offering the more specialised services that local authorities may not have available.

Whether or not the issue of how best to help disabled children and their families becomes more pressing will depend upon the future prevalence and severity of disabling conditions and this, in its turn, will be affected by the course of medical science. Over and above these matters, however, there remains the question of the classification of 'disabilities' – what is, or is not, covered. Much of that discussion turns on whether emotional and behavioural problems should be included, many of which present themselves in conjunction with other disabilities. Clearly, how the scale of disability is assessed depends upon the definitions employed.

In its 1986 study of disabled children in Great Britain the Office for Population Censuses and Surveys (OPCS) applied an inclusive definition to its analysis of disabled children in care.[31] In the more detailed exploration of these data that my colleagues and I undertook we found that in 1986 in England and Wales 26% (18,700) of children in care were disabled according to the OPCS definition. Of these 49% were in foster homes (compared with 53% of non-disabled children), 31% (against 23% of the non-disabled) were in residential care and 12% (compared with 17%) were 'home on trial'. A small proportion was in other forms of care. Furthermore, whereas 5.7% of all disabled children under 18 were in care the rate for those who were not disabled was 0.5%.[32]

These findings provide a useful benchmark, particularly since the Office for National Statistics (ONS) conducted a survey in 2002 of the mental health of young people between five and seventeen years of age who were looked after by English local authorities using the same International Classification of Diseases as was used in the OPCS survey.[33] Among the five- to ten-year-olds 42% had a mental disorder and in the 11 to 15 group, 49%. Among children who were not looked after the rates were 8% and 11% respectively. Given that the figure of 26% for disabled children in care in 1986 included *all* disabilities, the 2002 rate for mental disorder alone would indicate a considerable increase. However, the ONS also gathered data about the 'physical complaints' of looked-after children, the most common of which were sight problems (16%), followed by speech or language problems (14%), bed wetting (13%), difficulties with co-ordination (10%) and asthma (10%). Over three-quarters of the children with a mental disorder had at least one physical disorder as well.

In its 2002 survey the ONS differentiated between three broad conditions: emotional disorders, conduct disorders and hyperkinetic disorders. Conduct disorders dominated the picture. Among the five to ten-year-olds its prevalence rate was 36% and for the 11 to 15-year-olds, 40%, compared with 5% and 6% respectively among children who were not looked after. The prevalence rate for the emotional disorders suffered by looked-after children was around 12% in both age groups. Eleven per cent of the younger children suffered from hyperkinetic disorders and 7% of those who were older.

These results showed that, in 2002, looked-after children exhibited challenging rates of emotional and behavioural problems and that these rates had risen since the middle 1980s. What has happened since 2002? Unfortunately we have no data comparable with those of the earlier years but we do have some information. The 'outcomes' data now available in the local authority returns include evidence of the emotional and behavioural health of looked-after children based upon a strengths and difficulties questionnaire that was administered to those between the ages of four and sixteen. The 'scores' obtained were divided into three categories: normal, borderline and 'cause for concern'. In 2013 the rate for the last group was 36%. If those who were borderline are included the rate rises to 49%; and these proportions do not include disabled children who are looked after but who do not have emotional and behavioural problems. This would suggest an upward trend but also the growing importance of emotional and behavioural problems, hardy surprising in the light of the increasing number of children being looked after because of their neglect or abuse. It is harder to assess what has been happening with respect to other disabilities. The situation is difficult to untangle because of the overlapping of emotional and behavioural problems with other conditions.

Although we now have more information about disability among looked-after children we know less about its prevalence among those with whom the children's services work in their own homes. Furthermore, we have no accurate picture of the prevalence and character of disabilities among the parents of children in need or at risk. Without these further data the task of formulating preventive policies and planning the necessary services is that much harder. What is evident, however, is that disability currently figures prominently in the challenges that the children's services face and that there is no indication that it will become less pressing. Nonetheless, much will depend upon the preventive and treatment measures that are taken. These are considered later; but first we turn to certain issues of gender.

Gender

Some things about the pattern of gender-related differences among looked-after children are so familiar that they attract little attention. For example, as was pointed out in Chapter 7, there have always been more boys than girls 'in care'. In 1952 the proportions were 55% and 45% respectively.[34] The figures were the same in 2013.[35] Although familiar, these longstanding differences have only been explained in rather superficial ways: in particular that boys are more 'troublesome' than girls. But that hardly explains why (with occasional exceptions) there are more boys than girls being looked after at *all* ages.

Although differences between boys and girls will have been taken into account in work with individual children it is by no means clear that these differences have raised questions at policy levels. Today most policies appear to be gender-neutral in contrast to many of those adopted in the past. Yet we now have data which suggest that more attention should be paid to the *dissimilarites* in the patterns of needs as between boys and girls. One important source of such information is the 'outcomes' material to be found in the statistics gathered by the Department for Education to which reference has already been made.

Consider first the emotional and behavioural health of four to sixteen-year-old looked-after children as determined by the strengths and difficulties questionnaire. Overall, in 2013 40% of the boys obtained a score that was considered to be a 'cause for concern' compared with 32% of the girls. However, this is only part of the picture. The peak age for the boys whose scores gave 'cause for concern' was eight whereas that for the girls was twelve. Furthermore, the widest difference was at age seven where 42% of the boys had 'cause for concern' scores by contrast to 28% of the girls. Although these are disturbing results for both it is notable how extensive the problems are among boys of primary school age. This is surely a cause for concern.

Important further differences were exposed in the ONS survey of the mental health of looked-after young people that was undertaken in 2002. Overall 49% of the boys in the sample were considered to have a mental disorder compared to 39% of the girls. However, it will be recalled that the results were divided into emotional disorders, conduct disorders and hyperkinetic disorders. The prevalence of emotional disorders was similar for boys and girls (10% and 14%) but whereas it decreased with age among boys it increased for the girls (to 20% for the 16- to17-year-olds). Conduct disorders were more common among the boys (42%) than the girls (31%) although the widest difference was in the five- to ten-year-old age group where 44% of the boys were so classified compared with 27% of the girls. The overall rate for hyperkinetic disorders was comparatively low (7%) but significantly greater among the boys than the girls and especially so among the five to tens (16% of boys to 5% of girls).

Taking these two sources of information about the emotional and behavioural health of looked-after children together several conclusions stand out. One is that there are substantial differences between boys and girls in the prevalence of disorder as well as in the types of problems that each suffers. Furthermore, both of these factors vary according to the children's ages. Two other noteworthy conclusions (among many in the reports) are that young boys from five to ten exhibit worrying levels of disorder and that the prevalence of emotional disorders among girls rises quite steeply as they get older. Do our present policies and practices within the children's services, the mental health services and in the schools adequately reflect these gender differences and what, in any case, do they foreshadow for the future?

There are, however, other differences between looked-after boys and girls that are discernible in the Department for Education's 'outcomes' data, particularly the educational attainment results at Key Stages 2 and 4.[36] Although the attainments of looked-after children were substantially poorer than other children, the general differences between boys and girls still existed. For example, whereas at Stage 2 in 2012 66% of looked-after girls achieved the expected level in English the rate for boys was only 54% and, for the first time since 2009, girls also out-performed boys in mathematics. At Key Stage 4 19% of looked-after girls achieved the 'basics' (English and Mathematics at grades A–C). The rate for boys was 12%. As the Department for Education pointed out, 'For children looked after continuously for 12 months during the year ending March 2012 a higher proportion of girls achieved the expected level in all subjects compared with boys.'[37] The Social Exclusion Unit's report on the education of looked-after children made the further point that 'girls…outperform boys by a greater margin than is seen in the rest of the population'.[38]

Other outcomes data also reflect certain gender differences. For example, whereas 5% of looked-after boys were identified as having a problem of substance misuse, the rate for the girls was 3%; and while 9% of the looked-after boys between the ages of 10 and 17 had been convicted of an offence, made subject to a final warning or reprimand during the year, the rate for the girls was 4%.

Few of these many differences seem to cause surprise and almost appear to be regarded as a fact of life; but they are substantial differences, especially at the younger ages. Little attention is devoted to the analysis of gender differences in the published statistics or in more general commentaries on the issues that preoccupy those concerned with the children's services.[39] This was not always the case, possibly because, in the past, there was a more pronounced physical separation of boys and girls – in residential provision and in schools. A consequence of this was that clearly identified clusters of boys and girls existed that encouraged both their distinctive enumeration and study. This was particularly evident in the former approved school system (later community homes with education) and led to separate publications such as Gittins' *Approved School Boys*[40] and Richardson's *Adolescent Girls in Approved Schools*.[41]

Although those who work with them will pay careful attention to the different needs of boys and girls there is scant mention of these differences in policy statements or practice guidance. Only when children's well-being is imperilled by actual or feared sexual exploitation do questions of gender appear to come into play. For the sake of both boys and girls the future will require more attention to be devoted to their differing needs and to the manner in which these differences are manifested in different contexts, by age, by behaviour and by public and professional attitudes.

III The quest for prevention

The prevention of social ills has been a longstanding and widely held aspiration. There have been numerous initiatives in both the public and in the voluntary sectors. Some have been found to be ineffective, some have faded away for want of support or because there was considered to be something better. Even so, it would be a mistake to conclude that the children's services have been unsuccessful in their preventive activities; but their achievements have tended to be obscured. First, because there has been a tendency to view preventive schemes (nowadays 'programmes' or 'projects') as something additional to the day-to-day activities of social workers, health visitors, clinics, schools and other services. Yet these must surely have prevented some family disintegration and child suffering, albeit that it is hard to know how much. This is closely connected to a second reason why some preventive work is liable to go unacknowledged; that is, because it means different things to different people and in different contexts. Furthermore, greater significance (and approbation) tends to be attached to primary prevention (to borrow from the public health vocabulary) than to later stages in the preventive process (the secondary or tertiary interventions). That is not to say that early intervention should not be sought, only that there are notable difficulties to its realisation as, indeed, there are to the successful pursuit of subsequent stages of prevention in the children's services. What, then, are the difficulties that still have to be confronted?

Identification and scale

If the ills that befall certain children are to be forestalled those children need to be identified. That poses a number of problems. In the first place identification largely depends upon them *already* being regarded as 'in need' or 'at risk'; and that implies that they have already passed the point at which primary preventive measures might have been taken. It makes more sense, therefore, to think simply of 'early intervention', as advocated in the Allen report.[42]

Even so, there are three ways in which candidates for that early intervention may be recognised. One is by their membership of known (or assumed to be known) need or risk groups. A second is by the screening of child populations.[43] The third is by responding to particular events that cause sufficient concern to lead to a notification or referral. The first of these approaches allows services to be aimed at certain *categories* (specified by considerations of factors such as age, living conditions, area or behaviour). The second depends upon survey-like sweeps that are only likely to be done from time to time and in particular areas. The third requires that specific steps be taken to ensure that a *particular* child is adequately protected. All three ways forward satisfy the terms of the Children Act 1989 that oblige every local authority to 'take reasonable steps to identify the extent to which there are children in need within their area'.

The 'Children in Need' censuses that followed this requirement have provided an idea of the scale of that need.[44] As was indicated in Chapter 7 593,500 children were referred to the children's services in England in 2012–13 as potentially 'in need'. After investigation it was deemed necessary to conduct 441,500 'initial' assessments that, in their turn led to 232,700 more searching 'core' assessment being made and then to 52,700 children being made subject to a protection plan.

At the end of March 2013 about 3.5% of the child population (as it was enumerated in the 2011 Census) was recorded as being 'in need'.

This picture prompts at least three questions with regard to securing more early intervention. First, were all the children who were referred and then not considered to be in need actually not in need or were their needs not judged to be sufficiently great to warrant further action? Did they fail to reach the threshold of seriousness that was being used? If that threshold is moved, even a little, the number 'in need' could be rather different. The second question concerns the extent to which children's needs do not become visible and therefore do not lead to a referral. We do not know how large that hidden component is. There are various estimates. For example, the NSPCC's 2013 report *How Safe are our Children?* maintained that about 520,000 children were abused or neglected at home each year, only some one in nine of whom (57,800) it was concluded were known to the children's services.[45] The third of these questions about early intervention is this: if the available figures reflect the number falling into the need or risk category how is that defined and then how have those who are included been identified?

Early intervention depends on either a child or family being considered to be in need or at risk. However, that identification often relies upon someone having sufficiently close contact with a child and their family to be concerned about a child's circumstances and then being prepared to act on that disquiet; and that applies whether or not they are professionals. Nevertheless, there are a number of reasons why action is not taken or not taken in a timely fashion, most of which derive from dilemmas of uncertainty. People may be unsure about the severity of what they see or hear, they may conclude that what worries them is an isolated incident (particularly in the case of physical abuse), they may decide that what they are told or hear (rather than see) is exaggerated, they may feel a misplaced sympathy for, or loyalty to, the presumed perpetrator, they may assume that someone else (or some other agency) will be dealing with the matter or they may be anxious about the consequences that might follow were they to take action, especially should their fears be unfounded. In short, they are either unconvinced that a situation is serious enough to act or undecided about what they should do and when.

Such uncertainties are illustrated in the data that the NSPCC collected about how long it took for callers to their helpline (whose concerns warranted a referral) to make these calls.[46] During 2012–13 48% had waited more than a month and 25% more than six months, prompting the exhortation 'don't wait until you are certain'. However, there are signs of a growing willingness to comply with this injunction, perhaps as a result of the spate of cases of historic abuse that have come to light. For example, in 2012–13 the NSPCC's helpline received 15% more contacts from adults concerned about children than in the previous year[47] and Childline provided 18% more counselling sessions than the year before, with sharp increases in cases of self-harm and attempted or threatened suicide (mostly among girls), but not in physical or sexual abuse.[48]

There is also more and clearer guidance for professionals about the identification and assessment of children in need or at risk and about what should be done thereafter. The most comprehensive document and *statutory* guidance is *Working Together to Safeguard Children* that was published in 2013 and in which considerable emphasis is placed upon providing prompt help.[49] There are some 20 organisations that have to follow its instructions. One interesting requirement is placed upon Local Safeguarding Children Boards; namely, that they have to draw up and publish a threshold document that sets out criteria for determining when a case should be referred to local authority children's services. Together with the principal document (of 95 pages) there are supplementary guidelines for specific situations; for example, child trafficking, female genital mutilation, forced marriage, sexual exploitation and so on. As well as these documents other guidelines have been produced by a number of organisations; for instance, by the National Collaborating Centre for Women's and Children's Health that published *When to Suspect Child Maltreatment* as well as other guidelines on conditions such as autism and childhood spasticity.[50] In short, there is a growing volume of guidance about the identification of childhood need and risk that should help in the quest for improved prevention.

The better identification of children in need or in jeopardy may, however, create its own problems. If more such children are discovered then referrals to the children's services could grow considerably. In the face of declining budgets and the likelihood that the areas where today's hidden needs are greatest are those in which resources are most stretched, a significant increase in referrals may accentuate existing problems. Should that happen the threshold for deciding that further action is required could be raised or, if not, the services that are provided to those who are assessed as being 'in need' could be diluted. The other possibility is that resources would be diverted from other children's services activities.

And after identification?

It is all well and good identifying those in need or at risk but what is to be done then? There are two broad approaches: the general and the selective. The first of these makes certain services available to all (whether children or parents) who fall into wide categories defined by a presumption that they experience certain stresses and strains in common that are liable to lead to substantial and damaging problems in the future. Many of these preventive interventions lie beyond the usual boundaries of the children's services: in social security, in housing, in education, in health or in employment policies. One example that has already been mentioned is the entitlement to early education for all three- and four-year-olds that was introduced in 2007. Another could be the government's announcement that, as from September 2014, every child in reception and Year One and Two classes in state-funded schools will have the right to free school dinners, not only to improve their diet and to promote educational achievement but also to assist parents financially, all without the stigma of having to satisfy a poverty qualification.

It might be argued that such policies do little to prevent the worst instances of neglect and abuse, not least because there is no compulsion involved and that, without it, parents of the most vulnerable children will fail to take advantage of the opportunities to which their children have a right. That is certainly possible, but it would seem to be less likely when a universal service offers a material benefit to the parents, when there is little difficulty in using it and when no disapprobation is attached to its use. If services with these characteristics were to form a thought-out part of a preventive strategy in the future, albeit alongside more selective interventions, significant progress might be made. The political problems that this approach is liable to encounter are first, that it generally costs more than the provision of selective services, second, that it is hard to demonstrate that the most disadvantaged do actually benefit (although perhaps the children and the parents differently) and third, that when private enterprise and voluntary initiatives are favoured the development of universal services will not be high on the agenda.

The additional problem is that successful prevention is not achieved by any single intervention, whether universal or selective. It depends upon the cumulative effect of several, often small increments. Vulnerable children do not suddenly become profoundly vulnerable and neither do parents suddenly become abusive. The likelihood is that one problem has led to another in a worsening descent. It seems reasonable therefore to assume that if that descent is to be checked and then reversed it will be achieved by the creation of *accumulating* improvements, some of which depend upon improvements that derive from universal services. It is not an exact comparison but one might note the benefits that accrued to the poor (both adults and children) as a result of the sanitary reforms of the second part of the nineteenth century.[51]

So, in any preventive strategy in the coming years a sharp eye should be kept on the contribution that our universal services can make. However, most emphasis in recent years has been placed upon the part that selective interventions might make to the prevention of the ills that threaten children. Even so, there are many kinds and levels of this 'targeted' prevention.

Currently the most common of them aim to improve parenting and would qualify as 'early intervention'. Some are described as 'family intervention projects'; that is, 'local services which provide support to families with multiple social, economic, health and behavioural problems'. According to the Department for Education 4,870 families in England had been offered and accepted such a service between January 2006 and March 2010; 67% of those who had been referred.[52] Although the picture may have changed since 2010 it is unlikely that it has done so significantly. In short, the spread of such schemes is relatively limited, certainly set against the estimates of the size of the population that needed to be reached, estimates that have ranged from around 140,000 to half a million, although, of course, the figures depend upon the definitions being employed. The half a million, for example, was quoted by the Riots Communities and Victims panel that investigated the street riots of August 2011 and which referred to the 'forgotten families' who 'bump along the bottom of society'.[53] The Child Poverty Action Group, using figures from the Department for Work and Pensions' analysis of households below average incomes, concluded that there are currently 3.5 million children living in poverty, or about one in four.[54] The size of the 'problem' depends upon how it comes to be defined.

The successful advancement of preventive measures that are addressed to 'disadvantaged' families faces at least three challenges. The first of these, as the figures above suggest, is their coverage; and that turns on the availability of specific interventions and then upon the willingness of families to engage with them, an issue discussed more fully later.

The second obstacle arises from the fact families with multiple problems need a variety of services that are often fragmented and not easily and efficiently combined. For example, it was noted in the Social Exclusion Task Force report of 2007 that 53 family intervention projects were being 'rolled out' that would 'challenge and support families who are causing harm to the community'.[55] The Allen report lists 72 early intervention 'programmes' that address a variety of problems such as poor literacy, drug and alcohol abuse, conduct disorders, delinquency, parent–child relationships and parenting skills. Those aimed at children cover different ages. Some are geared to children 'in need' while others are more general. Many originate in the US, only some of which are being used in this country. With so many 'preventive initiatives' it becomes hard to keep track of what is being done, by whom, for whom and with what success,[56] although on this last count the Allen report offered an encouraging analysis of their effectiveness, as has the Department for Education; but with so many projects in play it is probably unsafe to generalise.

Thus, demonstrating that they 'work' constitutes a third challenge confronting these selective schemes and which, for the moment, dominate the quest for prevention in and around the children's services. There appear to be two broad answers to this question. One is that some clearly do work. The problem is that those that have been shown to work can only do so if the people for whom they are intended become involved and then do not drop out, but it seems likely that those who need the service the most are the ones least likely to use it. This, indeed, is the difficulty that runs through the history of preventive endeavours in many fields – now termed the problem of 'engagement'. The many reasons for this are well documented and spring from the very circumstances that give rise to the need for preventive measures in the first place: social isolation, poor education, poor health, few resources, lack of confidence and numerous other socially disabling factors.[57] Indeed, it is the very multiplicity of these factors, concentrated among 'those who need the service most' that has prevented prevention from realising its promise. Will more of that promise be realised in the years to come?

If it is, it will be because the key problems that have been discussed have been ameliorated and, possibly, because certain theoretical and practical 'breakthroughs' have been made, for example, in neurobiology[58] or in developmental psychopathology. However, whatever new insights that research and experimentation may provide, much will still depend upon the level of political commitment to an *integrated* pursuit of better prevention that includes across-the-board policies (such as those for the reduction of poverty and unemployment and for the improvement of standards in health and education) as well as specific initiatives aimed at those families whose children (at whatever age) are at risk of suffering in ways that profoundly blight their lives.

Notes and references

Preface
Hawkes, N. (2013) 'Sailing without a lookout', *British Medical Journal*, 347, f6739, 16 November, p 25.

Chapter 1: Introduction: patterns of change and continuity
[1] See Adcock, M., White, R. and Rowlands, O. (1982) *The Administrative Parent*. London: BAAF. Report to the DHSS.

[2] See, Owen, D. (1991) *Time to Declare*. London: Joseph; pp 231–2 and his 'The Objectives of the Children Act', in *A Review of the Children Act* [1975]: *10 years on*. London: National Foster Care Association. See also Castle, B. (1980) *The Castle Diaries: 1974–76*. London: Weidenfeld and Nicholson; pp 38–9.

[3] Discussed in Parker, R. (2010) *Uprooted: The Shipment of Poor Children to Canada, 1867–1917*. Bristol: Policy Press; pp 244–5.

[4] See Bullard, E. and Malos, E. (1991) *Custodianship: Caring for Other People's Children*. London: HMSO.

[5] This was section 1 of the Act.

[6] A good explanation of the status of regulations and rules is provided in Department of Health (DoH) (1989) *The Care of Children: Principles and Practice in Regulations and Guidance*. London: HMSO; pp 2–6.

[7] *Children and Young Persons (Boarding out) Rules* (1933), Statutory Rules and Orders 787.

[8] *Children and Young Persons, England, Boarding Out Rules* (1946), Statutory Rules and Orders 2083.

[9] *Children and Young Persons: The Boarding out of Children Regulations* (1955), Statutory Instrument (SI) 1377.

[10] *The Boarding-out of Children (Foster Placement) Regulations* (1988), Statutory Instrument (SI) 2184.

[11] DoH (1991) *The Children Act, 1989: Guidance and Regulations,* vol 3, 'Family Placements'. London: HMSO.

[12] See Loughran, F. and Parker, R. (1990) *Child Care Work Arising from Matrimonial, Domestic and Guardianship Proceedings*. Bristol University: Department of Social Policy. Report to the DoH.

[13] From annual statistics of *Children in Care of Local Authorities in England and Wales*. London: HMSO.

[14] See Parker, R. (ed.) (1999) *Adoption Now*. Chichester: Wiley; esp. ch 1.

[15] For example, until 1975 the annual statistics of children in care in England and Wales included two headings in the list of 'circumstances in which children came into care': 'family homeless because of eviction' and 'family homeless for other reasons'. These accounted for 2,410 admissions that year or 7% of all voluntary admissions (section 1).

DHSS and Welsh Office (1975) *Children in Care in England and Wales, March 1974,* cmnd 6147. London: HMSO; p 7.

[16] Home Office, Ministry of Health and Ministry of Education, Joint Circular (1950). *Children Neglected or Ill-treated in their own Homes.* London: Home Office (HO).

[17] *Ibid. Appendix to Circular.* Statement made by the Secretary of State to Parliament, 20.7.50; p 1.

[18] Department for Children, Schools and Families (DfCSF) (2010) *Working Together.* London: DfCSF. This guidance was updated in April 2013, Department for Education (DfE). *Working Together to Safeguard Children.*

[19] Nonetheless, local authorities usually observe the requirements in such documents. Indeed, failing to do so is likely to weigh heavily against them should serious shortcomings in their work come to light. However, it is not difficult to understand that confronted with so much advice and guidance local authorities may find it difficult to digest it all. As Chris Mullin wrote in his diaries about New Labour in general: 'We've got reviews, strategies, targets, action plans coming out of our ears.' Mullin, C. (2010) *A View from the Foothills.* London: Profile Books; p 156.

[20] Packman, J. (1986) *Who Needs Care? Social Work Decisions about Children.* Oxford: Blackwell; pp 11–12.

[21] On the other hand, emerging patterns of practice may remain unacknowledged or fail to be recognised by management or, indeed, by central government: witness the rapid increase in the number of committed children being allowed 'home on trial' in the 1960s and 1970s without any indication that this was a policy intention. See, Farmer, E. and Parker, R. (1991) *Trials and Tribulations: Returning Children from Local Authority Care to their Families.* London: HMSO; pp 4–7.

[22] For a general discussion see Parsloe, P. (1981) *Social Services Teams.* London: Allen and Unwin.

[23] As note 21, p 101.

[24] Packman, J. and Hall, C. (1998) *From Care to Accommodation: Support, Protection and Control in Child Care Services.* London: The Stationery Office (TSO).

[25] *Ibid.* ch 3.

[26] The Child Poverty Act 2010 set out interim targets and included the requirement that reports on progress should be made to the minister. One view is that in introducing this measure New Labour was able to switch the emphasis away from poverty in general.

[27] DfCSF (2007) *The Children's Plan: Building Brighter Futures,* Cm 7280. London: TSO; p 3.

[28] DfCSF (2003*) Every Child Matters,* cm 5860. London: TSO.

[29] HM Treasury and Department for Education and Skills (DfES) (2007) *Aiming High for Children: Supporting Families.* London: HMT.

[30] DfES (2007) *Every Parent Matters.* London: DfES.

[31] Office of the Prime Minister (OPM) (2003) *A Better Education for Children: Social Exclusion Report.* London: OPM.

[32] Cabinet Office: Social Exclusion Task Force (2007) *Reaching Out. Think Family: Analysis and Themes from the Families at Risk Review.* London: Cabinet Office (CO).

[33] See, Eisenstadt, N. (2011) *Providing a Sure Start: How Government Discovered Early Childhood*. Bristol: Policy Press.

[34] See, for example, Cliffe, D. and Berridge, D. (1991) *Closing Children's Homes: An End to Residential Childcare?* London: National Children's Bureau. This was a study of the repercussions of the decision of Warwickshire County Council to close all its children's homes. Although the authors were unable to establish a direct connection they did find 'that the closure of children's homes coincided with a significant increase in the number of pupils placed away from home in "educational and behavioural difficulties" schools' (p 231).

[35] See, for example, Land, H. (1975) 'Detention Centres: the Experiment that could not Fail', in Hall, P., Land, H., Parker, R. and Webb, A., *Change, Choice and Conflict in Social Policy*. London: Heinemann; pp 311–70. See also, for further background and history, Choppin, V. (1970) 'The Origins of the Philosophy of Detention Centres', *British Journal of Criminology*, 10 (2), pp 158–68.

[36] As note 4.

[37] Prime Minister Gordon Brown apologised in 2010 for the UK's 'child migrant programme'. This followed the Australian Prime Minister's apology the year before for his country's involvement.

[38] Levy, A. and Kahan, B. (1991) *The Pindown Experience and the Protection of Children*. Stafford: Stafford CC.

[39] Since not all problems surrounding vulnerable children can obtain the same political and professional priority, some, even though significant, get relegated in favour of others that are deemed to be more pressing. However, when that pressure subsides those that have received less attention may rise to prominence. Thus, there is not always a succession of *new* problems but a re-prioritisation of some that have been there in the background all the time.

[40] See, for example, Hendrick, H. (1994) *Child Welfare: England, 1872–1989*. London: Routledge; ch 3 and his (2003) *Child Welfare: Historical Dimensions, Contemporary Debate*. Bristol: Policy Press.

[41] Parker, R. (1969) 'Co-operation between Social Welfare Organisations', in Kellmer Pringle, M, *Caring for Children*. London: Longmans.

[42] Thomas Stephenson (a Weslyan minister) established his first 'cottage for boys in great need' in Lambeth (London) in 1868, an initiative that, soon after, grew into the National Children's Homes (now Action for Children). Thomas Barnardo opened his first home in London in 1870. In the same year Leonard Shaw established the Manchester and Salford Boys and Girls Refuges and Homes (now the Together Trust). The following year William Quarrier purchased his first home in Glasgow (now Quarrier's). In 1872 James Fegan began his first venture with a home for boys in south-east London (now Fegan's Child and Family Service). The Liverpool Catholic Children's Protection Society was formed in 1881 (now the Nugent Care Society). The same year saw the inauguration of the Church of England's Waifs and Strays Society (now the Children's Society). Numerous other initiatives were launched along the same lines, many to fall by the wayside or to be absorbed by larger organisations such as Barnardos or the Waifs and Strays.

[43] Section 1 (3) of the Act. Note that this only applied to children admitted to care on a voluntary basis. No such requirement applied to children committed to care on

a fit person order although a parent or local authority could apply to the court for the discharge of such an order.

[44] See, Parker, R. (2004) 'Children and the Concept of Harm', in Hillyard, P., Pantazis, C. Toombs, S. and Gordon, D. (eds) *Beyond Criminology: Taking Harm Seriously.* London: Pluto Press; pp 236–50. This discusses the tension between children seen as the victims of harm and children viewed as its perpetrators.

[45] One of the scandalous examples of this is to be found in the Irish government's *Inter-Departmental Committee's Inquiry to Establish the Facts of the State's Involvement with the Magdalen Laundries,* published in 2013. The laundries continued to operate into the 1980s and were important for the financial viability of the religious communities to which they were attached. Over 10,000 girls and women had spent time working in these institutional laundries since 1922; 879 had died there, the oldest being 95 (p xiii).

[46] The Adoption Act 1926 (1930 in Scotland) provided that adoption orders could be made by courts under prescribed circumstances and with the consent of the parent or parents, although this could be dispensed with if the court established that the parents could not be found, that there had been persistent neglect or a failure to contribute to the child's maintenance. Two committees of inquiry had preceded the Act, one in 1921 (the Hopkinson *Committee on Child Adoption,* cmd 1254) the other in 1925–26 (the Tomlin *Committee on Child Adoption* that published three reports: cmd 2401, cmd 2469 and cmd 2711, the last two in 1926). See, Triseliotis, J. (1970) *Evaluation of Adoption Policy and Practice.* Edinburgh: Department of Social Administration, Edinburgh University for a brief but excellent resume of the history (pp 8–13).

[47] Local Government Board (LGB) (1901) *Annual Report for 1900,* cd 746, pp lii and liv. It should be noted that the figure of 23% boarded-out is based upon a total 'in care' that excluded those children receiving 'indoor relief' but who were accompanied by their parents. It is assumed that these were not considered to be eligible to be boarded-out. Note also that 75% of those who were boarded-out were placed within the area of the receiving authority.

[48] See, Abrams, L. (1998) *The Orphan Country.* Edinburgh: Donald; esp. ch 3; also Currie, R. and Ramage, A. (nd) *The Policy of Boarding out Children in Scotland.* Glasgow: Caledonian University.

[49] Barnardos (1901) *Annual Report*; and Waifs and Strays (1901) *Annual Report.*

[50] Here, for example, is a flavour of what the committee had to say about residential establishments: 'We found…many places where the standard of child care was no better, except in respect of disciplinary methods, than that of say 30 years ago…[there] was a lack personal interest in and affection for the children which we find shocking. The child in these Homes was not recognised as an individual with his [sic] own rights and possessions, his own life to live and his own contribution to offer…he was without the feeling that there was anyone to whom he could turn who was vitally interested in his welfare or who cared for him in person.' *Report of the Care of Children Committee* (1946), cmd 6922 (Curtis). London: HMSO; p 134.

[51] Essentially, this was a case based upon the increased dangers of cross-infection in institutions, especially the large ones. Infections like conjunctivitis spread rapidly, as did highly contagious diseases such as measles. Of course, similar disquiet was expressed about the elementary schools and, indeed, hospitals in general and children's hospitals in particular. But schools could be and were closed when an outbreak struck and to some extent a degree of isolation was possible in hospitals. Although children's homes

might have provision for some isolation this could only go so far. A somewhat different argument in favour of boarding-out was that children's health would be improved were they to be placed in the countryside, away from pollution and with the benefits of fresh air. For a general discussion of the diseases that affected children in the latter part of the nineteenth and early twentieth century, see Smith, F. (1979) *The People's Health: 1830–1910*. New York: Holmes and Meier; esp ch 3.

[52] See, Oldfield, S. (2009) *Jeannie, an 'Army of One': Mrs Nassau Senior, 1828–1877. The First Woman in Whitehall*. Brighton: Sussex Academic Press; esp chs 11–15. She campaigned in particular against the institutional care of girls, a view shared by the *Royal Commission on the Poor Laws* (1909), vol I, cd 4499. London: HMSO; p 237.

[53] Home Office (HO) (1951) *Sixth Report on the Work of the Children's Department*. London: HMSO; table II, p 148.

[54] See, for example, *Sixth Report from the Select Committee on Estimates, Session 1951–52 (Child Care)* (1953), HC 328. London: HMSO. Also in the preliminary estimates for 1954–55 the cost per child week for those boarded-out was £1.11s.9d and for those in local authority homes £6.0s.8d; that is, the average cost of the latter was nearly four times more. HO (1954) *Children in the Care of Local Authorities in England and Wales, November 1953*, cmd 9146. London: HMSO; p 7. In 2011 the respective costs were £694 and £2,965, a somewhat wider difference (pssru.ac.uk).

[55] See, for example, Mason, M. (1922) 'The Boarded-out Children of the Poor', *The Nineteenth Century and After*, DXLIV (June); pp 1053–67. Mary Mason was the first Local Government Board (by 1922 the Ministry of Health) inspector of children boarded-out under the Poor Law. In her article, for instance, she wrote: 'Boarding-out is sometimes thought to be more successful than it really is merely because we do not hear of all the failures. Children are supposed to be happy because superficial inspection does not reveal ill-treatment' (p 2056). See also Horsburgh, M. (1983) 'No Sufficient Security: the Reaction of the Poor Law Authorities to Boarding-Out', *Journal of Social Policy*, 12 (1); pp 51–73.

[56] Under section 29 (i) of the Children Act 1948 it became unlawful for a voluntary home not to be registered with the Secretary of State. Before then registration had been incomplete.

[57] Most of the voluntary children's organisations adopted this practice, some into the 1960s. One girl, Daisy Peacock, describing her reaction to that separation in 1914 wrote: 'It broke my heart. I cried and cried. I couldn't eat or sleep.' She had been in her foster home for eight years. Record of interview in Corbett, G. (1981) *Barnardo Children in Canada*. Peterborough (Canada): Woodland; p 92.

[58] HO (1953) *Children in the Care of Local Authorities in England and Wales, November 1952*, cmd 8910; HO. (1962) *Children in Care in England and Wales, March 1961*, cmnd 1599; DfE, *Children Looked After in England, March 2013*, SFR 36/2013; table A1. It should be noted that the data are for England only. Had the Welsh rate been added (as earlier) the figure would have been slightly lower. By contrast, historically the rate in Scotland has been higher. In 1958, for example, it stood at 6.3 per 1,000 (Scottish Home Department (1959) *Children in the Care of Local Authorities in Scotland, November 1958*, cmnd 779. Edinburgh: HMSO).

[59] HO (1963) *Children in Care in England and Wales, March 1963,* cmnd 1876. London: HMSO.

[60] As note 58, 2013.

[61] DoH (2002) *Children Looked After by Local Authorities for Year Ending 31 March, 2001, England* (A/F 01/12) and *ibid.*

[62] *Ibid.* (2002) appendix A, table A 1 for mid-year population estimates.

[63] DoH (2001) *Children Looked After by Local Authorities, March 2000, England*, A/F 00/12.

[64] DfE. (2011) *Children Looked After by Local Authorities, England, March 2011*, SFR/21/2011.

[65] HO (1963) *Children in Care in England and Wales, March 1963*, cmnd 2240. London: HMSO.

[66] As note 58.

[67] The reduction in mothers' confinement as a reason for admission to care could also have been influenced by changes in the pattern of confinements; for example, shorter periods in hospital or better pre- and post-natal care. The balance between home and hospital births would also have to be looked at as a possible influence. When home births were more common did it lead to more admissions to care of the other children in the family?

[68] Nonetheless, various schemes have been introduced: for example, the Family-Nurse Partnership; the Incredible Years parenting project (linked with Children's Centres) and the school-based Promoting Alternative Thinking Strategies (PATHS). And, of course, there has been Sure Start. However, the emerging evidence suggests mixed results. See, Little, M., Berry V., Morpeth, L., *et al* (2012) 'The impact of three evidence-based programmes delivered in public systems in Birmingham, UK', *International Journal of Conflict and Violence*, 6 (12).

Chapter 2: Residential child care: an historical perspective

[1] Specifically, the English Poor Law as distinct from the Scottish. The Irish system resembled that in England. See, Webb, S. and B. (1963 reprint) *English Poor Law History, part II. The Last Hundred Years, vol I.* London: Cass (first published 1929). For more particular histories see Rose, M. (ed.) (1985) *The Poor and the City: The English Poor Law in its Urban Context, 1834–1914.* Leicester: Leicester University Press and for a more rural study, Digby, A. (1978) *Pauper Palaces.* London: Routledge and Kegan Paul.

[2] See, Crowther, M. (1981) *The Workhouse System: 1834–1929.* London: Batsford.

[3] See, Lowndes, G. (1937) *The Silent Social Revolution: an Account of the Expansion of Public Education in England and Wales, 1895–1935.* London: Oxford University Press; particularly pt 1; also, Hurt, J. (1979) *Elementary Schooling and the Working Classes: 1860–1918.* London: Routledge and Kegan Paul; Rich, E. (1970) *The Education Act 1870: A Study of Public Opinion.* London: Longmans, Green and Simon, B. (1965) *Education and the Labour Movement: 1870–1920.* London: Lawrence and Wishart.

[4] *Ibid.* Simon, esp. ch 2.

[5] See Parker, R. (1990) *Away from Home: a History of Child Care.* Ilford: Barnardos; esp. ch 3. For a fuller coverage of the issues see the *Report of the Royal Commission on Reformatory and Industrial Schools.* (1884), cd 3876 and the accompanying 'Minutes of Evidence', cd 3876–1. London: HMSO.

[6] Home Office (HO). (1925) *Third Report of the Children's Branch*. London: HMSO; p 58.

[7] *Seventeenth Report of the Inspector of Reformatory and Industrial Schools of Great Britain*. (1874), c 1058; pp 3–4 and 16. London: HMSO.

[8] The growth occurred principally in the industrial schools. Figures for 1883 are to be found in the *Twenty-seventh Report of the Inspector of Reformatories and Industrial Schools of Great Britain*. (1884), c 4147; p 5. London: HMSO.

[9] See HO (1923) *Report of the Work of the Children's Branch*. London: HMSO. This includes the 1919 circular which stated that: 'many of the forms of occupation that have hitherto been classified as "industrial training" must be abolished or curtailed'; p 26.

[10] For example, after the Second World War the Home Office encouraged an expansion of the system. Two reasons were given. One was that there was a need for more approved schools for girls because of 'war-time influences, including the presence of foreign troops in this country' that had 'led to a still greater increase in the number of girls of fifteen and sixteen falling into immoral ways...'. The second ground for expanding the number of approved schools was 'the war-time rise in delinquency ...'. Indeed, in 1948 the rate of juvenile delinquency was 30% above its pre-war level – 'the highest rate ever recorded...'. HO (1951) *Sixth Report on the Work of the Children's Department*. London: HMSO; pp 64 and 47.

[11] Children and Young Persons Act 1933.

[12] As note 5, pp 46–7 for fuller details of these changes.

[13] For accounts of these organisations see, for example, Rose, J. (1987) *For the Sake of the Children* [Barnardos]. London: Hodder and Stoughton; Wagner, G. (1979) *Barnardo*. London: Weidenfeld and Nicholson; Horner, F. (1919) *Shadow and Sun* [NCH]. London: Epworth/NCH; Magnusson, A. (1984) *The Village: a History of Quarriers*. Glasgow: Quarriers and Stroud, J. (1971) *Thirteen Penny Stamps: the Story of the Church of England's Children's Society from its Beginnings as 'Waifs and Strays'*. London: Hodder and Stoughton.

[14] Various devices for 'rationing' were introduced. One of the earliest was that adopted by the Coram Foundling Hospital. Mothers seeking the admission of their babies were required to dip into a bag containing white balls and black balls. Admission was only granted to those drawing a white one. See, Pugh, G. (2007) *London's Forgotten Children: Thomas Coram and the Foundling Hospital*. Stroud: Tempus.

[15] The Prevention of Cruelty to Children Act 1889.

[16] From about the 1870s information concerning the number of Catholic children in poor law provisions could be gathered from the creed registers that institutions were required to keep. For example, these indicated that at the beginning of 1873 there were almost 5,000 Catholic children in poor law homes in England and Wales and that during the previous year 359 had been transferred to Catholic residential homes. However, the Catholic children looked after by the poor law were heavily concentrated in certain areas: in 1873 some 42% in Liverpool and its vicinity. Another 22% were in London (particularly Kensington and the Strand and were probably children of domestic servants). The rest were to be found in the major cities: Manchester, Birmingham, Newcastle, Leeds and Sheffield. There were few elsewhere. *Children of Roman Catholic Parents: the number of children entered in the creed registers... in England and Wales on 1 January, 1873*. (1874); HL 33.

[17] See, Parker, R. (2008) *Uprooted: the Shipment of Poor Children to Canada, 1867–1917*. Bristol: Policy Press and Wagner, G. (1982) *Children of the Empire*. London: Weidenfeld and Nicholson.

[18] See, Barnardo, T. (1889) *Something Attempted Something Done*. London: Barnados/ Shaw. There he wrote that to secure 'the open door at the front' there had to be an 'exit door at the rear' (p 181).

[19] This issue was well discussed in a report of a committee of enquiry set up by the National Council of Social Services. (1967) *Caring for People: Staffing Residential Homes* (Williams). London: Allen and Unwin; esp. ch 7.

[20] See, *Sixth Report from the Select Committee on Estimates, 1951–1952*. (1952), HC 235. London: HMSO.

[21] The National Economy Act 1931 was an attempt by the second Labour government led by Macdonald to deal with the budget deficit arising from the 'slump'. It divided the Labour party and caused the downfall of Macdonald's administration.

[22] In 1920 there were 68,400 children in the care of the poor law in England and Wales. By 1939 (then the public assistance committees) the figure had fallen to 37,500, the reduction being most evident from 1932 onwards. See *Annual Reports of the Ministry of Health*. Those in the care of education departments and approved schools are not included. For a review of trends in residential care in general in the first half of the twentieth century see Donnison, D. and Ungerson, C. (1968) 'Trends in Residential Care, 1911–1961', *Social and Economic Administration*, 2 (2), and for a study of trends in child care numbers from the 1860s to the 1970s, see Loughran, F. and Parker, R. (1990) *Trends in Child Care: A Report to the Economic and Social Research Council*. Bristol: Department of Social Policy and Social Planning.

[23] See, for example, *Report of the Care of Children Committee* (Curtis). (1946), cmd 6922; esp. sect. II.

[24] As note 13 (Rose) for Barnardos' practice in this respect at pp 117 and 124.

[25] Knapp, M. (1979) *Cost Information and the Planning of Social Care Services: The Residential Care of Children in England and Wales*. Canterbury: University of Kent, PSSRU; paper 129.

[26] Using the retail price index as a guide to relative purchasing power (and therefore to costs) we find that in 1952 (England and Wales) the cost per child week in a local authority home was £4.18s.8d. The equivalent amount in 2010 (England) would have been £111; in fact, it was £2,767. Taking 1972 instead of 1952 the cost per child week was £23.98. That would have been equivalent to £247 in 2010; but it stood at £2,767. For 1952 and 1972 see HO (1953) *Children in the Care of Local Authorities in England and Wales, November 1952*, cmd 8910. London: HMSO and Department of Health and Social Security (DHSS) (1973) *Children in Care in England and Wales, March 1972*, cmnd 5434. London: HMSO. For 2012 see Department for Education (DfE), *Children's Homes in England Data Pack*; p 24. Calculations provided at www.measuringworth.com

[27] The rate was 42% in England and Wales in 1953 and 48% in 1969. But by 1973 it had fallen to 32%, a reduction largely attributable to the inclusion of older former approved school children in the 'in care' population. By 1985 it had recovered to 50% and for the last few years it has exceeded 70%.

[28] See, for example, Parker, R. (1966) *Decision in Child Care: a Study of Prediction in Fostering*. London: Allen and Unwin; also George, V. (1970) *Foster Care*. London: Routledge and Kegan Paul; and Berridge, D. and Cleaver, H. (1987) *Foster Home Breakdown*. Oxford: Blackwell.

[29] In 1949 in England and Wales there were some 25,200 children in homes run by voluntary societies of whom 17%, or 6,000, had been placed there by local authorities. (As note 10; pp 9 and 23.) By 1959 the overall figure had fallen to 15,000: HO (1959) *Children in Care in England and Wales, March 1959*, cmnd 914. London: HMSO. The figures for 1970 are from HO (1970) *Children in Care in England and Wales, March 1970*, cmnd 4559. London: HMSO and for 1978 Children and Young Persons Act 1969. (1980) *Children in Care in England and Wales March 1978*, HC 542. London: HMSO

[30] Heralded by the Labour Party's (1964) *Crime: A Challenge to us All*. London: Labour Party; then by two white papers once the party was in power after the 1964 general election: *The Child, the Family and the Young Offender* (1965) cmnd 2742, and *Children in Trouble* (1968) cmnd 3601. These led to the Children and Young Persons Act 1969 that gave legislative expression to the general direction of what had gone before. For a discussion of the issue see Packman, J. (1975) *The Child's Generation*. Oxford: Blackwell/Robertson; ch 6.

[31] As note 5; pp 54–5.

[32] See, for example, the *Report of the Royal Commission on the Law Relating to Mental Illness and Mental Deficiency, 1954–57*. (1957), cmnd 169. London: HMSO; Skull, A. (1979) *Museums of Madness: the Social Organisation of Insanity in Nineteenth Century England*. London: Allen Lane; Goffman, E. (1961) *Asylums: Essays on the Social Situation of Mental Patients and Other Inmates*. London: Penguin also Parker, R. (1988) 'An Historical Background to Residential Care', in Sinclair, I. (ed.). *Residential Care Reviewed* (vol II of the Wagner report). London: HMSO.

[33] One of the widely read contributions to this issue was Barton, R. (1959) *Institutional Neurosis*. Bristol: Wright.

[34] See Chapter 9 for fuller details and Corby, B. (2001) *Public Inquiries into Abuse of Children in Residential Care*. London: Kingsley.

[35] An excellent assessment of these issues and trends is provided in Kahan, B. (1994) *Growing up in Groups*. London: HMSO. See also Bullock, R., Little, M. and Milham, S. (1993) *Residential Care for Children: A Review of the Research*. London: HMSO.

[36] In England, for example, the number of children in care fell from 88,700 in 1982 to 54,500 in1992: Department of Health (DoH) (1995) *Children Looked After by Local Authorities, 14 October 1991 to 31 March 1993, England*, A/F 95/12.

[37] See, Bamford, T. (1967) *The Rise of the Public Schools: A Study of Boys' Public Boarding Schools in England and Wales from 1837 to the Present Day*. London: Nelson; p 18 and chs 2 and 7.

[38] It is notable that so many of the public schools had, and continue to have, a sectarian character: Anglican; Methodist; Quaker; Roman Catholic and Jewish.

[39] DoH (2001) *Children's Homes at 31 March 2000, England*. (Statistical Bulletin 2001/9). Definitions of the different categories of children's homes are to be found in this publication on p 8.

[40] Department for Education (DfE) (2013) *Children's Homes in England: Data Pack*.

[41] In 2011 the weekly cost of a place in the private sector was £2,472 and £2,767 in the public, DfE (2012) *Children's Homes Data Pack.*

[42] The potentially unpredictable nature of the future of residential children's services is illustrated by referring back to Berridge, D. (1984) 'Private Children's Homes', *British Journal of Social Work*, 14 (4) in which he concluded from recent research that 'the private children's homes sector is in decline' (p 350) although it was pointed out that there had been a 'considerable expansion' in special boarding schools, 'especially those catering for maladjusted children' (p 351).

[43] As note 41; table LAA 3.

[44] DHSS (1973) *Children in Care in England and Wales, March 1972,* cmnd 5434. London: HMSO. (England).

[45] For example, the number of children in care (looked after) will have affected the number in residential care and the former figure has varied considerably, having reached a peak of 101,158 (England and Wales) in 1977 from a low point of 46,372 in 1939 (including the approved school population). Secretaries of State for Social Services and for Wales (1979) *Children in Care in England and Wales, March 1977*, HC 129. London: HMSO. Also Ministry of Health (MoH) (1939) *Annual Report, 1938–9*, cmd 6089. London: HMSO; p 73 for earlier figures.

[46] As note 23; p 161.

[47] As note 10; p 21.

[48] *Ibid.* p 22. Guidance about the organisation of reception homes was contained in a memorandum issued by the HO (1949) for the *Guidance of Local Authorities and Voluntary Organisations on Provision of Accommodation for the Temporary Reception of Children.*

[49] Children and Young Persons Act 1969 (1976) *Children in Care in England and Wales, March 1975*, HC 595.

[50] DoH (1997) *Children Looked After by Local Authorities, Year Ending 31 March 1996, England*, A/F 96/12.

[51] DoH (1999) *Children Looked After by Local Authorities, Year Ending 31 March 1998, England*, A/F 98/12. For an interesting account of the much altered role of observation and assessment centres see Bullock, R. and Blower, S. (2013) 'Changes in the Nature and Sequence of Placements Experienced by Children in Care, 1980–2010', *Adoption and Fostering*, 37 (2).

Chapter 3: From boarding-out to foster care

[1] Barnardos had placed 27% of the children in their care in foster homes in 1900 (1901) *Annual Report for 1900* (excluding the auxiliary boarding-out scheme and those placed in Canada); the figure for the Waifs and Strays in the same year was 25%, *Annual Report for 1900* (1901) and the National Children's Homes 23% by 1908, *Annual Report for 1908* (1909).

[2] Poor Law Board. (1861) *Annual Report for 1860–61*, 2820 and for *1870* (1871), c 123. London: HMSO.

[3] Davenport Hill, F. (1868) *Children of the State: The Training of Juvenile Paupers.* London: Macmillan.

[4] The deputation that met the president, George Goschen, in May 1870 included: Hannah Archer, Louisa Bourcherett, Frances Power Cobbe and the sisters Florence and Joanna Davenport Hill.

[5] *Boarding-out of Pauper Children*, General Order 8 (1870).

[6] Appendix A to the *Annual Report of the Poor Law Board, 1870–1* (1871), c 396. London: HMSO; p iv.

[7] *Ibid*. p 15.

[8] As note 5, Regulation 16.

[9] *Annual Report of the Local Government Board, 1874–5*, (1875), c 1328; appendix B, report 15, 'Swansea Union – Boarding-Out of Pauper Children.' London: HMSO; p 172.

[10] *Annual Report of the Local Government Board, 1888–9* (1889), c 5813. London: HMSO; p xcvi.

[11] *Annual Report of the Local Government Board, 1876–77* (1877), c 1865. London: Eyre and Spottiswoode; pp xxxviii–ix.

[12] *Annual Report of the Local Government Board, 1886–87* (1887), c 5131. London: HMSO; pp lii–iii.

[13] *Annual Report of the Local Government Board, 1914* (1915), cd 7444. London: HMSO; p 78.

[14] As note 10.

[15] *Annual Report of the Local Government Board, 1912–13* (1913), cd 6980. London: HMSO; p xlvi.

[16] See, Hollis, P. (1987) *Ladies Elect: Women in Local Government, 1865–1914*. Oxford: Clarendon; esp. chs 4 and 5.

[17] *Report of the Departmental Committee to Inquire into the Existing Systems of Maintenance and Education of Children in the Charge of Managers of District Schools and Boards of Guardians in the Metropolis* (Mundella), vol I 'Report', c 8027 and vol II 'Evidence', c 8032 (1896). London: HMSO.

[18] Local Government Board, *Boarding-out Order, 1889 (Regulations)*.

[19] As note 13 and *Annual Reports of the Ministry of Health, 1920–1* (1922), cmd 932 (see Appendix II on boarded-out children; pp 128–9); *1925–26*. (1926), cmd 2724; p 121 and *1938–39*. (1939), cmd 6089; p 73. London: HMSO.

[20] As note 19 (Ministry of Health, 1922).

[21] As note 13.

[22] See for example, Middleton, N. (1971) *When Family Failed*. London: Gollanz; ch X. For a fuller discussion of the inter-connections between foster care and residential care, see Parker, R. (1988) 'Residential Care for Children', in Sinclair, I. (ed.) *Residential Care: The Research Reviewed*, vol 2 of the *Independent Review of Residential Care* (Wagner). London: HMSO.

[23] The Local Government Act 1929 abolished boards of guardians and poor law unions and transferred the functions of guardians to the councils of counties and county boroughs. The Poor Law Act 1930 basically consolidated existing poor law legislation.

[24] See, Honigsbaum, F. (1970) *The Struggle for the Ministry of Health.* London: Bell.

[25] See, *Annual Reports of the Ministry of Health* for the respective years. See also Middleton, note 22.

[26] *Annual Report of the Ministry of Health, 1931–32* (1932), cmd 4113. London: HMSO; p 208.

[27] *Annual Report of the Ministry of Health, 1934–5.* (1935), cmd 4978. London: HMSO; p 228.

[28] *Ibid.*

[29] See *Report of the Care of Children Committee* (1946), cmd 6922. London: HMSO; table III, p 25.

[30] *Ibid.* p 152.

[31] *Thirtieth Annual Report of the Board of Supervision for the Relief of the Poor and Public Health in Scotland, 1874–75* (1875), c 1382. Edinburgh: HMSO; appendix A, report 1. In this report, and in others of the period, one can find detailed accounts of both the development and the state of boarding-out in Scotland. It is a rich source.

[32] *Twentieth Annual Report of the Local Government Board for Scotland, 1914* (1915), cd 8041. Edinburgh: HMSO; appendix A, report 6.

[33] *Report of the Committee on Homeless Children* (1946) cmd 6911. Edinburgh: HMSO; calculated from appendix II.

[34] In her report for 1913, for example, Dr Mary Menzies (the 'lady medical inspector of boarding-out' appointed in 1910) wrote of boarding-out on small farms and crofts that: 'the children are not only employed early and late as small servants, but are treated as such. If…there is much work done by the child before school hours, as indeed is sometimes the case, the child is half-asleep at school'. *Nineteenth Annual Report of the Local Government Board for Scotland, 1913.* (1914), cd 7327. Edinburgh: HMSO; appendix A, report 6; p 18.

[35] *Report of the Royal Commission on the Poor Laws and the Relief of Distress* (1910), cd 5075. London: HMSO; appendix XXIII, 'Report to the Commission…on the Condition of Children who are in receipt of poor relief…in Scotland' (Parsons).

[36] *Annual Report of the Ministry of Pensions.* (1920), HC 35; pp 24 and 47. The War Pensions (Administrative Provisions) Act 1918 imposed a duty on the minister to provide care for children whose fathers had died from causes arising out of their military service or who were on active service where their mother was dead or unable to care for them, including their neglect.

[37] *Ministry of Health Annual Report, 1919–20* (1920), cmd 932. London: HMSO; p 128.

[38] Ministry of Pensions (1949) *Twenty-Fourth Report for the Period April 1948 –March 1949*, HC 260. London: HMSO; pp 21–2.

[39] By section 96 (1) of the Children and Young Persons Act 1933. See also the associated *Children and Young Persons (Boarding out) Rules*, Statutory Rules and Orders (1933) 787.

[40] As note 29, table IV, p 27.

[41] Calculated from Home Office (HO) (1951) *Sixth Report of the Children's Department.* London: HMSO; p 11.

[42] *Ibid.*

[43] For a fuller account, see Titmuss, R. (1950) *Problems of Social Policy.* London: HMSO.

[44] www.kindertransport.org/history04_Britain.htm

[45] See the *Report on the Circumstances which led to the Boarding-Out of Dennis and Terence O'Neill at Bank Farm, Minsterley, and the steps taken to supervise their Welfare* (1945), cmd 6636. London: HMSO.

[46] For a fuller account see Parker, R. (1983) 'The Gestation of Reform: The 1948 Children Act', in Bean, P. and MacPherson, S. (eds) *Approaches to Welfare.* London: Routledge and Kegan Paul.

[47] Among other things, in 1948 the Women's Group on Public Welfare had published *The Neglected Child and His Family.* Oxford: OUP. In this they had struck a rather negative note about foster care, writing that: 'The conditions that exist when a child is accepted by the foster-parents often change unfavourably to the child's happiness and lead to a serious breakdown after a few years' (p 52).

[48] As note 29.

[49] As note 33.

[50] As note 48; Appendix I, 'Training in Child Care'; p 184. For an account of the early location of social work training in universities in Britain, see Parker, R. (1972) 'Social Ills and Public Remedies', in Robson, W. (ed.) *Man and the Social Sciences.* London: LSE/Allen and Unwin.

[51] HO, circular 160/1948, 'Children Act 1948', 8.7.48; para 28.

[52] HO, circular 258/1952; para 2.

[53] *Children in the Care of Local Authorities in England and Wales* (1953 to 1965). London: HMSO.

[54] As note 41.

[55] As note 52.

[56] *Sixth Report from the Select Committee on Estimates, Session 1951–2 (Child Care)* (1952), HC 235. London: HMSO; para 14, p xiv.

[57] HO (1952) memorandum, *Departmental Reply to the Sixth Report of Session 1951–2 on Child Care*; para 1.

[58] HO (1953) *Children in the Care of Local Authorities in England and Wales, November 1952,* cmd 8910. London: HMSO.

[59] HO (1955 and 1966) *Children in the Care of Local Authorities in England and Wales, November 1954* and *March 1964–65,* cmd 9488 and cmnd 3063. Department of Health and Social Security (DHSS) (1975) *Children in Care in England and Wales, March 1974,* cmnd 6147. London: HMSO.

[60] See, Parker, R. (1990) *Safeguarding Standards.* London: National Institute for Social Work; ch 4.

[61] Gray, P. and Parr, E. (1957) *Children in Care and the Recruitment of Foster Parents.* London: Social Survey, SS 249.

[62] Holman, R. (1975) 'The Place of Social Work in Fostering', *British Journal of Social Work,* 5 (1).

[63] HO (1955) *The Boarding-Out of Children Regulations,* Statutory Instrument (SI) 1377.

[64] See, Donnison, D. (1960) *Housing Policy Since the War*. Welwyn: Codicote and Jephcott, P. (1971) *Homes in High Flats*. Edinburgh: Oliver and Boyd.

[65] Trasler, G. (1960) *In Place of Parents*. London: Routledge and Kegan Paul.

[66] Parker, R. (1966) *Decision in Child Care: A Study of Prediction in Fostering*. London: Allen and Unwin.

[67] George, V. (1970) *Foster Care*. London: Routledge and Kegan Paul.

[68] HO (1955) *Seventh Report of the Work of the Children's Department*. London: HMSO; p 8.

[69] HO (nd) *Children Act, 1948: Summary of Local Authorities' Returns of Children in Care at 31, March 1968*.

[70] Children and Young Persons Act 1969 (1976) *Children in Care in England and Wales, March 1975*, HC 595. London: HMSO; calculated from note 1, table I.

[71] DHSS (1974) *Report of the Committee of Inquiry into the Care and Supervision Provided in Relation to Maria Colwell*. London: HMSO. In relation to relatives the report referred to 'family feuds' and 'animosities'.

[72] DHSS (1988) *Children in the Care of Local Authorities in England and Wales, March 1985*. London: DHSS.

[73] See, Farmer, E. and Parker, R. (1991) *Trials and Tribulations: Returning Children from Local Authority Care to their Families*. London: HMSO.

[74] The data published for 1985 (as note 72) included lodgings and residential employment among the residential categories but did not provide any separate figures.

Chapter 4: The evolution of landmark legislation

[1] For good brief accounts of these events see Hay, J. (1975) *The Origins of the Liberal Reforms: 1906–14*. London: Macmillan as well as Aitkin, K. (1972) *The Last Years of Liberal England, 1900–1914*. London: Collins.

[2] 'Miles' (1902) 'Where to Get Men', *The Contemporary Review*, 433: pp 78–86.

[3] Maurice, F. (1903) 'National Health: A Soldier's Story', *The Contemporary Review*, 445, pp 41–56. Also the *Report of the Committee on Physical Deterioration* (1904), cd 2175. London: HMSO.

[4] For an account of the eugenics movement and its influence, see Searle, G. (1976) *Eugenics and Politics in Britain*. Leyden (NL): Sijthoff and Noordhoff.

[5] See, Searle, G. (1990) *The Quest for National Efficiency: A Study of British Politics and Political Thought (1899–1914)*. London: Ashfield; esp. ch 2.

[6] *Report of the Royal Commission on Physical Education (Scotland)* (1903), vol I 'Report', cd 1507 and vol II 'Evidence', cd 1508. Edinburgh: HMSO.

[7] As note 3, vol II 'Evidence', cd 2210. London: HMSO.

[8] Booth, C. (1892–97) *The Life and Labour of the People of London* (10 vols). London: Macmillan.

[9] Rowntree, B. (1902) *Poverty: a Study of Town Life*. London: Macmillan.

[10] It was preceded in 1905 by the *Report of the Inter-Departmental Committee on Medical Inspection of Children Attending Public Elementary Schools*, vol I, cd 2779. London:

HMSO. See, Dwok, D. (1987) *War is Good for Babies and Young Children: A History of the Infant Welfare Movement in England, 1889–1918;* esp. ch IV. London: Tavistock.

[11] As note 1 (Aitkin); pp 77–80.

[12] See Wasserstein, B. (1992) *Herbert Samuel: A Political Life.* Oxford: Clarendon.

[13] Samuel, H. (1945) *Memoirs.* London: Cresset.

[14] For example, in *Parliamentary Debates (Commons)*, Children Bill, 2R, 24.3.08.

[15] Subsequently she wrote a pamphlet (to which Samuel contributed a preface) entitled *The Children's Charter.* Inglis, M. (1909). Edinburgh: Nelson.

[16] He mentioned especially the NSPCC and the State Children's Association.

[17] For example, juvenile courts had already been established in parts of the US and Canada and in a number of British cities.

[18] For the history surrounding these events see Titmuss, R. (1950) *Problems of Social Policy.* London: HMSO and Longmans, also his essay 'War and Social Policy' in his *Essays on the Welfare State* (1958). London: Allen and Unwin.

[19] For a fuller account of the origins of the 1948 Act see Parker, R. (1983) 'The Gestation of Reform: The Children Act 1948', in Bean, P. and MacPherson, S. (eds) *Approaches to Welfare.* London: Routledge and Kegan Paul; also Cretney, S. (1998) *Law, Law Reform and the Family.* Oxford: Clarendon; ch 9.

[20] At *Public Record Office (PRO)*, MH 102/1390. A final statement was issued in 1946 as the *Report of the Committee on the Break-up of the Poor Law.* (1946), SS (46) 13.

[21] At *PRO*, MH 102/1293/20.

[22] *The Times*, 15.7.44.

[23] At *PRO*, MH 102/1161/17. War Cabinet Reconstruction Committee, Joint Memorandum (1944) *Enquiry into Methods of Providing for Homeless Children*; p 17.

[24] *Report of the Care of Children Committee* (1946), cmd 6922. London: HMSO.

[25] *Report of the Committee on Homeless Children* (1946), cmd 6911. Edinburgh: HMSO.

[26] *Report on the Circumstances that led to the Boarding-out of Dennis and Terence O'Neill at Bank Farm, Minsterley, and the Steps taken to Supervise their Welfare* (1945), cmd 6636 (Monckton). London: HMSO.

[27] For an excellent account see Parton, N. (1985) *The Politics of Child Abuse.* London: Macmillan; esp. chs 3 and 4.

[28] *Report of the Committee of Inquiry into the Care and Supervision Provided in Relation to Maria Colwell.* (1974). London: HMSO.

[29] Department of Health and Social Security (DHSS) (1970) *The Battered Baby*, CM 02/70.

[30] Rowe, J. and Lambert, L. (1973) *Children who Wait.* London: Association of British Adoption Agencies.

[31] Jones, R. (2009) 'Children Acts, 1948–2008: The Drivers for Legislative Change in England over 60 Years', *Journal of Children's Services*, 4 (4).

[32] As note 27; p 116.

[33] *First Report from the Select Committee on Violence in Marriage*. (1975) vol I, HC 533. London: HMSO.

[34] *First Report from the Select Committee on Violence in the Family: Violence to Children* (1977), HC 329; p xlviii. London: HMSO.

[35] Cretney, S. and Mason, J. (1990) *Principles of Family Law* (5th edn). London: Sweet and Maxwell; p 590.

[36] *Ibid*. pp 590–1.

[37] *Second Report from the Social Services Committee: Children in Care*. (1984), HC 380. London: HMSO; p xvi.

[38] DHSS (1987) *Review of Child Care Law: Report to Ministers from an Interdepartmental Working Party*.

[39] For an account of the political ups and downs of the Law Commission see Cretney note 19; ch 1.

[40] Eekalaar, J. and Dingwall, R. (1990) *The Reform of Child Care Law: a Practical Guide to the Children Act 1989*. London: Tavistock/Routledge; p 19.

[41] Harris, P. (2006) 'The Making of the Children Act: a Private History', *Family Law*, Dec, p 2057.

[42] *The Law on Child Care and Family Services*. (1987), cm 62. London: HMSO; p 2.

[43] The limit was imposed by the Future Legislation Committee of the Cabinet.

[44] Hendrick, H. (1994) *Child Welfare, 1872–1989*. London: Routledge and his revised (2003) *Child Welfare: Historical Dimensions, Contemporary Debate*. Bristol: Policy Press.

[45] de Saint-Exupéry, A. (1976) *Southern Mail/Night Flight*. Harmondsworth: Penguin; p 45.

[46] As well as her letters this may reflect the fact that, at much the same time, she published her pamphlet *Whose Children?* (nd c 1947). London: Simpkin Marshall. Furthermore, she was no stranger to political lobbying and had the kind of contacts that enabled it to be more effective. For example, she had already written to *The Times* about nursery education and had friends connected with the paper. She had written the Country Diary for the *Manchester Guardian* and had contacts there too. She knew Herbert Morrison who had been her house-guest as early as 1940. Prior to sending her letter to *The Times* she had written to various influential people and acquaintances in order to alert them to what she intended to do and encouraging them to keep the correspondence going with their own letters, which is what happened. See her autobiography (1975) *Memoirs of an Uneducated Lady*. London: Thames and Hudson; esp chs 12–14.

[47] As note 41; p 1059.

[48] These ideological differences have been discussed in Fox Harding, L. (1991) *Perspectives in Child Care Policy*. London: Longman.

Chapter 5: Getting started with the 1948 Children Act: what do we learn?

[1] Niechcial, J. (2010) *Lucy Faithfull: Mother to Hundreds*. Available from jfmniechcial@hotmail.com

[2] *Report of the Care of Children Committee* (1946), cmd 6922. London: HMSO; p 12.

[3] *Report of the Committee on Homeless Children* (1946), cmd 6911. Edinburgh: HMSO; p 7.

[4] This is made clear in section 96 (1) of the Children and Young Persons Act 1933.

[5] As note 2; p 18.

[6] As note 3; p 40.

[7] In Scotland, however, it was the poor law authorities that were responsible for supervising children subject to the Child Life Protection legislation.

[8] Home Office (HO) (1951) *Sixth Report of the Work of the Children's Department.* London: HMSO; p 36.

[9] See *Wallbridge and Another v. Dorset County Council* 2 W.L.R. 1068 (1954). However, the law was not actually changed until the Children Act 1958.

[10] The new children's committees did not become responsible for approved schools or remand homes. These remained controlled by their management committees and by the Home Office centrally.

[11] As note 2; p 36.

[12] See, Parker, R. (1983) 'The Gestation of Reform: The Children Act 1948', in Bean, P. and MacPherson, S. *Approaches to Welfare.* London: Routledge and Kegan Paul. The Home Office was especially keen to retain and acquire responsibility for children's services because these were regarded as important for softening the public image of its otherwise predominant responsibilities for law and order.

[13] As note 2; p 146.

[14] *Ibid.* p 148.

[15] As note 3. John Murphy (1992) argues in his *British Social Services: the Scottish Dimension* (Edinburgh: Scottish Academic Press) that the absence of any mention of the qualities needed in a children's officer in the Clyde report was a major weakness that 'was to prove adverse to the establishment of adequate children's departments' in Scotland in the early years (p 31). But this seems too simple an explanation: other factors were at work as well, not least the stronger opposition to the idea of separate children's departments in Scotland than in England and Wales.

[16] HO, circular 160/1948.

[17] As note 8; p 6.

[18] *Report of the Royal Commission on Local Government in England, 1966–69,* vol III, 'Research Appendices' (1969), cmnd 4040-II. London: HMSO; p 237.

[19] Winnicott, C. (1963) *Children's Officers Appointed in 1948,* unpublished, private communication.

[20] Brill, K. (1991) *The Curtis Experiment.* Birmingham University Phd; p 47. Unfortunately Brill gave no information about the source of this material but he had been children's officer in Croydon and in Devon and the long-serving secretary of the Association of Children's Officers.

[21] *Ibid.* pp 45–6.

[22] *Ibid.* p 55.

[23] *Ibid.* p 58.

[24] *Ibid.* p 48.

[25] See, Wedge, P. (2003) *Developing Notions of Children in Need*. Brighton: East Sussex Social Services Department/University of Sussex and Jackson, S. (2008) *Social Care and Social Exclusion: Can Education Change the Trajectory for Looked After Children?* Brighton: East Sussex Social Services Department/ University of Sussex.

[26] *PRO*, MH 102/1642.

[27] *Municipal Yearbook* (1938). London: Municipal Journal.

[28] *British Imperial Calendar and Civil Service List* (1946 and 54). London: HMSO.

[29] Until the Children and Young Persons Act 1933 (sect 94) there was no full record of the number of these institutions. Some had been inspected by the Ministry of Health, but most (estimated to be more than 1,000) were under no form of inspection (HO, 1938) *Fifth Report of the Children's Branch*. London: HMSO; pp 103–9).

[30] As note 20; p 47.

[31] Association of Directors of Children's Services, membership list, 2011.

[32] *Municipal Yearbook* (1948). London: Municipal Journal.

[33] *PRO*, HO 414/1.

[34] Scottish Home Department (1958) *Children in the Care of Local Authorities in Scotland, November 1957*, cmnd 461. Edinburgh: HMSO.

[35] Watkins, D. (1993) *Other People's Children: Adventures in Child Care*. Cornwall: Devoran; p 126.

[36] Holman, R. (1998) *Child Care Revisited: Children's Departments, 1948–71*. London: Institute of Childcare and Social Education; pp 33 and 53.

[37] As note 20; p 59.

[38] As note 35; p 129.

[39] As note 20; p 54.

[40] Wedge, P. (2011), private communication.

[41] *PRO*, MH 102/1642.

[42] *PRO*, MH 102/1644.

[43] As note 36; p 88.

[44] Kent County Council (1950) *Report of the Children's Committee, 1948–50*. Maidstone: KCC; p.7.

[45] As note 36; p 49.

[46] Holman, R. (1996) *The Corporate Parent: Manchester Children's Department, 1948–71*. London: National Institute for Social Work; p 53.

[47] Again, it is frustrating that Brill provided no information about where these records were to be found. My search in the Public Record Office failed to locate them there. However, the Home Office did keep a 'personal file' on all children's officers, but where this is or whether it still exists I do not know.

[48] As note 20; p 52.

[49] *Ibid.* p 101.

[50] *Ibid.* p 124

[51] *PRO*, MH 102/1642.

[52] As note 18; p 238.

[53] As note 8; p 33.

[54] *Ibid.* p 34.

[55] *Ibid.* p 35.

[56] See Parker, R. (1990) *Safeguarding Standards*. London: National Institute for Social Work; ch 4.

[57] As note 8; p 49.

[58] As note 34.

[59] *Report on the Circumstances that led to the Boarding-out of Dennis and Terence O'Neill at Bank Farm, Minsterley, and the Steps taken to Supervise their Welfare* (1945), cmd 6636. London: HMSO.

[60] *PRO*, MH 102/1642.

[61] *PRO*, HO 414/1.

[62] As note 8; p 19.

[63] *Ibid.* p 148.

[64] HO (1953) *Children in the Care of Local Authorities in England and Wales, November 1952*, cmd 8910. London: HMSO.

[65] As note 63.

[66] As note 1; pp 85–6.

[67] Like the ACO the ACCO was also created in 1949. In one of the series of essays in its commemorative report of 1970 Clare Winnicott pointed out that in its inaugural year there were just 12 members but that by 1970 there were 2,589. Furthermore, she emphasised its importance in creating a sense of professional identity and professionalism in child care, thereby, together with the ACO, laying a bedrock for an emerging social work profession and its parallel body, the British Association of Social Work (pp 74–5).

[68] Today those involved with the provision and development of children's services have a plethora of research and journals upon which to call. The first children's officers and those around them had hardly any. Indeed, it was not until the mid-1960s that these sources of information began to be available. See Parker, R. (2005) 'Then and Now: 40 Years of Research in the UK', in Axford, N., Berry, V., Little, M. and Morpeth, L. *Forty Years of Research, Policy and Practice in Children's Services*. Chichester: Wiley.

Chapter 6: Child care in the melting pot in the 1980s

[1] For instance, the number of children in private schools for the 'maladjusted' in England and Wales increased roughly from 4,500 in 1970 to 7,500 by 1981.

[2] For a general discussion of children's appointments see Davis, G., Macleod, A. and Murch, M. (1983) 'Undefended Divorce: Should Section 41 of the Matrimonial Causes Act of 1973 be Repealed?', *Modern Law Review*, 46 (2).

[3] Matrimonial care orders in England and Wales have been the fastest growing category of 'reasons for admission care', although they still only amount to some 500 or 600. But children so admitted stay for long periods and hence the total number of them in care grew.

[4] For example, in England and Wales the grand total in 1971 was 40,370 and in 1981 41,000. In 1971 private foster homes accounted for 25% of the total but in 1981 only 9%. Department of Health and Social Security (DHSS) *Children in Care in England and Wales*, annual statistical returns.

[5] See, Scottish Education Department, Social Work Services Group (nd) *A Longitudinal Study of Children in Care*. Edinburgh: SED; especially table 5.2, p 31. Also Rowe, J., Cain, H., Hundleby, M. and Keane, A. (1984) *Long-Term Foster Care*. London: Batsford.

[6] See DHSS (1984) *Children in Care in England and Wales, March 31 1982*; tables A1 and 2, pp 16–9.

[7] *Second Report from the Social Services Committee* (1984) Session 1983–84, *Children in Care*, vol 1, 'Report', HC 360–1.

[8] Later published as DHSS. (1987) *Review of Child Care Law: Report to Ministers from an Independent Working Party*.

[9] Discussed at length in the *Report of the Commission on One-Parent Families* (1974) London: HMSO, cmnd 5629; especially chs 13 and 14.

[10] As note 7; p xiii.

[11] Bowlby, J. (1951) *Maternal Care and Mental Health*. Geneva: WHO; but also the later *Deprivation of Maternal Care: A Reassessment of its Effects*. (1962) (various contributors). Geneva: WHO and Rutter, M. (1981) *Maternal Deprivation Reassessed*. Harmondsworth: Penguin.

[12] Note the politically sensitive implications of studies like Gill, O. and Jackson, B. (1983) *Adoption and Race*. London: Batsford.

[13] For a fuller discussion see, Martin, F. and Murray, K. (eds) (1982) *The Scottish Juvenile Justice System*. Edinburgh: Scottish Academic Press; esp ch 7.

[14] Millham, S., Bullock, R., Hosie, K. and Haak, M. (1986) *Lost in Care: The Problems of Maintaining Links between Children in Care and their Families*. Aldershot: Gower; p 47.

[15] See Dartington Social Research Unit (1983) *Place of Safety Orders*. Report to the DHSS.

[16] See the annual statistics *Children in Care of Local Authorities*. London: HMSO.

[17] See Fanshel, D. and Shinn, E. (1982) *On the Road to Permanency*. NY: Columbia University Press and their earlier report *The Child in Foster Care* (1979) NY: Columbia University Press.

[18] Calculated from the annual statistics *Children in Care*.

[19] See Office of Population, Censuses and Surveys, *Monitor*, 'Population Projections: mid-1982 based': PP2 83/1, March, 1983.

[20] As note 7, p xciii.

[21] See Parker, R. (ed.) (1980) *Caring for Separated Children*. London: Macmillan; especially ch 5 for a fuller discussion.

[22] See, for example, Parker, R. (1966) *Decision in Child Care*. London: Allen and Unwin.

[23] Packman, J., Randall, J. and Jacques, N. (1986) *Who Needs Care? Social Work Decisions about Children*. Oxford: Blackwell.

[24] See Scottish Education Department, Social Work Services Group, *Statistical Bulletin*, August, 1984.

[25] See annual statistics *Children in Care*.

[26] An information service produced by the All Party Parliamentary Group for Children.

[27] See de Jouvenel, B. (1967) *The Art of Conjecture*. London: Wiedenfeld and Nicholson.

[28] Wilson, C. (1978) *The Outsider*. London: Pan Books; esp ch 8.

Chapter 7: Trends, transitions and tensions: children's services since 1980

[1] Unless otherwise indicated the statistics throughout refer to England. Unfortunately, it is both difficult and time-consuming to assemble comprehensive data for the United Kingdom. Until 1986 combined figures were published for England and Wales, thereafter they were produced separately, as have the statistics for Scotland and Northern Ireland. These differences and the problems they create are well described in the 2009 edition of *Social Trends* (no 39, p 235).

[2] Department of Health and Social Security (DHSS) (nd) *Children in Care in England and Wales March 1980*; Department of Health (DoH) (1996) *Children Looked after by Local Authorities, Year Ending March 1994, England*. A/F 94/12 and Department for Education (DfE) (2013) *Children Looked after in England, March 2013*. SFR 36/2013. Subsequent figures for these dates derive from the same sources.

[3] There was a steady increase in committals to care in family proceedings in the 1960s followed by a period of rapid growth in the 1970s that paralleled the rise in divorce after the implementation of the Divorce Law Reform Act, 1969. In 1972 there were 1,500 children in care in England on matrimonial care orders; by 1976 there were 3,100 and by 1981 6,200. In 1985 the figure stood at 6,800. Despite these increases little attention was paid to the issue and, as the House of Commons Social Services Committee on *Children in Care* (1984, HC 360–I. London: HMSO) pointed out 'neither the Minister nor anybody else seem to have much idea as to why the number of matrimonial care orders is rising, although it has been doing so steadily for the last decade' (p lxi).

[4] All rates during this period (England and Wales) fell within the range 6.1 to 6.9 (adjusted to include the approved school population).

[5] One of the issues in determining the level of foster care revolves around how children who have been committed to care but are allowed to be in the care of their parents are to be classified. In these figures they have been excluded.

[6] The classification 'in residential care' has tended to vary or the categories have been grouped in different ways in the statistical returns. In 2013 these differentiated eight sub-categories. Most of the children in residential provisions were in 'homes or hostels' (73%) others were living in secure units, in care homes, in an NHS facility, in a family centre or mother and baby unit, in a young offenders institution or prison, in a residential school or in a refuge. Although the number of children in most of the categories, other than 'homes or hostels', was not large, taken together they accommodated just over a quarter of all children in 'residential care'.

[7] Sec. of State for Social Services (1980) *Children in Care in England and Wales, March 1978.* London: HMSO.

[8] See, for example, DoH, Welsh Office, Home Office and Lord Chancellor's Department (1993) *Adoption: The Future,* cm 2288. London: HMSO (Conservative administration) and DoH (1998) *Adoption – Achieving the Right Balance,* LAC (98) 20 (Labour administration).

[9] As note 2.

[10] But we now have the children in need surveys; for example, DfE (2013) *Characteristics of Children in Need, England 2012–13,* SFR45/2013. See also for a review of the issues and problems Parker, R., Ward, H., Jackson, S., Aldgate, J. and Wedge, P. (eds) (1991) *Assessing Outcomes in Child Care: The Report of an Independent Working Party Established by the Department of Health.* London: HMSO.

[11] As note 10.

[12] DoH (1993) *Children and Young People on Child Protection Registers Year Ending 31 March 1992, England.* A/F92/13.

[13] House of Commons, Second Report of the Social Services Committee, session 1983–84 (1984*) Children in Care,* vol I, HC 360–1. London: HMSO.

[14] *Report of the Tribunal of Inquiry into the Abuse of Children in the Care of Gwyndd and Clwyd since 1974* (2000) (Waterhouse), HC 201.

[15] Rowe, J. and Lambert, L. (1973) *Children Who Wait.* London: Association of British Adoption Agencies.

[16] See, Parker, R. (2005) 'Then and Now', in Axford, N., Berry, B., Little, M. and Morpeth, L. (eds) *Forty Years of Research, Policy and Practice in Children's Services.* Chichester: Wiley.

[17] See DoH (1989) *The Care of Children: Principles and Practice in Regulations and Guidance.* London: HMSO.

[18] As note 2, 2013; table A8.

[19] Eisenstadt, N. (2011) *Providing a Start: How Government Discovered Early Childhood.* Bristol: Policy Press.

[20] *Modernising Government* (1999) cm 4310. London: HMSO; p 17.

[21] Little, M. (2012) 'In the Shadows: Children's Social Policy in the Blair Years', *Adoption and Fostering,* 36 (1).

[22] DfE (2010) *Numbers of Sure Start Children's Centres as at 30 April 2010* (England), OSR14/2010.

[23] See, HC Education Committee (2013) *Foundation Years: Sure Start Children's Centres,* 5th report, session 2013–14. HC 364-I and II. However, there seemed to be some uncertainty about the figures.

[24] For an excellent account and discussion see Churchill, H. (2011) *Parental Rights and Responsibilities: Analysing Social Policy and Lived Experience.* Bristol: Policy Press; esp pt 2.

[25] *Ibid.* The Labour Party manifesto reinstated Labour's primary policy objectives: 'to reduce welfare reliance, promote employment opportunities and reduce child poverty'; p 98.

[26] DfE (2013) *Provision for Young Children Under Five Years of Age in England*; SFR 23/2013. Take up was less extensive among 'Black African, Pakistani and Bangladeshi mothers'; p 5.

[27] DfE (2011) *Post legislative assessments of the…Childcare Act 2006…* cm 8204; paras 193–4. London: HMSO.

[28] Department of Work and Pensions and the Cabinet Office (2011) *Early Intervention: The Next Step* (Allen). London: Her Majesty's Government (HMG).

[29] HMG (2011) *Early Intervention: Smart Investment, Massive Savings*. London: HMG; quotation from Allen's covering letter to the Prime Minister.

[30] DoH (2002) *Children Looked After by Local Authorities, 31 March 2001, England*. A/F 01/12; table M, p 56.

[31] As note 2.

[32] DfE (2013) *Children's Homes Data Pack*; p 43 (includes some data for 2014).

[33] As note 2.

[34] OFSTED (2011) *Fostering Datasets: Fostering Agencies and Fostering Services Survey, 2010–11: Independent Fostering Agencies*.

[35] As note 32; pp 43 and 45.

[36] As note 32.

[37] DfE (2014) *Children's Social Work Workforce…as at Sepember 2013*; SFR 08/2014.

[38] As note 32; p 24.

[39] As note 34.

[40] Independent Children's Homes Association (2012) *Commissioners' Handbook*. Figures calculated from entries.

[41] See, for a commentary on the early years, Bartlett, W., Popper, C., Wilson, D. and Le Grand, J. (eds) (1994) *Quasi-Markets in the Welfare State*. Bristol: Policy Press; esp. ch. 8.

[42] DoH, DfEE and HO (1999) *Working Together to Safeguard Children: A Guide to Inter-agency Working*.

[43] DH, DfEE and HO (2000) *A Framework for the Assessment of Children in Need and their Families*. London: TSO.

[44] DfE (2013) *Working Together to Safeguard Children: A Guide to Inter-agency Working*.

[45] DfE (2012) *Children Looked After by Local Authorities, England, March 2012*. SFR20/2012.

[46] *Ibid*.

[47] As note 7.

[48] As note 45, calculated from local authority tables.

[49] As note 2, 1980.

[50] As note 45.

[51] *Ibid*.

[52] *Statistics Relating to Approved Schools, Remand Homes and Attendance Centres in England and Wales for the Year 1968* (1969), HC 35. London: HMSO.

[53] As note 2, 2013, calculated from the Local Authority Tables.

[54] From children in care statistics 1960–69.

[55] Another factor may be differences in the duration of being looked after but the published statistics do not break this down by gender.

Chapter 8: Reflections on the assessment of outcomes in child care

[1] Parker, R. (ed.) (1991) *Assessing Outcomes in Child Care*. London: HMSO.

[2] Hicklin, M. (1946) *War-Damaged Children*. London: Association of Psychiatric Social Workers.

[3] Cornish, D. and Clarke, R. (1975) *Residential Treatment and its Effects upon Delinquency*. London: HMSO.

[4] Bartak, L. and Rutter, M. (1975) 'The Measurement of Staff–Child Interaction in Three Units for Autistic Children', in Tizard, J., Sinclair, J. and Clarke, R. *Varieties of Residential Experience*. London: Routledge and Kegan Paul.

[5] Quinton, D. and Rutter, M. (1988) *Parenting Breakdown*. Aldershot: Avebury.

[6] Parker, R. (1966) *Decision in Child Care*. London: Allen and Unwin.

[7] Farmer, E. and Parker, R. (1991) *Trials and Tribulations: Returning Children from Local Authority Care to their Families*. London: HMSO.

[8] McGuire, J., Stein, A. and Rosenberg, W. (1997) 'Evidence-Based Medicine and Child Mental Health Services', *Children and Society*, 11 (2).

[9] Gibbons, J., Gallagher, B., Bell, C. and Gordon, D. (1995) *Development after Physical Abuse in Early Childhood*. London: HMSO.

[10] See Department for Education (DfE) (2013) *Outcomes for Children Looked After by Local Authorities in England as at 31 March, 2013*. SFR 50/2013.

[11] Department of Health (DoH) (1994) *Key Indicators of Local Authority Social Services*. London: DoH.

[12] Audit Commission. (1994) *Seen But Not Heard: Co-ordinating Community Child Health and Social Services for Children in Need*. London: HMSO.

[13] As note 10. The indicators used by the DfE include: educational achievement, emotional and behavioural health, health care, offending, substance misuse, school exclusions and developmental progress for the under-fives.

[14] As note 7.

[15] Facey, A. (1981) *A Fortunate Life*. Australia: Penguin.

[16] Harrison, P. (1979) *The Home Children*. Winnipeg: Watson and Dwyer.

[17] However, there have been several important recent publications addressing the issue of children's well-being and how it is to be determined; for example, Axford, N. (2008) *Exploring Concepts of Child Well-being*. Bristol: Policy Press; and Bradshaw, J. (2006) 'The Use of Indicators of Child Well-Being in the United Kingdom and the European Union', in Ben-Arieh, A. and George, R. (eds) *Indictors of Children's Well-being*. Dordrecht, NL: Springer.

[18] Thoburn, J. (1980) *Captive Clients: Social Work with Families and Children Home on Trial*. London: Routledge and Kegan Paul.

[19] Treseliotis, J., Borland, M., Hill, M. and Lambert, L. (1996) *Teenagers and the Social Work Services*. London: HMSO.

Chapter 9: The role and function of inquiries

[1] Health Select Committee Third Report (1997) *The Welfare of Former British Child Migrants*, HC 755-I and II. London: HMSO.

[2] *Report of the Royal Commission on the Funding of Long-term Care for the Elderly*. (1999), cm 4192. London: HMSO.

[3] See, for examples Sinclair, R. and Bullock, R. (2002) *Learning from Past Experience: A Review of Serious Case Reviews*. London: Department of Health (DoH). Also, Brandon, M., Bailey, S. and Belderson, P. (2010) *Building on the Learning from Serious Case Reviews: A Two-year Analysis of Child Protection Database Notifications, 2007–2009*. London: Department for Education (DfE).

[4] *Report by Sir Walter Monckton, KC on the circumstances which led to the boarding-out of Dennis and Terence O'Neill at Bank Farm Minsterley and the steps taken to supervise their welfare* (1945), cmd 6636. London: HMSO.

[5] Home Office (HO) (1967) *Administration of Punishment at Court Lees Approved School: Report of Inquiry by Mr Edward Brian Gibbens, QC*. London: HMSO.

[6] On the latter see, Morris, A. (1970) *The Growth of Parliamentary Scrutiny by Committee: A Symposium*. Oxford: Pergamon.

[7] Wheare, K. (1955) *Government by Committee: An Essay on the British Constitution*. Oxford: Clarendon.

[8] Rhodes, G. (1975) *Committees of Inquiry*. London: Allen and Unwin; esp. ch 2.

[9] Corby, B, Doig, A. and Roberts, V. (2001) *Public Inquiries into Abuse of Children in Residential Care*. London: Kingsley.

[10] Hall, P., Land, H., Parker, R. and Webb, A. (1975) *Change, Choice and Conflict in Social Policy*. London: Heinemann; esp. ch 15.

[11] Herbert, A. (1936) *Mild and Bitter*. London: Methuen; but also his *Anything but Action? A Study of the Uses and Abuses of Committees of Inquiry* (1960). London: Institute of Economic Affairs.

[12] For example, as note 2.

[13] *Residential Care: A Positive Choice. Report of the Independent Review of Residential Care* (1988) London: HMSO. Also, see particularly, Kahan, B. (1994) *Growing up in Groups*. London: HMSO; pp 45–54.

[14] Department of Health and Social Security (DHSS) (1974) *Report of the Committee of Inquiry into the Care and Supervision Provided in Relation to Maria Colwell*. London: HMSO.

[15] London Borough of Brent (1985) *A Child in Trust: The Report of the Panel of Inquiry into the Circumstances Surrounding the Death of Jasmine Beckford*. London: London Borough of Brent.

[16] Levy, A. and Kahan, B. (1991) *The Pindown Experience and the Protection of Children*. Stafford: Stafford County Council.

[17] DoH and HO (2003) *The Victoria Climbié Inquiry: Report of an Inquiry by Lord Laming*, cm 5730. London: HMSO. See also Health Select Committee's review of the report *The Victoria Climbié Inquiry Report,* sixth report, session 2002–3, HC 570. London: HMSO.

[18] As note 3, Brandon; p 3.

[19] See, for example, Axford, N. and Bullock, R. (2005) *Child Deaths and Significant Case Reviews: International Approaches.* Edinburgh: Scottish Education Department, *Insight* 19.

[20] See, for example, Parker, R. (1967) *The Problems of Reform*. London: Family Welfare Association.

[21] For example the report on the death of 'Baby P' explains on its first page that it 'was written by an independent author commissioned by Haringey Local Safeguarding Children Board' Haringey: LSCB (2008) *Serious Case Review – Child 'A'*. London: London Borough of Haringey/DfE.

[22] For example, Olive Stevenson's note of dissent in the Colwell report; as note 14.

[23] See, Hall, P. (1976) *Reforming the Welfare: The Politics of Change in the Personal Social Services.* London: Heinemann. 'Frederic Seebohm decided that the best strategy for his committee to adopt was to keep the financial and manpower implications of its proposals vague' (p 76).

[24] A good illustration of the importance of such committees in influencing the direction of policy in children's services is to be found in the *Sixth Report from the Select Committee on Estimates* (1952) session 1951–52, 'Child Care', HC 235. London: HMSO. Its publication strengthened the case for more foster care, particularly on financial grounds.

[25] Audit Commission. (1994) *Seen but not Heard: Co-ordinating Community Child Health and Social Services for Children in Need.* London: HMSO.

[26] Joseph, K. (1971) 'Future Policy for Mental Health', in *Minds Matter* (Annual Conference Report). London: National Association for Mental Health; p 39.

[27] Denham, A. and Garnett, M. (2001) *Keith Joseph.* Chesham: Acumen; p 213. It should be noted that, as Secretary for State for Social Services, Joseph was responsible for setting up the committee of inquiry into the death of Maria Colwell in 1973, although it was Barbara Castle to whom it reported in April 1974, following Labour's election victory the month before.

[28] See, Parker, R. (1969) 'Co-operation between Social Welfare Organisations', in Kellmer Pringle, M. (ed.) *Caring for Children*. London: Longmans.

[29] Munro, E. (1999) 'Common Errors of Reasoning in Child Protection Work', in *Child Abuse and Neglect*, 23 (8).

[30] Reder, P. and Duncan, S. (2004) 'From Colwell to Climbié : Inquiring into Fatal Child Abuse', in Stanley, N. and Manthorpe, J. (eds) *The Age of Inquiry: Learning and Blaming in Health and Social Care*. London: Routledge; pp 108–9.

[31] Munro, E. (2004) 'The Impact of Child Abuse Inquiries Since 1990', in Stanley and Manthorpe, as note 30.

Chapter 10: Evidence, judgement, values and engagement

[1] Bowlby, J. (1951) *Maternal Care and Mental Health*. Geneva: WHO.

[2] Parker, R. (1966) *Decision in Child Care*. London: Allen and Unwin.

[3] Trasler, G. (1960) *In Place of Parents*. London: Routledge and Kegan Paul.

[4] See, for a summary of this finding, Wolkind, S. and Rushton, A. (1994) 'Residential and Foster Family Care', in Rutter, M., Taylor, E. and Hersov, L. (eds) *Child and Adolescent Psychology*. Oxford: Blackwell, 3rd edn; p 160.

[5] Knapp, M., Bryson, D. and Matthews, J. (1982) 'Child Care Costs and Policies', in *Social Work Service*, 32 (winter).

[6] For example, Lloyd, E. (ed.) (1999) *Parenting Matters: What Works in parenting Education?* Ilford: Barnardos.

[7] Meltzer, H., Smyth, M. and Robus, N. (1989) OPCS surveys of disability in Great Britain, Report 6, *Disabled Children: Services, Transport and Education*. London: HMSO and Gordon, D., Parker, R. and Loughran, F. (2000) *Disabled Children in Britain*. London: TSO.

[8] Robinson, C. and Stalker, K. (1991) *Respite Care: Summaries and Suggestions*. Bristol: Norah Fry Centre.

[9] An illuminating discussion is offered in Vickers, G. (1965) *The Art of Judgement: A Study of Policy Making*. London: Chapman and Hall.

[10] For example, Quinton, D. and Rutter, M. (1988) *Parenting Breakdown*. Aldershot: Avebury.

[11] Wilkins, L. (1963) *Social Deviance*. London: Tavistock; p 3.

[12] See, *An Enquiry into the Social Science Research Council* (1981), cmnd 4814. London: HMSO.

[13] Donnison, D. (2014*) 'On Tap But Not On Top'*. Dartington: Centre for Social Policy; pp 8–9. At: darti-whg.vispweb3.userarea.co.uk/csp/index.asp?p=papers

[14] *Ibid*. p 11.

Chapter 11: Emerging issues: looking ahead

[1] See, for example, Silver, N. (2012) *The Signal and the Noise: The Art and Science of Prediction*. London: Penguin.

[2] Department for Education (DfE) (2012) *Private Fostering Arrangements in England, Year Ending 31 March, 2012*.

[3] Department of Health (DoH) (2002) *Children Looked after by Local Authorities, Year Ending 31 March, 2001, England*. A/F 01/12; p 56.

[4] DfE (2013) *Children Looked After by Local Authorities, Year Ending 31 March, 2013, England*. SFR 36/2013.

[5] OFSTED (2011) *Fostering Datasets: Fostering Agencies and Fostering Services Survey, 2010–11: Independent Fostering Agencies*.

[6] As note 4.

[7] NAFP is the trade association for independent and voluntary foster services providers and was established in 2008, www.napf.co.uk

[8] See Fostering Networks (2012) *Transfer of Foster Carers Protocol*, www.rbkc.gov.uk/pdf/transfer%20of%20foster%20carers.pdf

[9] DoH (2001) *Children's Homes at 31 March, 2000, England*; table A.

[10] DfE (2013) *Children's Homes Data Pack, March, 2013, England*; p 15.

[11] *Ibid.*

[12] *Ibid.* p 11.

[13] DfE (2012) *Children's Homes Data Pack, March, 2012*, supplementary p 2.

[14] *The Fostering Services (England) Regulations 2011*, regs 14, 33, 34. Statutory Instrument (SI) 2011/581. *The Children's Homes Regulations 2001*, reg. 39. Statutory Instrument (SI) 2001/3967.

[15] See, for example, NAFP, ICHA and the National Association of Independent Schools and Non-Maintained Special Schools. (2012) *Death by Paperwork? The impact of Local Authority procurement on voluntary and private children's services providers*, www.nafp.co.uk

[16] As note 10.

[17] As note 5.

[18] DfE (2014) *Powers to Delegate Children's Social Care Functions* (consultative paper).

[19] For example, letters to the *Guardian*, 16.5.14.

[20] As reported in the *Guardian*, 21.5.14.

[21] As notes 3 and 10. The 'ethnic designations' employed in the text are those used in the published statistics and are indicated by inverted commas.

[22] As note 3; table A7.

[23] As note 4.

[24] As note 3.

[25] As note 4.

[26] DfE (2012) *Children Looked After by Local Authorities at 31 March, 2012, England*; local authority tables.

[27] *Ibid.* hand count.

[28] As note 4.

[29] Children Act 1989 (1991) *Guidance and Regulations, vol 6: Children with Disabilities*. London: HMSO.

[30] DoH (2003) *Children Looked After by Local Authorities at 31 March, 2002, England*, table C and note 3.

[31] Office for Population Censuses and Surveys (1989) *Surveys of Disability in Great Britain, report 6: Disabled Children: Services, transport and education* (Meltzer, H., Smyth, M. and Robus, N.). London: HMSO.

[32] Gordon, D., Parker, R. and Loughran, F. (2000) *Disabled Children in Britain*. London: The Stationery Office (TSO); p 153.

[33] Office for National Statistics (ONS) (2003) *The Mental Health of Young People Looked After by Local Authorities in England: Summary Report* (Meltzer, H., Corbin, T., Gatward, R., Goodman, R. and Ford, T.). London: HMSO.

[34] Home Office (1953) *Children in the Care of Local Authorities in England and Wales, November, 1952,* cmd 8910. London: HMSO.

[35] As note 4.

[36] As note 28.

[37] Figures from DoH (1991) *Children in Care of Local Authorities, Year Ending 31 March, 1988, England.* A/F88/12.

[38] Office of the Deputy Prime Minister (2003) *A Better Education for Children in Care*: Social Exclusion Unit. London: SEU; p 10.

[39] There are some exceptions such as Oakley, A. (2000) *Experiments in Knowing: Gender and Method in the Social Sciences.* Cambridge: Polity Press.

[40] Gittins, J. (1952) *Approved School Boys.* London: HMSO.

[41] Richardson, H. (1969) *Adolescent Girls in Approved Schools.* London: Routledge and Kegan Paul.

[42] HMG (2011) *Early Intervention: The Next Steps. An Independent Report to HMG.* London: HMG.

[43] See for example, the child well-being survey in Perth and Kinross at www.pkc.gov.uk/article/4899/Evidence2Success

[44] DfE (2012) *Children in Need in England…2011–12* (Children in Need Census).

[45] Harker, L., Jütte, S., Murphy, T., Bentley, H., Miller, P. and Fitch, P. (2013) *How Safe Are Our Children?* London: NSPCC.

[46] NSPCC (2013) *Helpline Highlights 2012/13.* London: NSPCC; p 18.

[47] *Ibid.*

[48] Childline (2012) *Saying the Unsayable: What's Affecting Children in 2012?* www.nspcc.org.uk/news-and-views/our-news/child-protection-news/12-12-04-childline-report/saying-the-unsayable-pdf_wdf93130.pdf

[49] HMG (2013) *Working Together to Safeguard Children: A Guide to Inter-agency Working to Safeguard and Promote the Welfare of Children.*

[50] National Collaborating Centre for Women's and Children's Health (2013) *When to Suspect Child Maltreatment.* London: National Institute for Health and Clinical Excellence.

[51] See, for example, Morris, J. (1975) *Uses of Epidemiology* (3rd edn). London: Churchill Livingstone; also DHSS (1975) *Prevention and Health: Everybody's Business.* London: HMSO.

[52] DfE (2010) *Monitoring and Evaluation of Family Intervention Projects to March 2010*; table 1.1.

[53] The Riots Communities and Victims Panel (2012) *Final Report of the Riots Communities and Victims Panel.* London: RCVP; p 7.

[54] At cpag.org.uk/child-poverty-facts-and-figures

[55] Cabinet Office, Social Exclusion Task Force (2007) *Reaching Out: Think Family. Analysis and Themes from the Families at Risk Review.* London: CO; p 6.

[56] However, there are now numerous on-line databases internationally that not only list these various projects, but that also endeavour to assess how well grounded they are on evidence. See www.blueprintsprograms.com

[57] See, for example, Axford, N., Berry, V., Little, M. and Morpeth, L. (2012) 'Engaging Parents in Parenting Programs: Lessons from Research and Practice', *Children and Youth Services Review*, 34; p 2061. Also, British Psychological Society (2012) *Technique is Not Enough: A Framework for Ensuring that Evidenced-based Parenting Programmes are Socially Inclusive.* Leicester: BPS; p 5.

[58] See, for example, Woolgar, M. (2013) 'The Practical Implications of the Emerging Findings in the Neurobiology of Maltreatment for Looked-After and Adopted Children: Recognising the Diversity of Outcomes', *Adoption and Fostering*, 37 (3).

Bibliography

Books and pamphlets

Abrams, L. (1998) *The Orphan Country*. Edinburgh: Donald.

Adcock, M, White, R. and Rowlands, O. (1982) *The Administrative Parent*. London: British Agencies for Adoption and Fostering.

Aitkin, K. (1972) *The Last Years of Liberal England, 1900–1914*. London: Collins.

Allen, M. (c 1947) *Whose Children?* London: Simpkin Marshall.

Allen, M. (1969) *Planning for Play*. London: Thames and Hudson.

Allen, M. (1975) *Memoirs of an Uneducated Lady*. London: Thames and Hudson.

Axford, N. (2008) *Exploring Concepts of Child Well-being*. Bristol: Policy Press.

Axford, N. and Bullock, R. (2005) *Child Deaths and Significant Case Reviews: International Approaches*. Edinburgh: Scottish Executive.

Bailey, S. and Belderson, P. (2010) *Building on the Learning from Serious Case Reviews: A Two-year Analysis of Child Protection Database Notifications, 2007–2009*. London: Department for Education.

Bamford, T. (1967) *The Rise of the Public Schools: A Study of Boys' Public Boarding Schools in England and Wales from 1837 to the Present Day*. London: Nelson.

Barnardo, T. (1889) *Something Attempted Something Done*. London: Barnardos/Shaw.

Bartlett, W., Propper, C., Wilson, D. and Le Grand, J. (eds) (1994) *Quasi-Markets in the Welfare State*. Bristol: Policy Press.

Barton, R. (1959) *Institutional Neurosis*. Bristol: Wright.

Berridge, D. and Cleaver, H. (1987) *Foster Home Breakdown*. Oxford: Blackwell.

Booth, C. (1892–97) *The Life and Labour of the People of London*. London: Macmillan.

Bowlby, J. (1951) *Maternal Care and Mental Health*. Geneva: WHO.

Brill, K. (1991) *The Curtis Experiment*. PhD thesis. Birmingham: University of Birmingham.

British Imperial Calendar and Civil Service List (1946 and 1954). London: HMSO.

British Psychological Society (BPS) (2012) *Technique is Not Enough: A Framework for Ensuring that Evidence-based Parenting Programmes are Socially Inclusive*. Leicester: BPS.

Bullard, E. and Malos, E. (1991) *Custodianship: Caring for other People's Children*. London: HMSO.

Bullock, R., Little, M. and Millham, S. (1993) *Residential for Children: A Review of the Research*. London: HMSO.

Callaghan, J. (1987) *Time and Chance*. London: Collins.

Castle, B. (1980) *The Castle Diaries: 1974–76*. London: Weidenfeld and Nicholson.

Childline (2012) *Saying the Unsayable: What's Affecting Children in 2012?* www.nspcc.org.uk/childline

Churchill, H. (2011) *Parental Rights and Responsibilities: Analysing Social Policy and Lived Experience*. Bristol: Policy Press.

Cliffe, D. and Berridge, D. (1991) *Closing Children's Homes: An End to Residential Childcare?* London: National Children's Bureau.

Corbett, G. (1981) *Barnardo Children in Canada*. Peterborough (Canada): Woodland.

Corby, B., Doig, A. and Roberts, V. (2001) *Public Inquiries into Abuse of Children in Residential Care*. London: Kingsley.

Cornish, D. and Clarke, R. (1975) *Residential Treatment and its Effects upon Delinquency*. London: HMSO.

Cretney, S. (1998) *Law Reform and the Family*. Oxford: Claredon.

Cretney, S. and Mason, J. (1990) *Principles of Family Law*, 5th edn. London: Sweet and Maxwell.

Crowther, M. (1981) *The Workhouse System: 1834–1929*. London: Batsford.

Currie, R. and Ramage, A. (nd) *The Policy of Boarding out Children in Scotland*. Glasgow: Caledonian University.

Dartington Social Research Unit (DSRU) (1983) *Place of Safety Orders*. Dartington: DSRU.

Davenport Hill, F. (1868) *Children of the State: The Training of Juvenile Paupers*. London: Macmillan.

de Jouvenel, B. (1967) *The Art of Conjecture*. London: Weidenfeld and Nicholson.

de Saint Exupéry, A. (1976) *Southern Mail/Night Flight*. Harmondsworth: Penguin.

Denham, A. and Garnett, M. (2001) *Keith Joseph*. Chesham: Acumen.

Digby, A. (1978) *Pauper Palaces*. London: Routledge and Kegan Paul.

Donnison, D. (1960) *Housing Policy Since the War*. Welwyn: Codicote.

Dwok, D. (1987) *War is Good for Babies and Children: A History of the Infant Welfare Movement in England, 1889-1918*. London: Tavistock.

Eekaleer, J. and Dingwall, R. (1990) *The Reform of Child Care Law: A Practical Guide to the Children Act 1989*. London: Tavistock/Routledge.

Eisenstadt, N. (2011) *Providing a Start: How Government Discovered Early Childhood*. Bristol: Policy Press.

Facey, A. (1981) *A Fortunate Life*. Australia: Penguin.

Fanshel, D. and Shinn, E. (1979) *The Child in Foster Care*. New York: Columbia University Press.

Fanshel, D. and Shinn, E. (1982) *On the Road to Permanency*. New York: Columbia University Press.

Farmer, E. and Parker, R. (1991) *Trials and Tribulations: Returning Children from Local Authority Care to their Families*. London: HMSO.

Fox Harding, L. (1991) *Perspectives in Child Care Policy*. London: Longman.

Freeman, M. (1980) *The Child Care and Foster Children Acts 1980*. London: Sweet and Maxwell.

George, V. (1970) *Foster Care*. London: Routledge and Kegan Paul.

Gill, O. and Jackson, B. (1983) *Adoption and Race*. London: Batsford.

Gittins, J. (1952) *Approved School Boys*. London: HMSO.

Goffman, E. (1961) *Asylums: Essays on the Situation of Mental Patients and Other Inmates*. London: Penguin.

Gordon, D., Parker, R. and Loughran, F. (2000) *Disabled Children in Britain*. London: The Stationery Office.

Gray, P. and Parr, E. (1957) *Children in Care and the Recruitment of Foster Parents*. London: Social Survey.

Hall, P., Land, H., Parker, R. and Webb, A. (1975) *Change, Choice and Conflict in Social Policy*. London: Heinemann.

Hall, P. (1976) *Reforming the Welfare: The Politics of Change in the Personal Social Services*. London: Heinemann.

Harker, L., Jütte, S., Murphy, T., Bentley, H., Miller, P. and Fitch, P. (2013) *How Safe are our Children?* London: NSPCC.

Harrison, P. (1979) *The Home Children*. Winnipeg: Watson and Dwyer.

Hay, J. (1975) *The Origins of the Liberal Reforms: 1906–1914*. London: Macmillan.

Hendrick, H. (1994) *Child Welfare, 1872–1989*. London: Routledge.

Hendrick, H. (2003) *Child Welfare: Historical Dimensions, Contemporary Debate*. Bristol: Policy Press.

Hicklin, M. (1946) *War-Damaged Children*. London: Association of Psychiatric Social Workers.

Herbert, A. (1936) *Mild and Bitter*. London: Methuen.

Herbert, A. (1960) *Anything but Action? A Study of the Uses and Abuses of Committees of Inquiry*. London: Institute of Economic Affairs.

Herbert, T. (ed.) (2000) *The British Brass Band: Musical and Social History*. Oxford: Oxford University Press.

Hollis, P. (1987) *Ladies Elect: Women in Local Government, 1865–1914.* Oxford: Clarendon.

Holman, R. (1996) *The Corporate Parent: Manchester Children's Department, 1948–71.* London: National Institute for Social Work.

Holman, R. (1998) *Child Care Revisited: Children's Departments, 1948–71.* London: Institute of Child Care and Social Education.

Honigsbaum, F. (1970) *The Struggle for the Ministry of Health.* London: Bell.

Horner, F. (1919) *The Shadow and the Sun.* London: Epworth/NCH.

Hurt, J. (1979) *Elementary Schooling and the Working Classes: 1860–1918.* London: Routledge and Kegan Paul.

Independent Children's Homes Association (ICHA) (2012) *Commissioners' Handbook.* Sutton Coldfield: ICHA.

Inglis, M. (1909) *The Children's Charter.* Edinburgh: Nelson.

Jackson, S. (2008) *Social Care and Social Exclusion: Can Education Change the Trajectory for Looked-After Children?* Brighton: East Sussex Social Services Department (SSD)/University of Sussex.

Jephcott, P. (1971) *Homes in High Flats.* Edinburgh: Oliver and Boyd.

Kahan, B. (1994) *Growing up in Groups.* London: HMSO.

Knapp, M. (1979) *Cost Information and the Planning of Social Care Services: The Residential Care of Children in England and Wales.* Canterbury: University of Kent, Personal Social Services Research Unit (PSSRU).

Labour Party (1964) *Crime: A Challenge to us All.* London: Labour Party.

Levy, A. and Kahan, B. (1991) *The Pindown Experience and the Protection of Children.* Stafford: Stafford CC.

Lloyd, E. (ed.) (1999) *Parenting Matters: What Works in Parenting Education.* Ilford: Barnardos.

Loughran, F. and Parker, R. (1990) *Child Care Work Arising from Matrimonial, Domestic and Guardianship Proceedings.* Bristol: Bristol University Department of Social Policy.

Loughran, F. and Parker, R. (1990) *Trends in Child Care: A Report to the ESRC.* Bristol: Bristol University, Department of Social Policy.

Lowndes, G. (1937) *The Silent Social Revolution: an Account of the Expansion of Public Education in England and Wales, 1895–1935.* Oxford: Oxford University Press.

Magnusson, A. (1984) *The Village: a History of Quarriers.* Glasgow: Quarriers.

Martin, F. and Murray, K. (eds) (1982) *The Scottish Juvenile Justice System.* Edinburgh: Scottish Academic Press.

Meltzer, H., Smyth, M. and Robus, N. (1989) *Disabled Children: Services, Transport and Education.* London: HMSO.

Middleton, N. (1971) *When Families Failed.* London: Gollanz.

Millham, S., Bullock, R., Hosie, K. and Haak, M. (1986) *Lost in Care: The Problems of Maintaining Links Between Children in Care and Their Families*. Aldershot: Gower.

Morris, A. (1970) *The Growth of Parliamentary Scrutiny by Committee: A Symposium*. Oxford: Pergamon.

Morris, J. (1975) *Uses of Epidemiology*, 3rd edn. London: Churchill Livingstone.

Mullin, C. (2010) *A View from the Foothills*. London: Profile Books.

Municipal Journal (1938 and 1948) *Municipal Yearbook*. London: MJ.

Murphy, J. (1992) *British Social Services: The Scottish Dimension*. Edinburgh: Scottish Academic Press.

National Collaborating Centre for Women's and Children's Health (2013) *When to Suspect Child Maltreatment*. London: National Institute for Health and Clinical Excellence.

National Council of Social Services (1967) *Caring for People: Staffing Residential Homes*. London: Allen and Unwin.

National Society for the Prevention of Cruelty to Children (NSPCC) (2013) *Helpline Highlights*. London: NSPCC.

Nationwide Association of Foster Care Providers, Independent Children's Home Association and The National Association of Independent Schools and Non-maintained Special Schools (2012) *'Death by Paperwork?' The Effect of Local Authority Procurement on Voluntary and Private Children's Services Providers*. www.nafp.co.uk

Niechcial, J. (2010) *Lucy Faithful: Mother to Hundreds*. Self published: Niechcial.

Oakley, A. (2000) *Experiments in Knowing: Gender and Method in the Social Sciences*. Cambridge: Polity Press.

Oldfield, S. (2009) *Jeannie, an 'Army of One': Mrs Nassau Senior, 1828–1877. The First Woman in Whitehall*. Brighton: Sussex Academic Press.

Owen, D. (1991) *Time to Declare*. London: Joseph.

Packman, J. (1975) *The Child's Generation*. Oxford: Blackwell/Robinson.

Packman, J. (1986) *Who Needs Care? Social Work Decisions about Children*. Oxford: Blackwell.

Packman, J. and Hall, C. (1998) *From Care to Accommodation: Support, Protection and Control in Child Care Services*. London: The Stationery Office.

Parker, R. (1966) *Decision in Child Care: A Study of Prediction in Fostering*. London: Allen and Unwin.

Parker, R. (1967) *The Problems of Reform*. London: Family Welfare Association.

Parker, R. (ed.) (1980) *Caring for Separated Children*. London: Macmillan.

Parker, R. (1990) *Away from Home: A History of Child Care*. Ilford: Barnardos.

Parker, R. (1990) *Safeguarding Standards*. London: National Institute for Social Work.

Parker, R. (ed.) (1999) *Adoption Now*. Chichester: Wiley.

Parker, R. (2010) *Uprooted: The Shipment of Poor Children to Canada, 1867–1917*. Bristol: Policy Press.

Parker, R., Ward, H., Jackson, S., Aldgate, J. and Wedge, P. (eds) (1991) *Assessing Outcomes in Child Care*. London: HMSO.

Parsloe, P. (1981) *Social Service Teams*. London: Allen and Unwin.

Parton, N. (1985) *The Politics of Child Abuse*. London: Macmillan.

Pugh, G. (2007) *London's Forgotten Children: Thomas Coram and the Foundling Hospital*. Stroud: Tempus.

Quinton, D. and Rutter, M. (1998) *Parenting Breakdown*. Aldershot: Avery.

Rhodes, G. (1975) *Committees of Inquiry*. London: Allen and Unwin.

Rich, E. (1970) *The Education Act 1870: A Study of Public Opinion*. London: Longmans Green.

Richardson, H. (1969) *Adolescent Girls in Approved Schools*. London: Routledge and Kegan Paul.

Robinson, C. and Stalker, K. (1991) *Respite Care: Summaries and Suggestions*. Bristol: Norah Fry Centre.

Rose, J. (1987) *For the Sake of the Children*. London: Hodder and Stoughton.

Rose, M. (ed.) (1985) *The Poor and the City: The English Poor Law in its Urban Context, 1834–1914*. Leicester: Leicester University Press.

Rowe, J. and Lambert, L. (1973) *Children who Wait*. London: Association of British Adoption Agencies.

Rowe, J., Cain, H., Hundleby, M. and Keane, A. (1984) *Long-Term Foster Care*. London: Batsford.

Rowntree, B. (1902) *Poverty: A Study of Town Life*. London: Macmillan.

Rutter, M. (1981) *Maternal Deprivation Reassessed*. Harmondsworth: Penguin.

Searle, G. (1976) *Eugenics and Politics in Britain*. Leyden (NL): Sijthoff and Noordhoff.

Searle, G. (1990) *The Quest for National Efficiency: A Study of British Politics and Political Thought (1899–1914)*. London: Ashfield.

Skull, A. (1979) *Museums of Madness: The Social Organisation of Insanity in Nineteenth Century England*. London: Allen Lane.

Silver, N. (2012) *The Signal and the Noise: The Art and Science of Prediction.* London: Penguin.

Simon, B. (1965) *Education and the Labour Movement: 1870–1920.* London: Lawrence and Wishart.

Sinclair, I. (ed.) (1988) *Residential Care: The Research Reviewed,* vol 2 of *Residential Care: A Positive Choice.* London: HMSO.

Sinclair, R. and Bullock, R. (2002) *Learning from Past Experience: A Review of Serious Case Reviews.* London: Department of Health.

Smith, F. (1979) *The People's Health: 1830–1910.* NY: Holmes and Meier.

Stroud, J. (1971) *Thirteen Penny Stamps: The Story of the Church of England's Children's Society from its Beginnings as the 'Waifs and Strays'.* London: Hodder and Stoughton.

Thoburn, J. (1980) *Captive Clients: Social Work with Families and Children Home on Trial.* London: Routledge and Kegan Paul.

Titmuss, R. (1950) *Problems of Social Policy.* London: HMSO.

Titmuss, R. (1958) *Essays on the Welfare State.* London: Allen and Unwin.

Trasler, G. (1960) *In Place of Parents.* London: Routledge and Kegan Paul.

Triseliotis, J. (1970) *Evaluation of Adoption Policy and Practice.* Edinburgh: Department of Social Administration.

Triseliotis, J., Borland, M., Hill, M. and Lambert, L. (1996) *Teenagers and the Social Work Services.* London: HMSO.

Vickers, G. (1965) *The Art of Judgement: A Study of Policy Making.* London: Chapman and Hall.

Wagner, G. (1979) *Barnardo.* London: Weidenfeld and Nicholson.

Wagner, G. (1982) *Children of the Empire.* London: Weidenfeld and Nicholson.

Watkins, D. (1993) *Other People's Children: Adventures in Child Care.* Cornwall: Devoran.

Wasserstein, B. (1992) *Herbert Samuel: A Political Life.* Oxford: Clarendon.

Webb, S. and Webb, B. (1963 reprint) *English Poor Law History: The Last Hundred Years, vol I.* London: Cass.

Wedge, P. (2003) *Developing Notions of Children in Need.* Brighton: East Sussex Social Services Department (SSD)/University of Sussex.

Wheare, K. (1955) *Government by Committee.* Oxford: Clarendon.

Wilkins, L. (1963) *Social Deviance.* London: Tavistock.

Wilson, C. (1978) *The Outsider.* London: Pan Books.

Women's Group on Public Welfare. (1948) *The Neglected Child and His Family.* Oxford: Oxford University Press.

Articles and chapters

Axford, N., Lehtonen, M., Tobin, K., Kaoukji, D. and Berry, V. (2012) 'Engaging parents in parenting programs: Lessons from research and practice', *Children and Youth Services Review*, 34, p 2061.

Bartak, L. and Rutter, M. (1975) 'The Measurement of Staff-Child Interaction in Three Units for Autistic Children', in Tizard, J., Sinclair, I. and Clarke, R. (eds) *Varieties of Residential Experience*. London: Routledge and Kegan Paul.

Berridge, D. (1984) 'Private Children's Homes', *British Journal of Social Work*, 14 (4).

Bradshaw, J. (2006) 'The Uses of Indicators of Child Well-Being in the United Kingdom and European Union', in Ben-Arieh, A and George, R. (eds) *Indicators of Child Well-being*. Dordrecht (NL): Springer.

Bullock, R. and Blower, S. (2013) 'Changes in the Nature and Sequence of Placements Experienced by Children in Care, 1980–2010', *Adoption and Fostering*, 37 (2).

Cawson, P. (1985) 'Intermediate Treatment'. *Journal of Child Psychology and Psychiatry*, 26 (5).

Choppin, V. (1970) 'The Origins of the Philosophy of Detention Centres', *British Journal of Criminology*, 10 (2).

Davis, G., MacLoed, A. and Murch, M. (1983) 'Undefended Divorce: Should Section 41 of the Matrimonial Causes Act of 1973 be Repealed?' *Modern Law Review*, 46 (2).

Donnison, D. and Ungerson, C. (1968) 'Trends in Residential Care, 1911–1961', *Social and Economic Administration*, 2 (2).

Donnison, D. (2014) *'On Tap but not on Top'*. Dartington: Centre for Social Policy.

Harris, P. (2006) 'The Making of the Children Act: A Private History', *Family Law*, December.

Gibbons, J., Gallagher, B., Bell, C. and Gordon, D. (1995) *Development after Physical Abuse in Early Childhood*. London: HMSO.

Hawkes, N. (2013) 'Sailing Without a Lookout', *British Medical Journal*, 347, f6739, 16 November.

Holman, R. (1975) 'The Place of Social Work in Fostering', *British Journal of Social Work*, 5 (1).

Horsburgh, M. (1983) 'No Sufficient Security: The Reaction of the Poor Law Authorities to Boarding-Out', *Journal of Social Policy*, 12 (1).

Jones, R. (2009) 'Children Acts, 1948–2008: The Drivers for Legislative Change in England Over 60 Years', *Journal of Children's Services*, 4 (4).

Joseph, K. (1971) 'Future Policy for Mental Health', in *Minds Matter*. London: National Association for Mental Health.

Knapp, M., Bryson, D. and Matthews, J. (1982) 'Child Care Costs and Policies', *Social Work Services*, 32 (Winter).

Land, H. (1975) 'Detention Centres: The Experiment that could not Fail', in Hall, P., Land, H., Parker, R. and Webb, A. *Change, Choice and Conflict in Social Policy*. London: Heinemann.

Little, M. (2012) 'In the Shadows: Children's Social Policy in the Blair Years', *Adoption and Fostering*, 36 (1).

Little, M., Berry, B., Morpeth, L. *et al* (2012) 'The Impact of Three Evidence-based Programmes Delivered in Public Systems in Birmingham, UK', *International Journal of Conflict and Violence*, 6 (12).

Mason, M. (1922) 'The Boarded-out Children of the Poor', *The Nineteenth Century and After*, DXLIV (June).

Maurice, F. (1903) 'National Health: A Soldier's Story', *The Contemporary Review*, 445 (41–56).

McGuire, J., Stein, A. and Rosenberg, W. (1997) 'Evidence-Based Medicine and Child Mental Health Services', *Children and Society*, 11 (2).

'Miles' (1902) 'Where to Get Men', *The Contemporary Review*, 433 (78–86).

Munro, E. (1999) 'Common Errors in Reasoning in Child Protection Work', *Child Abuse and Neglect*, 23 (8).

Munro, E. (2004) 'The Impact of Child Abuse Inquiries Since 1990', in Stanley, N. and Manthorpe, J. (eds) *The Age of Inquiry: Learning and Blaming in Health and Social Care*. London: Routledge.

Owen, D. (1985) ' The Objectives of the Children Act', in *A Review of the Children Act* [1975] *10 Years On*. London: National Foster Care Association.

Parker, R. (1969) 'Co-operation Between Social Welfare Organisations', in Kellmer Pringle, M. (ed.) *Caring for Children*, London: Longmans.

Parker, R. (1972) 'Social Ills and Public Remedies', in Robson, W. (ed.) *Man and the Social Sciences*. London: LSE/Allen and Unwin.

Parker, R. (1983) 'The Gestation of Reform: the 1948 Children Act', in Bean, P. and MacPherson, S. (eds) *Approaches to Welfare*. London: Routledge and Kegan Paul.

Parker, R. (1988) 'Residential Care for Children', in Sinclair, I. (ed.) *The Research Reviewed*. vol 2 of *Residential Care: A Positive Choice*. London: HMSO.

Parker, R. (2004) 'Children and the Concept of Harm', in Hillyard, P., Pantazis, C., Tombs, S. and Gordon, D. (eds) *Beyond Criminology: Taking Harm Seriously*. London: Pluto Press.

Parker, R. (2005) ' Then and Now: 40 Years of Research in the UK', in Axford, N., Berry, V., Little, M. and Morpeth, L. (eds) *Forty Years of Research, Policy and Practice in Children's Services*. Chichester: Wiley.

Reder, P. and Duncan, S. (2004) 'From Colwell to Climbié: Inquiring into Fatal Child Abuse', in Stanley, N. and Manthorpe, J. (eds) *The Age of Inquiry: Learning and Blaming in Health and Social Care*. London: Routledge.

Woolgar, M. (2013) 'The practical implications of the emerging findings in neurobiology of maltreatment for looked after and adopted children', *Adoption and Fostering*, 37 (3).

Wolkind, S. and Rushton, A. (1994) 'Residential and Foster Care', in Rutter, M., Taylor, E. and Hersov, L. (eds) *Child and Adolescent Psychiatry*, 3rd edn. Oxford: Blackwell.

Select list of official publications (omitting annual reports, Acts, Bills, secondary legislation and statistics)

Reports of committees of inquiry or review (by date)

Report of the Royal Commission on Reformatory and Industrial Schools (1884) cd 3876 and 'Evidence', cd 3876-I. London: HMSO.

Report of the Departmental Committee to Inquire into the Existing System of Maintenance and Education of Children in the Charge of Managers of District Schools and Boards of Guardians in the Metropolis (1896) vol I 'Report', c 8027 and vol II 'Evidence', c 8032. London: HMSO.

Report of the Royal Commission on Physical Education (Scotland) (1903) vol I 'Report', cd 1507 and vol II 'Evidence', (1904) cd 2210. Edinburgh. HMSO.

Report of the Committee on Physical Deterioration (1904) cd 2175. London: HMSO.

Report of the Inter-Departmental Committee on the Medical Inspection of Children Attending Public Elementary Schools (1905) vol I, cd 2779. London: HMSO.

Report of the Royal Commission on the Poor Laws (1909) cd 4499 and 'Appendices' (1910) cd 5075. London: HMSO.

Report of the Committee on Child Adoption (1921) cmd 1254. London: HMSO.

Report[s] (3) *of the Committee on Child Adoption* (1926) cmd 2401, 2469 and 2711. London: HMSO.

Report on the Circumstances which led to the Boarding-out of Dennis and Terence O'Neill at Bank Farm, Minsterley, and the Steps Taken to Supervise their Welfare (1945) cmd 6636. London: HMSO.

Report of the Committee on Homeless Children (1946) cmd 6911. Edinburgh: HMSO.

Report of the Care of Children Committee (1946) cmd 6922. London: HMSO.

Sixth Report from the Select Committee on Estimates (Child Care) (1953) HC 328. London: HMSO.

Report of the Royal Commission on the Law Relating to Mental Illness and Mental Deficiency, 1954–7 (1957) cmnd 169. London: HMSO.

The Administration of Punishment at Court Lees Approved School: Report of Inquiry by Mr Edward Brian Gibbens, QC (1967) London: HMSO.

Report of the Royal Commission on Local Government in England, 1966–9. (1969) vol III 'Appendices', cmnd 4040-II. London: HMSO.

Report of the Committee of Inquiry into the Care and Supervision Provided in Relation to Maria Colwell (1974) London: HMSO.

Report of the Commission on One-Parent Families (1974) cmnd 5629. London: HMSO.

Prevention and Health: Everybody's Business (1975) London: HMSO.

First Report from the Select Committee on Violence in Marriage (1975) vol I, HC 533. London: HMSO.

First Report from the Select Committee on Violence in the Family: Violence to Children (1977) HC 329. London: HMSO.

Report of a Longitudinal Study of Children in Care (Scotland) (nd, c 1980) Edinburgh: Scottish Education Department.

Report of an Inquiry into the Social Science Research Council (1981) cmnd 4814. London: HMSO.

Second Report of the Social Services Committee, Children in Care (1984) HC 360-I. London: HMSO.

Brent (London Borough) (1985) *A Child in Trust: The Report of the Panel of Inquiry into the Circumstances Surrounding the Death of Jasmine Beckford.* London: London Borough of Brent.

Review of Child Care Law: Report to Ministers from an Independent Working Party (1987) London: DHSS.

Seen but not Heard: Co-ordinating Community Child Health and Social Services for Children in Need: a report by the Audit Commission. (1994) London: HMSO.

Third Report of the Health Select Committee: The Welfare of Former British Child Migrants (1997) 'Report' HC 755-I and 'Evidence' HC 755-II. London: HMSO.

Report of the Royal Commission on the Funding of Long-term Care for the Elderly (1999) cm 4192. London: HMSO.

Report of the Tribunal of Inquiry into the Abuse of Children in the Care of Gwyndd and Clwyd since 1974 (2000) HC 201. London: HMSO.

The Victoria Climbié Inquiry: Report of an Inquiry by Lord Laming (2003) cm 5730. London: HMSO.

Sixth Report of the Health Select Committee on the Victoria Climbié Report (review) (2003) HC 570. London: HMSO.

The mental health of young people looked after by local authorities in England (2003) Office for National Statistics (Meltzer, H., Corbin, T., Gatward, R., Goodman, R. and Ford, T.). London: HMSO.

Serious Case Review: Child 'A' (London Borough of Haringey) (2008) London: Department for Education.

Early Intervention: The Next Step (report to HMG) (2011) London: HMG.

Early Intervention: Smart Investment, Massive Savings (report to HMG) (2011) London: HMG.

Final Report of the Riots Communities and Victims Panel (report to PM) (2012) London: RCVP.

Inter-Departmental Committee's Inquiry to Establish the Facts of the State's Involvement with the Magdalen Laundries (2013) Dublin: Irish Government.

Report of the Education Select Committee on Foundation Years: Sure Start Children's Centres (2013) HC 364-I and II. London: Department for Education.

White Papers (by date)

Children Neglected or Ill-treated in their own Homes (1950) London: Home Office.

The Child, the Family and the Young Offender (1965) cmnd 2742. London: HMSO.

Children in Trouble (1968) cmnd 3601. London: HMSO.

The Law on Child Care and Family Services (1987) cm 62. London: HMSO.

Adoption: The Future (1993) cm 2288. London: HMSO.

Adoption: Achieving the Right Balance (1998) LAC (98) 20. London: Department of Health.

Modernising Government (1999) cm 4310. London: HMSO.

Reports and statements from government departments (by department alphabetically)

Cabinet Office, Social Exclusion Task Force (2007) *Reaching Out: Think Families. Analysis and Themes from the Families at Risk Review.* London: CO.

Department for Children, Schools and Families (DfCSF) (2003) *Every Child Matters*, cm 5860. London: The Stationery Office (TSO).

DfCSF (2007) *The Children's Plan: Building Brighter Futures*, cm 7280. London: TSO.

DfCSF (2010) *Working Together*. London: DfCSF.

Department for Education (DfE) (2011) *Post Legislative Assessment of the Childcare Act 2006*, cm 8204. London: TSO.

DfE (2013) *Working Together to Safeguard Children: A Guide to Inter-agency Working*. London: DfE.

DfE (2013) *Outcomes for Children Looked After by Local Authorities in England as at March 2013* (SFR 50/2013). London: DfE.

DfE (2013) *Powers to Delegate Children's Social Care Functions*. London: DfE.

Department for Education and Schools (DfES) (2007) *Every Parent Matters*. London: DfES.

Department of Health (DoH) (1989) *The Care of Children: Principles and Practice in Regulations and Guidance*. London: HMSO.

DoH (1994) *Key Indicators of Local Authority Social Services*. London: HMSO.

DoH et al. (1999) *Working Together to Safeguard Children: A Guide to Inter-agency Working*. London: DoH.

DoH et al. (2000) *A Framework for the Assessment of Children in Need and their Families*. London: TSO.

HM Treasury et al. (2007) *Aiming High for Children: Supporting Families*. London: HMT.

Office of the Prime Minister (OPM), Social Exclusion Task Force (2003) *A Better Education for Children*. London: OPM.

National Archives

PRO, MH 102/1161/17. War Cabinet Reconstruction Committee (1944) *Enquiry into Methods of Providing for Homeless Children*.

PRO, MH 102/1390. *Report of the Committee on the Break-up of the Poor Law* (1946).

Miscellaneous reports and papers (by date)

Barnardos (1900 and 1901) *Annual Reports*. London.

Waifs and Strays Society (1900) *Annual Report*. London.

National Children's Homes (1908) *Annual Report*. Harpendon.

The Times, 15.7.44.

Kent County Council (KCC) (1950) *Report of the Children's Committee, 1948–50*. Maidstone: KCC.
Wallbridge and Another v. Dorset County Council (1954) WLR 1608.
The Guardian, 16.5.14 and 21.5.14.

Index

V

violence in families 61–2
Violence to Children 62
voluntary organisations
  decline of 29
  and foster care 27
  and residential care 23–9, 43, 44, 83,
    110, 112

W

war orphans 44–5
Watkins, D. 75, 76
'welfare to work' 109
Wheare, K. 128
Who Needs Care? (Packman, J.) 6–8
Wilkins, L. 142
Winnicott, C. 72
women, and senior posts 72, 73–84
Women's Group on Public Welfare 47
workhouses 19–20
Working Together to Safeguard Children 113,
  163

Y

young offenders 29, 57, 63